THE BRITISH POLICEWOMAN:
HER STORY

Ex-nurse and policewoman Joan Lock has written seven Victorian crime fiction titles and eight non-fiction police/crime books, including three on Scotland Yard's first detectives. She has also written short stories, radio plays and radio documentaries, as well as working as a columnist on the leading police journal, *Police Review*, and *Red Herrings*, the magazine of the Crime Writers' Association.

By the same author

Scotland Yard's First Cases
The Princess Alice Disaster

THE BRITISH POLICEWOMAN:
HER STORY

Joan Lock

ROBERT HALE • LONDON

ISBN 978-0-7198-1422-8

Robert Hale Limited
Clerkenwell House
Clerkenwell Green
London EC1R 0HT

www.halebooks.com

A catalogue record for this book is available from the British Library

2 4 6 8 10 9 7 5 3 1

Printed in Great Britain by Berforts Information Press Ltd

Contents

Illustrations

the Chief Constable, Sir Phillip Lane (centre), was not in favour of uniformed women police he pioneered their use in detective work. Alongside him here, far left to right: Policewoman Parker, Woman Inspector Charlotte Storey, Assistant Chief Constable W. Trubshaw, Woman Inspector Lilian Naylor (reputed to have been active in "special" anti-IRA work), Superintendent Gregson and Woman Sergeant Jackson. Behind them are twelve PWs (Policewomen) and four SPWs (Specials).

11. Members of the Women Police Service, probably in Paddington in 1918.

12. Some things don't change much! A post-Second World War Metropolitan Woman Police Constable.

13. Transport not provided. WPC Lodge, Forest Division, Gloucestershire Constabulary, with her own motorcycle, an AJS 350cc, in 1928. When riding it on duty she was allowed 1½d a mile in expenses.

14. Getting motorized. Commandant Margaret Damer Dawson comforts a rescued child whilst Sub Commandant Mary Allen drives them to safety. By 1918 the Women Police Service were equipped with four motorcycles (three with side-cars) which appear to have been largely for the use of the senior officers, mainly for inspection purposes.

15. Jubilee, 1935. The redoubtable Mabel Read of Hove receives her Jubilee Medal.

16. Just practising. A Metropolitan WPC demonstrating self-defence on a male colleague.

17. Specialist branches open up for women. Here, a Metropolitan WPC escorts the Guards to Buckingham Palace.

18. One of the first two Metropolitan women dog-handlers with her drug-detecting golden Labrador.

19. Pauline Clare, who in 1995 became the UK's first female chief constable when she was appointed to lead Lancashire Constabulary.

20. Chief Superintendent Shirley Becke in friendly conference with Yard colleagues. Becke, who became the first woman to attain the rank of Commander, guided the Metropolitan Women Police towards integration.

Acknowledgements

When this book was first published in 1979, I found myself indebted to the following people: Pat Plank of the Metropolitan Police Library for her assistance and encouragement, and for checking through the manuscript as far as one is able considering there was no other history with which to cross-check. Thank you also to her obliging staff and that of the Metropolitan Police Press and Publicity Library for helpfulness on the picture front. Finally to Mike Down and Linda Bell of the (then) Publicity Branch, for putting me in touch with these departments.

I am deeply grateful to all my friends in that treasure house of women's history, the Fawcett Library, for their interest and informed assistance, and also to the staff at the Imperial War Museum Reference Departments (Printed Books, Documents and Photographs) and the London Museum (Suffrage Collection) who were always most obliging on my less frequent visits there.

I would also like to thank the following members of the Metropolitan Women Police Association; Jean Bottel, Alice Lusher, Carol Gibson, Ethel Woods, Shirley Becke, Sally Hubbard, Wini Gould, and, especially, Ivy Sumner (née Robinson), Irene Williams, Eileen Anderson (née O'Leary), Barbara Bohane, Elizabeth Bather, Beatrice Wills and her daughter Ruth Russell, and Audrey Mattinson. Also the Chief Constables of Lancashire, North Yorkshire and Gloucestershire for allowing their officers, Woman Chief Inspector Lena Gelder, Inspector Peter N. Walker and Chief Inspector Jack Cratchley respectively, to search out so ably material and photographs for me. Also various other members of diverse police forces who knowingly, and sometimes unknowingly, provided me with snippets of useful opinion and information.

The relatives of Edith Watson (her son, Bernard John) and Ellen Harburn (her niece, Dr Sylvia Hatfield) were most kind and helpful and I am grateful to them for information and photographs.

I would like to thank my brother, Eric Greenslade, for research help and advice and my husband, Bob, for checking through the MS for typing and spelling errors; helping me to do similarly with the proofs; compiling the index, and for three years' tolerance of a home knee-deep in women police data.

For assistance with this edition's revised penultimate chapter and new final chapter I would like to add to the previous list: Sioban Clark, Linda Bailey and Beverley Edwards. Also, once again, various other members of the Metropolitan Women Police Association and the BAWP (now renamed the British Association for Women in Policing).

J.L.

1

The Wrong Side of the Law

1909: MARY ALLEN

As the horse-bus clip-clopped through Parliament Square, Mary Allen stood up in a determined manner. This time she must do it. Already she had travelled the route three times, trying to pluck up courage for her lone deed. This time she must do it. Her nerve held as she descended the rocking staircase. The bus stopped. She was out on the almost deserted pavement. Gripping her umbrella in one shaking hand, she reached through her skirt placket with the other and pulled a brown-paper-wrapped stone from the dorothy bag which was slung around her waist.[1] Striding purposefully towards the Home Office, she raised her arm high and flung the missile through the cool and silent windows. Mary had been a semi-invalid as a child and still suffered from uncertain health, but she felt better now.

The crash of the impact, and the tinkling of the glass as it fell, echoed deafeningly through the quiet street. Suddenly there were people everywhere. It was almost as though they had been waiting for her to act before they could make an entrance. Soon most of them had gathered around Mary and were staring at her closely but not touching her or saying anything. Mary found this more unnerving than being violently repelled, as she certainly would have been if she had been part of the House of Commons raiding-party at that moment. She stood quietly and waited. Ahead of her the previously empty Home Office windows were filled with astonished and curious faces, all with their eyes on her. After what seemed like hours, a large Metropolitan Police Constable arrived, took her arm and led her away.[2]

The magistrate thought it a lamentable thing to see a respectable woman charged with the same sort of offence as small hooligan boys and felt there could be no justification for women parading through the streets armed with stones and breaking windows.[3] When he asked Mary whether she had anything to say in answer to the charge of wilful and malicious damage, she said no, except that she did it intentionally. When she saw women arrested she did it as a protest against Mr Asquith's refusal to receive their members.[4] She had not meant it to come out so jumbled, but she was nervous standing up there with everyone listening. She had always been rather nervous, so it must have come as a shock to her father when he had told her she would have to give up all this suffrage nonsense Annie Kenney had put into her head, or leave home, and she had said, "Very well," and left.[5]

Mary Allen and the thirteen other women who had smashed so much of Whitehall's glass that afternoon and evening, were fined £5 plus 2/6d costs, or a month in the Second Division. Of course there was no choice. Prison it must be, again. The first time had been quite an ordeal for Mary: plank beds, prickly, coarse straw pillows, foul food and no toothbrushes, hairbrushes or mirrors. True, some of the poorer suffragettes had been delighted to have a room to themselves, time to read and regular food,[6] but Mary was one of the many who had been brought up in great comfort and hygiene and so felt rather differently. Worse than any of the deprivations, however, was the silence. They had managed to communicate in other ways, for instance by sewing messages onto scraps of material left over from the shirts they had been hemming, but the silence had remained and Mary hated it.

This time Mary knew that prison was going to be different. She and several of the others had already decided they were going to follow Marion Wallace Dunlop's lone example a week before. They were going to resist being treated like criminals and demand to be regarded as political prisoners; until that right was conceded, they would refuse all food.

The delicious aroma assailed Mary's nostrils long before she saw the delicate slices of chicken breast nestling in a savoury brown gravy. Then she heard ice tinkling in a glass. She turned her back. Tea-cups were clattered with great deliberation, and the nectar was poured slowly, very slowly, into the cups. Mary did not move. She was in the prison hospital, having been transferred there from the punishment cells where she and several others had been placed after breaking their ordinary cell windows. Mary knew she had already starved past Marion's record. She and Gladys Roberts had shouted the news jubilantly to each other when they realized they had done over ninety-six hours. After sixty more hours without food, Mary Allen was released.[7]

At her next public speech Mary did herself more credit. She was the first to be presented with the Hunger-Striker's Medal by her beloved Mrs Pankhurst. "Dear soldier in the woman's army", Mrs Pankhurst called her, Mary, who had been such a sickly child. Mary replied by saying how grateful she was to Mrs Wallace Dunlop for showing the way and told how she had fainted from hunger in her cell and, when she woke up, cold and weary, had sung 'The Women's Marseillaise' to cheer herself up. A shout of "Bravo" had come from the next cell. It was Gladys Roberts, who joined in the anthem, and they had sung it right through together. That went down quite well, even though Mary was aware that she was no speaker, not like Annie Kenney whose oratory had so changed Mary's life.[8]

Less than a month after her release, she was inside again, this time as a guide to no less a person than Herbert Gladstone, the Home Secretary. Keir Hardie, who was also in the inspection party, had persuaded him to make the visit so as to see for himself the conditions about which the suffragettes were complaining.[9]

On Saturday, 3rd September 1909 Mary and a fellow hunger-striker (and breaker of the Treasury windows), Mrs Dove Willcox, went home to Bristol. "'HUNGER STRIKERS' RETURN", exclaimed the *Bristol Evening News*, "BRISTOL SUFFRAGISTS BACK FROM HOLLOWAY". Alas, 'the venerable clerk' did not realize the importance of the occasion and allowed it to rain, the paper reported:

> Had it been fine and the sun shining, the proceedings could not, however, have been more interesting, and, in spite of the unpleasant conditions overhead and underfoot, there was an enthusiastic little gathering on the No. 1 platform at Temple Meads Station in time to welcome the three o'clock train from London. Mrs Dove Willcox and Miss Mary Allen were soon sighted by the Bristol contingent, who made a rush for their compartment. Affectionate greetings between the ladies followed.

> Leading the contingent of ladies was Annie Kenney, West of England Organizer for the WSPU and expecting to be 'taken' herself at any moment.[10]

> Most of the ladies were decorated with sashes and rosettes of the familiar tri-colour hues, and carried bouquets of similarly coloured flowers ...
>
> As soon as the salutations and the hand-shakings had been got over, the two heroines of the hour – both of whom, it must have been noticed by the many passengers who were attracted to the spot, were looking wonderfully well, and were tastefully attired – together with Miss Kenney and one or two others, posed for the benefit of the ever-present

photographer, and were then pounced on by an *Evening News* man and several kindred colleagues.

"What is it you want to know?" asked Mrs Dove Willcox, who acted as spokeswoman on her own and her companions' behalf, Miss Allen being content to silently acquiesce in the other's statements.

1913: NINA BOYLE AND EDITH WATSON

It was a droll sight. A middle-aged woman making an impassioned speech while struggling to keep her balance on the roof of a motor-launch cabin. Her astonished audience had been peacefully taking yet another gracious tea on the terrace of the Houses of Parliament when the launch had sped up the Thames, stopped abruptly and drawn alongside. Four women passengers had immediately unfurled the flag of the Women's Freedom League; then two of them had jumped onto the cabin roof. The speaker was Miss Nina Boyle, author, journalist, one-time actress, fighter for the rights of native women in South Africa where she had lived, and the Political and Militant Organizer of the Women's Freedom League. She proved most eloquent, despite intermittent turbulence from passing barges.

"You are quite ready," she pointed out to the MPs, "to accept the help of women at election times and yet, when elected, just as ready to refuse them their rights!"

She continued to upbraid them and tell them just how ridiculous she thought they were. They cheered her roundly for her pains, and they were not merely jibing cheers – there was a distinct element of admiration in them. Admiration for her spirit, audacity and excellent oratory. In fact everyone was thoroughly enjoying themselves. Everyone, that is, except the police, who had already hissed sternly, "You must go away!", to no effect and were now standing waiting, impatient and impotent, for the hastily summoned police launch to put in an appearance. They were not the only ones keeping watch. The other two women on the boat were not there for decoration.

Finally, and to humiliatingly ironical cheers, the police boat was spotted approaching the other side of Westminster Bridge. One of her lookouts signalled Miss Boyle, who drew her speech to its close. Her companion, young Mrs Edith Watson, then rose, smiled brightly at the now packed terraces and graciously thanked the members for their attention and appreciation. She also assured them that, were it thought necessary to complete their education on this subject, the Women's Freedom League would return. Throwing them some leaflets, which also had this purpose in mind, she then signalled the captain, who by now had the engine chugging over, and the motor-launch *La Reine* sped off towards Chelsea, its laughing occupants cheered on from the terraces.

The timing was perfect. The police launch, arriving just a second too late, did not attempt pursuit. The police, as the Press did not hesitate to point out, had been caught napping.[11]

The Women's Freedom League, led by Mrs Despard, was a breakaway group from the Pankhursts' WSPU, preferring a democratic to autocratic organization. Though they declared themselves non-violent, they had led many active campaigns, some of which were later to be credited to the WSPU. Their policy was: if there had to be damage, it should be to government property, since it was the government with whom they had their quarrel. Hampering officialdom was also part of their strategy – this included the police.

Nina Boyle believed in having many projects going at once, so that, at the same time as they were making the police look foolish at Westminster, they were campaigning for reform of the vans which, intermittently, took them to prison. The vans were then communal and carried both sexes, and, while the WFL were not prudish, they did feel that it was going too far when, en route to Holloway, one of their number had to witness an 'orgy of indecency' between a prostitute and a male prisoner.[12] Another thing they were agitating for was women police.[13]

1909-1914: MARY ALLEN

Shortly after Mary Allen's first hunger strike, she had gone to prison again. While finding conditions improved "since you ladies have been coming", she also found that force-feeding had been introduced for hunger-strikers, so not only did the ordeal last much longer, it was more painful. Mary's delicacy reasserted itself. She became very ill and nearly died after release.

Once nursed back to health, she was told by Mrs Pankhurst that enough was enough and forbidden to risk imprisonment again. She was appointed an organizer, which, while not exactly risk-free, was a less hazardous occupation. Organizing was also less fun and involved less limelight and less action. Mary did not like this, for, although nervous, she did like action.

Organizers were paid a wage and sent where needed, but the former was not important to Mary. Her father, the Manager of the Great Western Railway, had not stopped her allowance when he required her to leave his house; he had, in fact, increased it.[14]

Once in their given areas, organizers were expected to acquaint themselves with the local police, leaders of society and authorities. This was partially with an aim to influencing these people but also so that, when the WSPU did organize something, from breaking windows to setting fire to derelict buildings, these same people were in no doubt as to who had done the deed and why. Organizers also sought out the best pavements to chalk with messages and notices of coming meetings and the best street-corners from which to harangue passers-by.

1914: NINA BOYLE AND EDITH WATSON

By 1914 Edith Watson had been 'sitting in' on court cases for two years and reporting the results in her column 'The Protected Sex' which featured in *The Vote*, the official organ of the Women's Freedom League.

She had some pretty horrifying tales to tell. She found that, whether women or children made their appearances as accused, witnesses or victims, they got a rough passage and precious little justice. Worse, in cases involving 'indecency', where they were usually the victims, the judge or magistrate would become very gallant and clear the court of all other women, and then, somehow, the victims would become the accused. Even small children would be forbidden the company of their mothers when they faced the onslaught of counsel who frequently implied that they were already sexually experienced and had lured the poor innocent male.

Edith Watson, by dint of her brave and persistent presence, and Nina Boyle, through complaining to the Home Office about the illegality of such a practice, helped limit this exclusion. But there were many pockets of stubborn resistance, in particular one Frederick Mead, magistrate at Marlborough Street Police Court, who, when he felt that the prosecution was inadequate in suffrage cases, would sometimes take on the cross-examination himself. He was absolutely determined that women would not listen to "filthy and disgusting cases" in his court.[15] As for the Home Office, they had only agreed to do what they could about the problem, and, since women had no vote, it did not matter if that conveniently turned out to be not much.[16]

While Edith was present, things did improve for women in court, but she could not be everywhere and, even where she was, grossly biased judgements and sentences continued: nine months' hard labour for soliciting (there was no similar offence for men who propositioned women, and there still is not) but three months in the second division for a man who committed grievous bodily harm on a woman – this was duly reported in her columns.

The Women's Freedom League pressed for better treatment for women in courts and police stations and from the Home Office. They wanted women working in all these areas, acting mainly as watchdogs. They also wanted police protection while they said their piece at Speakers' Corner,[17] like everyone else, but, since their pleas fell on deaf ears, Nina Boyle decided it was time to take action again.

Five women huddled together in the waiting-room of Marlborough Street Police Court, which was then occupying temporary premises in Francis Street, W1. They tried to prevent the chain from rattling as they passed it through the rings in the leather belts around their waists, in case the police were alerted before they were ready. The other end of the chain was attached to the door of the court room and, when they were finished, they effectively blocked passage of witnesses to and fro and thus brought proceedings to a halt.

When arrested, the women gave their names as Ann Smith, Edyth Smythe, Lilian Smith, Annunziata Smith and Louisa Smith. In court Ann Smith asked the magistrate to refrain from talking into his waistcoat but to speak up so that they all could hear. Then she admonished a police sergeant: "I know it is not fashionable in this court to tell the truth, but do try."[18] Edyth Smythe, who appeared surprisingly familiar with court proceedings, cross-examined the police witnesses to great effect and to their embarrassment, though not to an acquittal. In reality they were, of course, Nina Boyle and Edith Watson respectively. The idea was to hold up court business for as long as possible, and this they managed admirably over several sittings.[19]

"The first of the Obstruction Protests ... was successful beyond our wildest dreams," reported Nina Boyle in *The Vote* of 24th July 1914.

2

The Volunteers

Seven days after Nina Boyle announced the success of her first Police Court Protest, the Germans declared war on Russia. Two days later, on August Bank Holiday Monday, they declared war on France. The Cowes Regatta was abandoned and, the following day, Britain was at war with Germany.

A week later the Home Secretary proposed a remission of suffragette prison sentences, and the Women's Freedom League decided to abstain from all forms of active militancy for the duration and to organize a Women's Suffrage National Aid Corps, whose chief aim would be to render help to women and children.

Soon there was a national call for special constables, and Nina Boyle wrote to Sir Edward Ward, the gentleman organizing, asking if he would consider able-bodied women for these posts. While awaiting his reply, she advised women to offer themselves as 'specials' locally, and, at Sandgate in Kent a Miss Mumford and Mrs Burke were enrolled. Their main tasks were to "keep a look out for suspicious persons and lights on the beach".[1] She also advertised in *The Vote* for recruits to work four hours a day as Women Volunteer Police.

It was essential, she insisted in the advertisement, that the volunteers should be "healthy, self-reliant and reliable, punctual and regular and not undersized". She hoped that, by degrees, a uniform costume would be adopted, consisting of a useful blue serge skirt, Norfolk jacket of the same with pockets, straw hat (Panama style) with a blue ribbon, and a white armlet with WPV thereon in bold lettering. Nina Boyle had by no means been swept along willy-nilly on the current tide of frantic patriotism; she was looking way ahead. In a letter to her members she remarked: "If we *now* equip every district in the country with a body of women able and willing to do this class of work, it will be very difficult for the authorities to refuse to employ women in such capacity after the war."[2] She was very quick to see this potential. It was going to become obvious to others later, but she made this statement only three weeks after the war started.

Sir Edward Ward decided that, since he had been instructed by the Home Office to raise twenty thousand able-bodied *men*, he could not go outside his instructions.[3] Miss Boyle was disappointed, but she went on recruiting.

One evening that same busy August, Miss Margaret Damer Dawson, a wealthy, thirty-nine-year-old philanthropist, was waiting at a London railway station to greet the latest batch of Belgian refugees who were streaming over the Channel in the vanguard of the German advance. Miss Damer Dawson was acting as Head of Transport in a committee formed by "Chelsea people", as she called them, to assist women refugees to find lodgings and make a new life. As she waited, she saw another woman hovering in the background. She thought she recognized the woman – surely there was something familiar, and yet she was not sure.

Later, when Damer Dawson finally got her group together and was ushering them towards her fleet of cars, she caught the woman trying to persuade two of the flock away with her. But by then she had remembered why the woman rang such a bell. She had indeed seen her twice before that evening, but on those occasions her clothes had been different and so had the colour of her hair. Damer Dawson also remembered that she had mysteriously lost two of her group on a previous mission. It was then, she later claimed, that she realized that to do this kind of work and keep white-slavers at bay, she must have a trained and uniformed body of women. Women police in fact.[4]

But the idea of women police was not really new to her. She was connected with the Criminal Law Amendment Committee and the National Vigilance Association, both of which bodies had been pressing for women police help in the fight against the white-slave traffic, and she had even assisted in the return of some prostitutes to their homes on the Continent: one of the NVA's pre-war schemes.

The 'wealthy and well-connected' Margaret Damer Dawson was a curious mixture of a woman in both her interests and character. Scholarly and artistic, particularly fond of music, having studied at the Royal Academy, she also liked horse-riding, mountaineering, gardening and motoring – which in those days was classed as a pastime. Before joining the fight against white slavery, animal welfare had been her ruling passion. In 1906 she had organized an international congress for the protection of animals, and later she received decorations for this work from Finland and Denmark. Her home, Danehill, at Lympne in Kent, was a refuge for overworked horses and other animals in need.[5] Her character seems to have been an amalgam of upper-class silliness and tactlessness, shyness and gentleness, high intelligence and toughness, over-confidence and, above all, utter determination. Her friends called her "Fighting Dawson".[6] She had some humour and cannot have been without charm considering the vast amounts of money she managed to spirit out of wealthy friends to support her aims. Women appear to have liked her better than men, probably since she seemed unable to play up to the latter.

She commenced recruiting 'women police' in September 1914, but soon she and Nina Boyle learned of each other's plans and, to avoid the current sin of 'overlapping' and to strengthen their hands through greater numbers, they met and amalgamated. Damer Dawson became Chief and Nina Boyle her deputy. According to Mary Allen, Damer Dawson's leadership "brought to her aid women of similar calibre, social standing and education, mentally and physically above average" – for example Mary Allen and her sister Mrs Hampton.[7]

When war broke out, Mary Allen had been busy organizing WSPU militancy in Edinburgh. Offering herself for war work, she was invited to join a needlework guild, a prospect which filled her with horror: she wanted action. While in this state of limbo, she overheard two people on a bus discussing the risible idea of women police. Mary was enchanted by the notion and immediately investigated and volunteered.[8]

The leadership of the Women Police Volunteers worked out the way it did because Damer Dawson was prepared to devote all her time and energies to establishing women police, whereas Nina Boyle, a less single-minded person, both had and wanted other projects in hand.[9] Also it is probable they were both aware that Damer Dawson's respectable, non-suffrage background would stand them in greater stead with the authorities. That was certainly the case when she went to see the Commissioner of Police of the Metropolis, Sir Edward Henry, to ask his permission for the Women Police Volunteers to train and patrol in London, on a purely voluntary basis.

Only a couple of months earlier, Sir Edward had said, when pressed, that he did not regard the idea of women police with favour, "especially in view of the strained relationships between the sexes, or some portion of the sexes, in connection with the agitation over the suffrage questions."[10] The Metropolitan Police had, of course, borne the brunt of the "suffrage question". But it was wartime now, and

Margaret Damer Dawson found him "not at all averse to the idea", though he was doubtless relieved that the women were not asking to be taken on by the Metropolitan Police. He was, however, most averse from Nina Boyle, whom he considered "an intransigeante and in opposition to constituted authority"[11] and besides had made fools of his police on numerous occasions. But Commandant Damer Dawson reminded him that the suffragettes had signed a truce for the duration, and, somewhat mollified, he gave his permission. The Commissioner made no suggestions as to what work they could do but did give them the titles of text-books they could study and put them in touch with an ex-sergeant of his who drilled them and taught them to give evidence, render first aid, keep to beats and even practise a little ju-jitsu.[12] "The only attribute of a good officer we amateurs had any real trouble to acquire," said Mary Allen, "was the correct, slow police step."[13] Of course there is really no such thing: policemen merely learn to walk slowly to avoid tiring themselves out.

The intention of the WPV was to show how good they were so that police forces would then wish to take them on their staff,[14] and, while training, they continued their work with Belgian refugees and other women at railway stations and patrolled the streets giving help and advice to women and children.

The first person to appear in public in the WPV uniform was probably Edith Watson, who, in September 1914,[15] was still plugging away with her column, 'The Protected Sex'. Indeed Nina Boyle had insisted that an important part of the training should be learning details of police and criminal court procedures, the rules of evidence and the rights of the public, and she was keen that keeping a watching brief on the courts should be very much part of the new WPV duties. When Edith, a young married woman from an ordinary Cockney background who had educated herself, appeared in her full regalia at the Old Bailey, she attracted a great deal of attention and was photographed and interviewed by the gentlemen of the Press.[16]

Soon full uniform became the order of the day for most recruits. A new hat, designed by a friend of Damer Dawson, Miss St John Partridge, was brought into use for winter wear. It was "a ladies riding hat slightly modified", Damer Dawson said later. "We thought it would stand the weather and might stand a fairly sharp knock on the head if necessary."[17] They were ready for action. The question was, where?

Areas where huge army camps had been rapidly set up were soon having public order problems. They attracted many prostitutes, and even local girls were carried away by the sight of so many uniformed men who might brighten their limited lives. Unlike the wealthy, they often had nowhere private to fulfil the passions so aroused, so there was soon much 'public concern' about their activities.

It was largely this concern which prompted the arrival on the scene of yet another body of women with police duties in mind: the Voluntary Women Patrols. Initially supported by a mixed array of organizations, which included the Mothers' Union, the Church Army, the Girl's Friendly Society, the YWCA and the National Union of Women's Suffrage Societies, the backbone and main organizers were the National Union of Women Workers.[18] The latter were not quite so much of the proletariat as their name suggests and were certainly organized by largely upper- and middle-class women, most of whom did not need to work. They were, indeed, soon to change their name to 'The National Council of Women'.

Their president, Mrs Creighton, widow of a bishop of London, also became president of the Women's Patrol Committee. She had represented most of the aforementioned societies on the July 1914 deputation which pressed for the employment of women police and was a prominent member of the International Bureau for the Suppression of White Slave Traffic. She also liked giving talks on purity[19] and had been active against women's suffrage though had by now begun to modify her views on this a little.[20] The aims of the women patrols were unambiguous. They wanted to influence and, if need be, restrain the behaviour of women and girls who congregated in the neighbourhood of the camps and to safeguard "our girls from the results of the very natural excitement produced by the abnormal conditions now prevailing."[21] They had the support of the current Bishop of London who announced that it was women's duty to "send out the young men in the right spirit, free from moral stain". He had heard sad stories, though he believed many of them to be nonsense, of how women haunted the camps. He thought women should promote prayer, temperance and purity among the young men in training. And there were many soldiers' wives who were just now better off than they had ever been (separation allowances being often higher than their wages had been), and he had been told that there was increase of drinking among them. Here was work for women. Let them go among the wives of the men at the front, make friends with them and encourage them to save against coming times of difficulty.[22]

A question in rather sharper tones was put in Parliament by Lord C. Hamilton. He asked whether the Government would pass a measure empowering magistrates to issue warrants for the summary arrest of "women of notorious bad character who were infesting the neighbourhood of the various military camps." The Home Secretary replied that he recognized the serious nature of the evil to which the noble Lord alluded but feared it would be impossible to deal with it effectively by such legislation. They would have to rely on the organized efforts being made by voluntary women workers and on the firm enforcement of the existing law.[23]

Nina Boyle viewed the growing anti-female propaganda with alarm. She was already making speeches all over the country advocating the use of women police, and she soon began adding warnings against the moves men were making to curtail current 'problems'. She was not being alarmist. Her worst fears were soon realized when Plymouth Watch Committee proposed that the infamous Contagious Diseases Acts be revived.[24] Nina Boyle and Mrs Despard went straight to the Prime Minister. He could not see them, but they were received politely by Mr Bonham Carter, something that would never have happened a few months before. Eventually they were persuaded to lay the facts before him in writing, which they did. Nina Boyle suggested dryly that perhaps the soldiers themselves could be prevailed upon to exercise a little elementary self-control for a while, and that maybe their COs could call upon them to preserve discipline and good behaviour in camps, barracks and cantonments? Then she dashed off to wage war in Plymouth. The Plymouth Town Council eventually decided to defer the move 'for consideration', and the Prime Minister quickly assured the women they had nothing to fear – such a move would require an Act of Parliament. Danger had been averted.[25]

On 16th November 1914 Nina Boyle spoke stirringly at Sheffield on the need for vigilance over women's rights and the need for women police. The following day Grantham was treated to her rousing oratory.[26] Grantham had a large dose of the current problems due to the huge new Belton Park Camp which had suddenly swelled its population by twenty thousand. Now it just so happened that Damer Dawson's brother-in-law was a staff captain at Belton Park. Shortly afterwards the Women Police Volunteers received an invitation to send two of their women to Grantham.

3

Women in Uniform

Fellow-passengers stared uninhibitedly at the crisp navy blue uniforms worn by the three women leaving London by train one foggy November morning in 1914. Two of the women, Mary Allen and Ellen Harburn, wore the regulation pudding-basin-style hats designed by Miss St John Partridge, but the third, Margaret Damer Dawson, sported a peaked cap, as befitted her rank of Commandant.

When the news of the pending selection of two recruits for Grantham had leaked out, Mary had taken fright and absented herself from headquarters, but Damer Dawson had taken a liking to her and selected her in her absence.

The fifty-year-old Miss E. F. Harburn was another seasoned suffrage campaigner. From a middle-class Manchester family, she had been an intimate of the Pankhursts in the early days but had preferred democracy when the split came and had gone with the Women's Freedom League. Education was her particular province, having worked as a school manager for the LCC and been involved with schools for the deaf and mentally handicapped. As well as coping with a new job, the sensible, outspoken Ellen Harburn was also coping with a new surname: it had been Haarbliecher, but current violent anti-German feeling had forced a name change on her.[1]

The thick skins she and Mary Allen had acquired during their suffrage days were put to the test when they arrived at Grantham, where crowds gathered to gape in astonishment and inform them 'in trenchant terms', of their approval or otherwise. Mostly otherwise. They donned, Mary Allen reported, "the proscribed official demeanour of stony unconcern",[2] but their hearts were not lifted by the industrial squalor they perceived as they trudged through mud puddles and pouring rain en route to their lodgings, pursued by a crocodile of small boys and wondering adults.

The Chief Constable had told the women that he did not care what they did as long as they kept out of the way. The Provost Marshal at least greeted them kindly but gave them very vague instructions. They were to "keep an eye on alleys, courts, yards and passages" and the roads leading to the camp, where an amazing conglomeration of stalls and temporary shops had sprung up to serve the needs of the soldiery and where a lot of trouble occurred between customers and stallholders.

They soon found that, as Nina Boyle had suggested,[3] attitudes to service recruits in those early days of the war were very indulgent. Late one night, when Damer Dawson was driving home, she came across a helplessly drunk soldier propped up against a wall by his lamenting mother. As they managed him into her car, the mother told her, "He's like this almost every night, and the magistrate won't give him anything because he's a soldier!"[4]

At first, the new policewomen were too nervous to take any action, especially since their every move was monitored by the populace. Whenever they halted in one spot for a moment, a crowd would gather. But Ellen Harburn had been given an additional duty to 'keeping an eye' – the more concrete 'public house inspection'. A turning-point in their confidence came when she first put her instructions into practice, as Mary Allen related in her book *The Pioneer Policewoman*.

Wondering what her reception would be like, she entered in fear and trembling. Public houses, it may be inferred, had not entered into her previous experience. The necessity to conceal an extreme nervousness gave her manner an incisiveness not at all characteristic of her somewhat airy and inconsequential approach, and she was quick to perceive not only that she had impressed the publican but that he was, if anything, more frightened than she was, most anxious to meet her halfway, eager to demonstrate that all in his power was being done to keep his place in order. ... No resistance to the inspection was ever again anticipated, nor was any ever offered.

They were learning that the combination of uniform and the assumption of authority often worked even with no power to back it up. Confidence was the key. Confidence and class. For, another thing Mary had noticed, was that "the rougher elements of mankind are more easily controlled by women than the so-called upper classes". It did not seem to occur to her, however, that it was their education and class, not their sex, which made the working classes obey them. They found they often got short shrift when they tried to interfere in the pleasures of the officers.

So, armed with class, education, confidence and courage, they became quite successful in quelling the activities of the class of people who were meant to be quelled, but they also lent a guiding hand to drunken ladies who got into difficulties with squads of soldiers; looked for missing girls; gave advice to parents to keep their young daughters away from the camps, and patrolled the camp areas looking for those same young girls when they managed to get through to the danger area. The young girls were, in fact, the main reason they were there. Their financial support came from the local Association for the Help and Care of Girls.[5]

Meanwhile, Nina Boyle had discovered that the 'threat to women' had not quite been averted. It reasserted itself with a vengeance after the passing of DORA (the Defence of the Realm Act) which gave the military and police extraordinary powers. According to one contemporary commentator, "Dora was a very real and terrible person."[6] Local commanding officers, pressured by Press and Church to do something about the public order problems, got quite carried away with their new powers but brought them largely into play against women.

On 29th November, two days after the three women had left for Grantham, the following report appeared in the *People*:

OUT AFTER HOURS
Court Martial on Women at Cardiff
Yesterday a novel court martial was held at Cardiff, when five women of a certain class were tried under the Defence of the Realm Act, 1914, for being out of doors between the hours of 7 pm and 8 am – An order had been issued by Colonel East, commanding the Severn Defences, closing public houses in the city to women customers between the hours of 7 pm and 6 am. Accused women, who pleaded guilty, had been arrested in various parts of the city during prohibited hours.

Liable to Three Months
It was stated that officers who served notices upon the women read and explained the order to those who were themselves unable to read. "The president pointed out that the women were liable to punishment not exceeding three months' imprisonment. It was intimated that the sentences of the court would be submitted to the General commanding the district and would be promulgated in the due course, the women being meanwhile detained in custody."

And it was not just that they were not allowed in pubs during this period: they were not allowed out of their houses – a curfew! Nina Boyle was furious and immediately wrote a scathing leader in *The Vote*, heading it "The Prime Minister and 'a scrap of paper' ", which has a familiar ring. The scrap of paper to which she was referring was the one on which Asquith assured the Women's Freedom League that the Contagious Diseases Acts were not to be reintroduced. Now, she declared, here they were being reintroduced in a new form. She went on:

> The sight of women, and women whom a hypocritical cant calls 'unfortunate', tried by a court martial in England – all this distance from the seat of active operations; their poor rights snatched away from them, their persons pilloried in ways that no man consents to for his own sex, is utterly sickening and makes one wonder how military men can so degrade their uniform and stain their boasted record as 'officers and gentlemen'. Let us remember that, when the Criminal Law Amendment suggestions tried to provide more safety for girls of sixteen, gentlemen in office protested on behalf of men who might be blackmailed; but none of these gentlemen protest against power being put in the hands of men to blackmail girls to provide safety for – not boys of sixteen but grown men! The trade called 'unfortunate' was not called into being by women; no woman has contributed one penny to its profits; it has been defended, when its practice was convenient, as 'necessary' and has received official sanction, official protection from prosecution, and official encouragement of every sort.[7]

Now it just so happened that Brigadier General Hammersley, commanding officer at Belton Park Camp, liked the idea of a curfew for women of a certain class and copied it. Since he also liked the work being done by the Women Police Volunteers, he conferred upon them what Mary Allen termed "their first mark of confidence", to wit, the right to enter any house, building or land within six miles' radius of the Army Post Office. The purpose of these powers was, as Damer Dawson later admitted, "to help keep the girls in their houses". But even that, it seems, was not enough. They soon began accompanying the military on deserter raids into those houses. Mary Allen admits that they realized the opportunities this gave them "to acquire merit" and held that "no order, however distasteful, could be shirked". That too has a familiar ring. She graphically describes how: "Women answering the sharp military knock on their doors would assume an air of shocked and surprised indignation, vehemently denying that any men so much as crossed their thresholds, while dimly discernible in the background, huddled in some corner, would be overcoats, unmistakenly masculine and military. Myriads of nephews and first cousins sprang up, and were claimed by women or girls with angelic faces of injured innocence."[8]

They did not rely entirely on the military for seeking out immorality but instigated their own 'cases' as well. A WPV Report describes some of these:

(4) On visiting the house of a woman suspected of being of bad character, married, with seven children, whose husband is a soldier at the front, the policewoman found a soldier in the house. The woman was alarmed and promised to send the man away directly after supper. The policewoman left, but returned to the house at 11 pm, and, finding the man still there, drove him in front of them out of the house, cautioning him not to return.

(7) The policewomen observed a drunken soldier enter a house which they knew to be occupied by a woman whose husband had just left for the front. This house had been previously suspected by them. They fetched the military picket, who came at once to the house, and with some difficulty forced an entrance. The soldier was caught and arrested. Several children found in the house in a dirty and diseased condition were taken care of by the policewomen and handed over to the NSPCC inspector. The woman escaped before the picket could enter, by means of a trap-door which connected with three other houses, and has not yet been found.[9]

When the women's suffrage organizations found out about these activities, the WPV were 'much criticized'.[10] Nina Boyle was furious and demanded Damer Dawson's resignation. The Commandant defended herself, saying that by assisting with the curfew they could at least find out whether it was working and, if it was not, get it stopped. It did not work; the women were managing to get more men and drink into their houses than they would have done if they had been allowed out in the streets. They told the authorities this, and the ban was lifted, Damer Dawson later claimed.[11] But the lifting of the ban probably had as much to do with the furore created by Nina Boyle and Sylvia Pankhurst and the fact that it had been declared illegal.[12]

After it was all over, Nina Boyle still insisted that Damer Dawson resign. She refused and called a meeting of the corps, who were asked to vote on the issue. The Commandant had worked much more closely with the recruits than had Nina Boyle, and she was a leader who inspired great loyalty. What is more, she was doubtless sincere in her fight against prostitution, having seen the risks of social ostracism, the then much less curable venereal diseases and unwanted pregnancy. There was a strong element of patriotism in their actions too, but, strongest justification of all, those actions had secured some 'official recognition' they needed for their women police. On hearing of the possibility of their withdrawal from Grantham, Hammersley had written to them saying that he trusted this was not the case, since their services had proved of great value and they had removed sources of trouble to the troops in a manner that the military police could not attempt. Moreover, he had no doubt whatever that the work was a great safeguard to the moral welfare of young girls in the town.[13]

The vote brought overwhelming victory for Damer Dawson and a stunning defeat for Nina Boyle. Out of about fifty women, all except three voted for "co-operation with the men". These three were Nina Boyle, Edith Watson and Eva Christy.[14] Damer Dawson decided to drop the name 'Women Police Volunteers' and reform the group as 'The Women Police Service'.

Three months after the split, which occurred in February 1914, the Women Police Service were invited to send two of their members to Hull. Replacements were found for Mary Allen and Ellen Harburn at Grantham, and in May 1915 they left to blaze the trail once again. This time they were to be directly under the control of the Chief Constable who, shortly after their arrival, held a meeting in the Town Hall and handed over to them control of the forty-strong local women patrols already working there. "WOMEN POLICE. LONDON OFFICERS TO ORGANISE HULL FORCE," announced the *Eastern Daily Post* on 24th May 1915. A short, sharp message from the central Women's Patrol Committee 'deprecated' this move.[15]

Though not sworn in as constables, the women were allowed to arrest, charge and give evidence in cases concerning women, Mary Allen claims, but, whenever they exercised this power, excited crowds followed them.

Shortly after their arrival, the first Zeppelin raids took place, giving the Commandant "the first opportunity of testing the grit of the policewomen".[16] By all accounts the huge dirigibles were an awesome sight. In her second book, *Lady in Blue*, Mary Allen vividly describes the first raid:

... The first I knew of the trouble was that a girl on the opposite pavement stopped, stared up into the grey sky and shouted: "Look! There's an airship." Far above us, like a silver cigar, stately and almost motionless,

hovered the form of the Zeppelin. I recognized it from illustrations I had
seen but strove to still the stab of terror the sight gave me. Surely it could
not be a raider, here without opposition, just looking down on us like that?
It *must* be a British airship! ...

There came a muffled roar from a street a quarter of a mile away. The
first bomb! It seemed that the town was instantly full of screaming people,
running to and fro, pointing upwards and madly piling furniture and
knick-knacks out of windows and doors into prams and trucks and
handcarts. There came the whine and crash of another bomb. Already I
was running towards the place where I judged that the first explosion had
occurred, and soon I reached it. Some old houses had been blown down
across the street; already, policemen had drawn a cordon to prevent
people rushing in amongst the still smoking and collapsing ruins.

Outside the barrier of blue heaved a mass of struggling, screaming
people, some in aimless terror, some feverishly trying to escape with their
pitiful household goods. I was allowed because of my uniform to pass
through the police cordon and assist in picking up the writhing or still
figures among the dusty brickwork, and help in getting them to waiting
cars. Overhead, the Zeppelin had already disappeared.

The Women Police Service then tried to calm people who were
running in and out of the houses which were still intact, carrying piles
of furniture, food, clothing and toys.

"I saw one old lady start off down the street, half running, shoving
a bumping pram filled with salvage, perched on top of which was a
canary in a cage, shrilling wildly. The woman had left behind her,
whimpering at the door of the house she had just left, a tiny girl of two
or three years old. The canary was being saved, but her own
grandchild was forgotten!"

As the raids continued, though they were of course nowhere near as
frequent or destructive as those of the Second World War, this trend
grew. People felt safer in the open air, and when the sirens blared or a
raid was rumoured, out would come the prams and handcarts and off
they would rush to the parks, which soon became littered with birds in
cages, pictures, ornaments and bedding. Worse, "sleeping in crowds in
this haphazard fashion inevitably led to disorderly conduct" – which
the WPS did their best to curtail. They also concentrated on calming
and organizing the women and children during the raids and helped
to keep order once the euphorically relieved crowds returned home
afterwards.[17]

Even in this kind of work, their education stood them in good stead.
Once, when patrolling after a raid, they came across a knot of excited

people standing on a street corner and assured them it was now safe to return home as the Zeppelins had left, whereupon some soldiers remonstrated with them, pointing to a light in the sky which, they said, was obviously a bomb dropping. The educated policewomen were able to reassure them that it was not, in fact, any such thing. It was the planet Venus rising.[18]

4

On Patrol

In contrast to the WPS, who wanted to work full time and were prepared to go wherever they were sent, the women patrols of the NUWW were purely voluntary and were required to work locally for only two or three hours a week. They wore no uniform, merely 'dark and unobtrusive clothing', an armlet and a numbered badge around their left wrists.[1] Like the Women Police Volunteers, their leaders had contacted the Commissioner and asked his advice and help, adding that, should he sanction them, provincial Chief Constables would probably do the same. Very flattering, but it did not take into account the traditional attitude of most constabularies towards the Metropolitan Police, which would probably make them want to do the opposite.

The Commissioner agreed to help them and issued them with identification cards, similar to those given to the Women Police Volunteers, which requested police to render them any necessary assistance. Mrs Creighton then had "a very satisfactory interview" with the Home Secretary, Mr McKenna, who expressed great sympathy with their aims and promised to inform chief constables that he had no objection to them. He kept his promise and went further, telling the police chiefs that the NUWW organization was one "to command confidence" and that the Commissioner had arranged to sign their cards.[2]

Their reactions were mixed. J. Farndale of Bradford thoroughly disapproved, feeling that the women were "in great danger of being insulted by indecent loafers, if not outraged", but he signed just the same, as did most of the others.[3] The Chief Constable of Manchester adamantly refused to recognize women patrols and maintained this position throughout the war, while Reading's was finally induced to do so only if he could add to the cards, "I the undersigned, am in no way responsible for the conduct of this patrol," which did tend to invalidate them.[4] When the question of the employment of militant suffragists as women patrols arose, the central committee hedged a little. "The first responsibility of the selection of women patrols must rest with the local committees," they advised, but warned that "it would constitute a grave difficulty to appoint women as patrols who had been arrested and might consequently be objected to by the police." They were unequivocal about one issue: militant suffragists were *not* eligible for the posts of women patrol organizers.

In fact, the very appointment of paid organizers was reminiscent of suffragette tactics. Those of the NUWW were sent out to any of their branches considering starting women patrols. They were paid £3 a week, plus travelling expenses, and were expected to ask for 'local hospitality'. Mrs Creighton herself offered to pay the salary of the first appointee, Mrs Hartwell, but the others were to be paid for by the central Women's Patrol Committee, who had already raised £1,500 from an early appeal in *The Times*.[5]

Mrs Hartwell went to Grantham on 27th October 1914 but must scarcely have had time to get her patrols going before the fully-trained Women Police Volunteers appeared on the scene a month later. Dublin and Cape Town were also among the first cities to ask for organizers. Soon Dublin was reporting unspecified 'difficulties', but the central committee must have known what they were for they advised that the Dublin patrols should always be two-thirds Catholic "to overcome the religious difficulty".

Despite strong backing from religious bodies as a whole and the Bishop of London in particular, not all clergymen gave their blessing, as the *Daily Express* reported on 3rd November 1914: "The organization of women patrols is warmly opposed by the Vicar of Southport, the Rev. W. Hodgson. 'Surely,' he says, 'This is an unnecessary precaution, which is un-English, and savours of German espionage, besides interfering unduly with the liberty of the subject. Much better to appeal to mothers to guard their daughters against all possible dangers and temptation, and to instil into them true ideals of modesty and self restraint'." Nevertheless, *The Times* was soon reporting that the women patrols acted "quietly and without parade", which was to be expected since they were "directed by a committee of ladies experienced in social work". The report also mentioned the clubs and guilds which had been opened by them.[6] This was a sensible early move since there were few places of amusement for the young, especially the poor young.

Mrs Carden, the central committee's Hon. Sec., followed Mrs Creighton's lead and kept the Home Secretary respectfully informed of their work, emphasizing that it was preventative and not rescue, and that women of all classes were needed.[7] She also began sending him copies of their monthly *Extracts from Organisers' Reports*, many of which concerned the efforts of the patrols to separate young girls from the company of soldiers – though not always soldiers:

> Two of our Patrols went on duty at 8 pm; they were walking on one of the paths when a military policeman came to them evidently very perturbed, he said he had been watching a couple (man a civilian) for some time, and would the lady patrols try to get the girl away?
>
> The Patrols thought they must do what they could, so went to the place pointed out by the MP. They found the couple indicated partly screened by bushes but with other couples all around and in a disgraceful position. After a time they moved off, the patrols followed them, after a long tramp traced the girl to her home. The young man took her to the end of the street where a young sister met her, at 8.30, when the patrols passed this same place they noticed that all the couples, though lying on damp grass, were in decorous attitudes. The two patrols are high-minded women, fond of girls and anxious to help them. Some patrols might have caused a disturbance; I also fear that some of them are inclined to dwell too much on the seamy side, and unless they see evil, imagine they are doing no good. The girl mentioned above will be looked after by a Rescue Worker.

The reports also mentioned that some soldiers brought girls to them when they thought they needed guidance and that parents, who at first thought them "interfering toads", soon changed their minds and felt "it rather wonderful that we should leave our homes and go about so quiet and ladylike and that there must be some need for the work, so they set about keeping their girls at home in the evenings."

Some of the clubs also featured in the reports: "The Recreation Room, or Flag Club as it is called, averages ninety-six per week. Dumb-bell drill, singing, Folk and Morris Dancing are being taught on different nights. Letter-cases for soldiers have been made and most successful bandage rolling parties have been held. Some of the girls have been taught to cut out and make blouses." There were even one or two mixed clubs which, one organizer admitted, were badly needed, though the difficulty in their particular case was "the poverty of the Town, as it depends on its fish trade and that has entirely stopped for this year at any rate".[8]

Soon the public became confused by the proliferating 'women police' organizations. This confusion was not alleviated by their attempts to co-operate or by the formation of the Bristol Training

School for both women patrols and women police. Though the latter was formed by the Bristol women patrols, Damer Dawson was invited to sit on their board, and their leaders, Miss Joseph, Mrs Gent and Miss Peto, went to London to observe WPS training and work.[9]

On 12th March 1915 even the central Women's Patrol Committee decided to ask Damer Dawson to join them. But a little later, when, through 'some misunderstanding', the invitation had not been sent out, they decided to drop the idea on the grounds that there was already too much confusion in the public mind, which might be why they were currently suffering from lack of response to their Press Appeals. They also decided to hold a meeting at the Mansion House in the cause of general public enlightenment.

But it was not just the public who were confused. When Damer Dawson wrote asking permission to speak to women and girls in Hyde Park,[10] a local police inspector commented fractiously that, when they had been allowed into the park to patrol, they had undertaken to speak only to young girls. Now they wanted to take on women.[11] In fact it was the women patrols who had made this undertaking "to befriend those young girls who are excited by the abnormal conditions of the moment and whose efforts to attract the attention of soldiers have already brought them into contact with the police".[12] Superintendent Wells, an old campaigner from the days of the militant suffragists, recommended that the WPS should not be given permission to speak to women but be left to act on their own responsibility, which they were.[13]

Complaints soon began to come in from the recipients of all this concern. One alleged that the women patrols had been "flashing electric torches in the faces of respectable persons sitting on seats in Hyde Park after dark" and another that, when a woman was waiting for her naval officer husband outside Crystal Palace, she was stopped by two patrols who asked her if she was going to meet a sailor. The Women Police Service were accused of stopping a fourteen-year-old girl and telling her she ought not to crimp her hair and put her hat on straight. They also admonished her, it was alleged, for "dressing herself up and walking about to attract the attention of men".[14]

The women patrols were determined to learn from experience and were soon sending out private and confidential 'hints and suggestions'. These had largely been culled from organizers' reports, and in them the branches were reminded that, when speaking of the work, they must make it clear that it was rescue and not detective and aimed solely at befriending girls. Their leaders clearly had their image well in mind when they added: "It is most desirable that the patrol leader should keep in touch with the local clergy of all denominations, with the Chief Constable, the Commanding Officer, the Chaplain to the Forces, the Town Clerk, the Medical Officer of Health for the District, the Vigilance Associations, the Rescue Workers and the Presidents and Secretaries of all social organizations." Surprisingly, Sunday opening for clubs was advised wherever possible, on the grounds that many girls and men who never entered a church would go to a club, and a quiet evening with singing, talks and a few prayers had been found most attractive.

One hint suggested that they had certainly learned from their Hyde Park complaints – when patrolling after dark, the use of lanterns rather than flashlights was recommended. As for work, visiting of questionable places of amusement and reporting on any harmful entertainments was one idea put forward, as was patrolling the local railway station if the station master was in agreement.[15] Dorothy Peto, in her memoirs, tells of doing such duty at the request of the railway authorities in Bristol:

> On the station, we dealt with girls stranded for the night or loitering there for amusement; with distressed women seeing their husbands, sons or sweethearts off to the front, and other similar predicaments. At the weekends, our tour of duty was extended to 1.30 am, so as to enable us to cope with the noisy throngs who came to see off the midnight leave-trains, and whose emotions found vent, as the time drew on, in last drinks from beer bottles, and in dancing 'Knees up, knees up Mrs Brown' in serried ranks across the platform.
>
> When the train itself drew in, the stalwart patrols picked for this duty took up strategic position at the edge of the platform ready, when the train moved out and hysterical women – and even men – leaped onto the footboards for a last farewell, to seize and drag them back by main force to safety ... The only disaster which we could neither foresee nor prevent was the shooting of a woman by her husband or sweetheart one night from a departing train; on which occasion the patrols on duty found themselves witnesses at his subsequent trial for murder.

By 1916 the organizers' reports began to show that women were experiencing some difficulties due to their lack of official status, power and uniform. One organizer asked permission to adopt a uniform hat of black felt with the letters 'WP', 'Women Patrols', thereon. At a cost of only three shillings it would be, she declared, a great help in all the work. Another commented that, when they spotted girls and servicemen secreted in doorways, they would take up positions on nearby kerbs, maybe even with their backs towards the couple but *where their armbands could be seen.* This usually worked, and the couple moved off. They began to cling to any small mark of authority. One reported: "I would like to emphasize the importance that the Badge gives us, and its usefulness time after time. I notice that couples move on as soon as they see we are officials."[16]

The working classes were becoming less cowed as the life expectancy of the men shortened and the independence of the women grew. The Bristol Training School instruction booklet contained the following good advice: "If you tell a group of bystanders to move on, don't look back to see if you have been obeyed."[17]

By 1916 heartening evidence of more interest in child welfare also began to emerge. Several of the patrols were distressed to see so many children wandering around late at night, and that begging and child labour was so prevalent. In one case, crowds of children would beg stale bread from factory workers as they poured out of the gates at the end of the day, and many children were selling papers in the streets until 11 pm. "Two small boys of eight and nine years were found selling papers outside a wine shop one bitterly cold night (it was January), very ragged and without shoes and stockings." The patrols would attempt to see the parents and put the children in touch with a Sunday school and possibly inform the NSPCC. In one area they toyed with the idea of taking a large hall and holding "an attractive service" to cope with the crowds of over-tens wandering around late on Sunday evenings.

The growth of clubs continued apace: "The club has proved a success and filled a great need. ... The girls gave a splendid Xmas party to twenty-five wounded soldiers, they gave a very nice entertainment, collected and gave a gift of fruit and tobacco to every man, the whole tone was excellent." One branch even inaugurated "Pleasant evenings for Women". The primary object of these was to encourage thrift, but since they thought this subject would be distasteful to many of the women they wished specially to reach, they wrapped up their "friendly little talks" among musical items, patriotic songs with a chorus and talks on 'Life in the Colonies' and 'Women under Turkish Rule'. The latter had the added advantage, it was felt, of enlarging the outlook of the women and widening their interests.

The reports which Mrs Carden passed on to the Home Office always contained a good sprinkling of quoted complimentary remarks made by members of the public about the women patrols. "The country cannot afford to do without women patrols now," said one, "they made an incalculable difference to the state of the streets." Judges and police officers were also apparently showing their appreciation. One Chief Constable went so far as to say, "I do not know what we shall do when you ladies give up your work," and went on to add the hope that they were forerunners of trained women. Conveniently, and perhaps I am doing them an injustice here, these quotes, like all of the reports, were from unnamed sources and venues.[18]

Pressure for some official women police continued, mainly from the Women Police Service and their friends, and the Church. In July 1916 Frank W. Perkins MP, who had been on the 1914 deputation for women police and was a persistent fighter in the cause, wrote to the Home Secretary setting out a long memorandum on the reasons women police should be appointed, sworn in and given power of arrest. He recommended that provision for such appointment could be made in the Police Miscellaneous Provisions Act then before Parliament. The reply of the Home Secretary (by then Sir Herbert Samuel) pointed out that the women did, in fact, already have considerable powers of arrest, as did all members of the public. He admitted that there were many offences not covered by these general powers but thought that it would not be helpful to women to give them powers which they would be physically incapable of exercising. He also felt that it would be repugnant to human nature to expect women to be exposed to the same risks as men. But the Home Office obviously knew that they were going to have to make some concessions and had already culled a run-down on the current 'women police organizations' from the Commissioner's reports and had acquired a memo on the subject from Sir Leonard Dunning, HM Inspector of Constabulary.

From the former they concluded that the Women Police Service performed similar duties but aimed at 'covering more ground' than the patrols of the NUWW whose work was strictly preventative. The Commissioner is quoted as saying that they should amalgamate with the women patrols, "whose governing body are wise enough to realize the limitations that should be put on the activities of their patrols". The WPS were mostly militant suffragettes, the report stressed, and their aspirations were much more ambitious than those of the NUWW. In fact, the former were "anxious to take on the duties of a constable and to have powers of arrest".

Sir Leonard Dunning felt that all the women had exaggerated ideas of the powers of police.[19] This was probably true – most members of the public are similarly misinformed even today – and the WPS at least had some good reason for their impression, many of them having seen police use the law as they saw fit when dealing with suffragettes. In fairness, one must admit that many policemen protected suffragettes from mob violence.[20] But the excessive powers DORA had bestowed on police and military must also have consolidated this notion.

Naturally the women patrols emerged from this examination as the softer option. They were less ambitious, easier to control – and get rid of – but they had recently informed the Commissioner that, unless they received some financial support soon, they might have to withdraw. When the 1916 Police Act was finally passed, it included a clause allowing for the employment of women on police duties. The Commissioner immediately announced that, with Home Office permission, he was going to employ a few women patrols, part-time, in an endeavour to check unseemly conduct in the Royal Parks and to assist him in making enquiries into the machinery for the sale of cocaine among women and soldiers.[21]

The central Women's Patrol Committee thought this a compliment, but they were not as unambitious for the appointment of women police as the men believed. They duly noted in their minutes the danger of paid patrols being considered an answer to the demand for women police but thought it advisable to run the risk in the hope that it would ultimately lead to such an appointment.

The new Special Patrols did not wear uniform, but their armlets were replaced by those of the regular police. Nor did they have any power of arrest, but they did acquire one entirely new accoutrement: a real live constable to escort them through the streets.[22]

5

Prudery and Prurience

Shortly after the inauguration of the Special Patrols, two of them, Mrs Bagster and Mrs Summerton, were patrolling Hyde Park with their escort constable when they came upon a shocking scene. A young man lying straddled on the ground while an older man leaned over him committing 'an act of gross indecency'. The offenders were duly arrested.

Acts of gross indecency between males were a bugbear to the Hyde Park police. About seventy-five per cent of the cases they brought were dismissed by the jury, due to the difficulty of convincing them "that such acts do take place in the open spaces of the Metropolis".[1]

If such acts were unbelievable to the twelve men on the jury (no women were allowed), they must have come as a double shock to Mrs Bagster and Mrs Summerton, but this was an opportunity to help the police, and they did not shirk it. They declared themselves willing, no – anxious, to attend court and give evidence.

There was only one problem. The magistrate who was to hear the case was Frederick Mead. After the arresting PC had completed his evidence, he told Mr Mead that there were two further witnesses, both of them women patrols. There is no record of Mead's initial response to this information, but we do know that he refused to hear the women, commenting that the prisoners had made no defence and had practically pleaded guilty. They had not, in fact, pleaded guilty, and he must have known that vigorous defences have a way of suddenly appearing once the case has reached the higher court whence this one was heading.

Mrs Hartwell, then the organizer of the London women patrols, promptly wrote to the Commissioner, Sir Edward Henry, and asked his advice. Sir Edward, in turn, consulted one of his Chief Constables, who asked the advice of the senior police officers in the areas where this offence most frequently took place. The Sub Divisional Inspector at Hyde Park was in no doubt: the women should be allowed to give evidence. They were both 'women of a mature age', and their statements, he felt, would have a powerful effect on the minds of the jury and probably secure a conviction. His Superintendent agreed; indeed he felt it was their duty to give evidence even though the details of such cases were usually "of an extremely unsavoury character".

Overwhelming evidence was necessary in such cases, the SD Inspector at Gipsy Hill commented. Moreover, he had always found Women Patrols very keen and willing to assist police: "They have attended court in this District in minor charges where women have been concerned: but up to the present have not been connected with more serious offences," but he saw no reason why they should not be.

It was not only the women patrols who culled a vote of confidence from this round-up. SD Inspector Jackson of Richmond said that they had no women patrols, but they did have policewomen belonging to the Women Police Service (one of them was Mary Allen's sister, Mrs Hampton), and he was sure they would not shrink from doing their duty, however repugnant, even if it meant stating in public details of filthy conduct. His Superintendent also felt that they should be heard even "on matters of a revolting nature". After all, they had known what they were letting themselves in for, and it was a sign of the times that work properly falling to men was being performed by women, "often with satisfactory results".

Harrow Road's Divisional Detective Inspector sent a reasoned report. It was up to the magistrate to decide whether he had heard enough evidence to send a case for trial, but persons placed in the witness box by police were usually heard, *except* in a case of such revolting details and where the witness was a woman. However, he also found it extremely difficult to convince jurymen "that men exist capable of committing such filthy acts", and, moreover, prisoners had able counsel to defend them. The difficulty could be got round, he suggested, by taking statements from the women patrols and handing them to the magistrates. His Superintendent felt very differently. He came out solidly behind Mr Mead, who had taken a very proper view of the matter. It was not desirable, he insisted, "to encourage women patrols to mix themselves up in these filthy cases". From his experience, women police were anxious to get themselves before magistrates only for the notoriety it brought them.

Sir Edward replied to Mrs Hartwell that the women would be allowed to give evidence at the Old Bailey in this case, and in any future cases the services of the police solicitors would be retained at Magistrates Court in any such case with women patrol witnesses.

Mr Mead was very much offended by this and had his clerk write to Chief Constable Major M.H. Tomlin, saying that he felt himself "in a certain atmosphere" about this, since the police order about the police solicitors had been issued "as a sort of sequel" to a case of his. Would Major Tomlin go to see him to clear it up? Major Tomlin did, and Mr Mead climbed down, telling him that if the women wished to justify their employment by being seen and heard in the witness box, he could, on occasion, take their evidence. "To be frank," Major Tomlin reported, "I think Mr Mead felt a little hurt, as he considered that his discretion was in some way questioned, and his dignity is ruffled." The women won that time, but they had made themselves an implacable enemy.

It is interesting to see how emotive was the language used by men on this subject even in official police reports. Prudishness is an accusation often levelled at the women of this time, and particularly the women patrols and WPS, but, if they were prudish, it is clear they were not alone.

To add a certain piquancy to the whole affair, several days after this incident a Mrs Salisbury and Miss Peebles reported for patrol duty at Hyde Park and enquired whether it was now considered necessary for them to attend court in cases of indecency. When told it was, they complained that they would not have come if they had known that, since they could not attend court but, as they were there, they might as well do a last evening's patrolling, as long as it was understood that they were to be kept out of any indecency charge. A constable accompanied them.

At 10.30 pm, ten minutes before the two ladies were due to go off duty, they came upon a soldier and a Harrod's clerk (female) having sexual intercourse. The constable duly arrested the couple, but, when the Station Sergeant tried to put the names of the women patrols down on the charge sheet as witnesses, they again protested that they could not attend court. Later the Acting Superintendent commented sourly that, unless they were prepared to attend court, the usefulness of the women patrols would be greatly impaired.[2] It is not clear whether Miss Peebles and Mrs Salisbury were Special or Voluntary Women Patrols. It seems likely that they were the latter, since they were unable to attend court; however the presence of the constable does put this in some doubt.

At about this time, the Special Patrols received an unexpected boost from a very unexpected quarter. As Sir Herbert Samuel, the Home Secretary, wrote to the Commissioner:

Lady Minto saw me last week at the Queen's request about the question of prostitution. You may like to see a copy of the statement I have sent her for the Queen's information. From what Lady Minto told me and from what I have heard from other quarters, I gather this question is being very much discussed at the present time, and there is a strong feeling that the police ought to be able to do more to check the evil. There was a proposal to hold a large meeting in the Albert Hall to call public attention to the matter, and no doubt the police would have come in for unmerited blame. Fortunately, this proposal has been dropped. One must not attach too much importance to unreasoning and unreasonable criticism, but I think public feeling would be reassured if some steps could be taken. I should be disposed to try the effect of employing a much larger number of women patrols in London, as, even if the experiment were not entirely successful, it would at least give women the opportunity of helping to cope with an evil which concerns their own sex as much as men. I notice you recently obtained sanction to pay a few women patrols, but I understand that you do not propose to employ more than about six. This seems to me far too small a number for a large area like London, and I should be disposed to try the experiment on a much bolder scale, by employing fifty or even a hundred women if you could find so many with suitable qualifications. Will you think this over and let me have your views as soon as you come back?[3]

The comment about the numbers was scarcely fair, since it was the Commissioner who had initiated their employment in the first place but, obviously, Sir Herbert needed someone to blame.

'Sitting in' at courts was a standard part of the training of both women patrols and the WPS, but, even after agreeing to hear some of the evidence of women patrols, Mr Mead's attitude to this did not change. He did not want females in his court during the hearings of 'charges of indecency'. He was not the only one. WPS Inspector Harburn had come up against this problem when she first went to Hull. She had been so interested in a court's proceedings that when the familiar call "All females out of court!" went up, she had not, she later claimed, realized it was directed at her and her trainees and sat on despite growing clamour. Eventually they were forced to leave but promptly complained to the Chief Constable, who gave them permission to remain in the future.[4] Mr Mead was not to prove so easy.

He made it plain that he was not worried about the effect of the proceedings on the women concerned. As he later pointed out: "They have already, in taking up this peculiar work, sterilized any maiden modesty they may have had."[5] He just thought it unpleasant and embarrassing for himself and the rest of the men in court to have these matters discussed in the presence of women. So when, in September 1916, the trainees began sitting in on indecency cases at Marlborough Street, there was a rumpus.

On the first occasion, he called them up to the witness box and questioned them, demanding to know by what right they were there. When they produced their cards and said they were in training, he expressed surprise that the Commissioner should sanction such a thing. He was particularly offended by the uniform of the Women Police Service, with its Sam Browne belt, whistle and black felt hat.

What particularly offended the women patrol concerned was that the Press, in reporting the incident, mixed them up with the Women Police Service! Mrs Carden promptly wrote to the Commissioner, pointing out that the women patrol "takes great exception to it". She had told her that she could do nothing about it: the usher had *distinctly* told the magistrates there were Women Police and women patrols, but the reporter had made a mistake. However, she had promised to write and ask his advice as to "making the magistrate aware that you were employing women patrols for this special sort of work particularly in Hyde Park".[6] Clever Mrs Carden.

In fact Mr Mead must have known about women patrols, after all the correspondence and interviews with regard to their giving evidence. Nonetheless, he was reminded, in a rather clever way, when *The Times* of 1st November 1916 reported:

WOMEN PATROLS IN HYDE PARK
Major Parsons, Chief Constable, Metropolitan Police, recently gave instructions to the Women Patrols who are being employed by the Commissioner to do special work in Hyde Park and other open spaces. He said, the Commissioner desired him to express appreciation of the work of the patrols, adding that they were especially deserving as the particular work in which they were engaged demanded exceptional tact, perspicuity and above all common sense. He referred also to the police court cases in which they had given evidence, mentioning that in one case praise had been accorded by the magistrate.

That was clear enough, but it made no difference. On 28th November, possibly encouraged by a current WPS publicity stunt which had enraged the police, Mr Mead wrote to the Commissioner complaining of the continued presence in his court of women "wearing a uniform imitating that of a police constable", and asserting that not only were they not qualified to become constables by virtue of their sex (this applied to women as solicitors, the Law Society had decided, so must apply even more so to women as constables), they were probably committing a criminal offence by purporting to be so. Of course he was right in that the legal position of the women was anomalous.[7]

Sir Edward Henry replied soothingly, saying he gave great weight to anything the learned magistrate said but adding that these were not normal times and it was best not to be too hasty in any actions they took. Mr Mead thought this answer very evasive and that Sir Edward was just trying to divert the attentions of militant suffragettes by letting them be policewomen.[8]

Ten days later, women patrols were present when a PC stated that a prostitute had shouted, "You fuck off!" at him, as prostitutes are wont to do. This was too much for Frederick Mead, who, immediately after sentencing the woman to a month's hard labour, called up the senior of the women present and asked her if she thought it benefited these young women to be brought there to listen to such "filthy and disgusting cases". She told him they were recruits, learning how to give evidence.

"I don't know what position you represent," he went on, "You represent to the public by your armlet that you are a constable, but you are not."

"We work with the police."

"I should have thought you would not have these young folk here to listen to this filth. How old are they?"

"One of them is thirty."

"Whatever the age, I should have thought your natural instinct would have revolted against a matter of this kind."

"Shall I remove them?"

"Please yourself about that. You can stay in court or leave."

"I am only obeying orders in coming here," she insisted, then left with her brood.[9]

Within a couple of weeks Mead was going to be even more embarrassed but, to his delight, was given reason to complain. Witnesses who have not yet given evidence in a case must stay outside the court until called, but Miss Freda Mackenzie, of the women patrols, was obviously unaware of this, for when she came forward, Mr Mead exclaimed, "This witness has been sitting in the court!" She was, however, allowed to give evidence, after which the magistrate took the opportunity to cross-question her about her duties and official position. But there was another woman witness, Mrs Frazer, who had remained outside court. Now Mrs Frazer was a less experienced witness than the PC but more graphic. While he had described the position of the accused and the disarray of their clothing, from which he deduced they were having sexual intercourse, Mrs Frazer added their *movements*: "backwards and forwards". Mr Mead's reaction to this shocking disclosure by one of these "abnormal women who seem to suffer from some sort of moral obliquity"[10] was to discharge the case, despite three eye-witnesses.[11]

6

Guarding the Munitionettes

At the end of 1915 Mrs Edith Smith, the policewoman who had replaced Mary Allen in Grantham, was sworn in and given power of arrest, making her the first official policewoman in the British Isles. Her acceptance onto the force proper was the result of a meeting at which Commandant Damer Dawson read a report of activities in Grantham and the local Bishop declared that policewomen deserved to be supported nationally and not just by local donations. The Chief Constable was also present, and he agreed, adding that he would like to take Mrs Smith on in an official capacity, and this he did after obtaining the permission of the Town Council and Watch Committee.[1]

The *Grantham Journal* felt that policewomen were "a distinct advantage to the town".[2] Certainly it was fortunate in acquiring someone of Mrs Smith's calibre. Dorothy Peto, who spent three weeks in her company when she went to London to observe WPS training and work, found her to be a woman of outstanding personality, fearless, motherly and adaptable. She tells how, when Edith Smith found couples wrapped around each other in the grass of Hyde Park, she would point out the dangers (which were then, of course, considerable) with motherly frankness and appeal to the men to be chivalrous towards the girls. Her manner was such, Miss Peto claims, as to make this perfectly acceptable, and they would respond with thanks and desist.[3]

Leonard Dunning, HM Inspector of Constabularies, said this swearing-in was not legal but, as I have pointed out, the constabularies are traditionally independent and were then more so. Even today the Home Office plays a mainly advisory role and usually has only the final say in matters of State security. The only real threat the Home Office can hold over constabularies is a curtailment of their government grant towards costs, but they do this only in extreme circumstances. The exception is the Metropolitan Police, which the

Home Office controls directly in lieu of a local police authority. This constabulary independence allows flexibility to local needs, but it also encourages extreme conservatism in some forces and daring innovation in others, according to the calibre of the men in control and their local police authorities. It is also liable to produce God-like tendencies in Chief Constables, and every now and then one of them is charged with corruption or misuse of funds, offences brought on as often by vanity as by greed. But, with the right sort of man, it can encourage enlightened progress – not that Dunning thought this was the case at Grantham. He felt that the Chief Constable had fallen into "the hands of some strong ladies" and added, defamatorily, "His senior woman police is perhaps a better man than he is." But the remark was safely under cover of a Home Office memo.[4]

The inauguration of the Special Patrols was an undoubted advance for the NUWW woman patrols, but the WPS received another opportunity to show their mettle at about the same time, in mid-1916. It was, however, a much more barbed opportunity.

Lloyd George, then Minister of Munitions, asked the Commissioner's assistance in forming a corps of trained policewomen to help control the rapidly increasing numbers of women workers in the munitions factories. Sir Edward, probably seeing a way to get the WPS out of his hair, passed the request on to Margaret Damer Dawson. She accepted the challenge immediately and entered into a most extraordinary agreement to supply, train and uniform 140 women, without any financial aid, for the first six months of the operation. Once they had trained the women and "proved the trustworthiness of the force", they would get some money, the Ministry told them.

Forty of the women were to go to a factory at Queensferry in Chester and the remaining hundred to the huge munitions township being erected on the Scotland/England border at Gretna. Around 3,500 people were to be employed there. Of these, over one thousand were construction workers and thirteen hundred women.

One of their main duties was to search the women workers going into the factories for cigarettes, pen-knives and hair pins, all apparently dangerous near explosives. They searched them again on their way out, looking this time for 'keepsakes' such as unexploded shells or cordite, which they were reputed to eat![5] Curbing 'larking about' in the vicinity of the explosives was also one of their duties, and, while on these patrols, they soon found themselves taking on many other duties: investigating petty thefts, acting as mother confessors to the young girl workers and keeping an eye open for a deepening in their already yellow skins, which signalled that they were about to be overcome by the cordite fumes.

It was difficult to persuade women operatives to keep their long hair covered. In her second book, *Lady in Blue*, Mary Allen relates with some relish the tale of a girl who, through letting her hair slip out from under her mob-cap,

... suffered for her omission by getting that hair caught in some whirling machinery. Before the scream of her neighbour at the bench had ended, before the victim had been dragged completely off her feet and while her head was still several inches from the pitiless whirring wheels, a policewoman had gripped the hair and cut it free with a slash from her clasp knife. Rescuer and rescued fell in a heap on the floor, while the machinery, giving a disappointed grind and grate, hungrily dragged the fair hair among its wheels and tore it tress from tress. But for the intervention that might have cost the policewoman her hands, or her life, had things gone wrong, those wheels would by that time have been cutting flesh and tissues into bits instead of hair.

Patrolling the perimeters of the township, six miles from end to end, and completely blacked out, the policewomen soon found that they needed powerful 'bull-dog lanterns', which turned out to be especially useful in guiding drunken navvies, still building the place, down the unlit steps of their canteen, to the cry of, "Lady Poleesh – God blesh them!" They also needed "good strong truncheons" in case they came upon burglars, snoopers around the women workers' hostels or the ever-expected spies, and their dress boots were soon found to be totally inadequate to cope with the ankle-deep mud and slush. As soon as they could, they changed them for 'K shooting boots and leggings' which were much more satisfactory. But, in November 1916 Damer Dawson wrote to the Commissioner in, for her, a rather wistful tone: "The weather conditions are very severe for patrolling work in the north, and we find it difficult to provide our women with rainproof clothes and boots. The things usually made for women are quite useless in such incessant rain."[6]

The policewomen worked in shifts of varying duration; 6 am to 4 pm; 10 am to 7 pm or 3 pm to 10.30 pm. In the evenings some of them patrolled Carlisle or looked after the 'women's side' of the police station office there.[7]

Their one-sided agreement with the Ministry of Munitions placed a huge financial burden on the WPS, especially since, with such large numbers needed, they could no longer restrict recruiting to women of private means. And the 'council of three' – Damer Dawson, Mary Allen and Isobel Goldingham, another ex-suffragette – had to devote so much of their time to selection, training and administering their new force that there was precious little time left for fund-raising speeches and 'at homes'. It was a bad time for them in another respect. They were great publicists but often went too far. On 26th November 1916 a long piece headed "WOMEN'S WEST END NIGHT PATROLS: How they are 'Cleaning the Streets'," appeared in the *Weekly Dispatch*:

Every night at eight o'clock a small procession starts out from the headquarters of the Women's Police Service in Little George Street, London. It is a quiet, unobtrusive procession, two or three women in neat, dark blue uniforms and a dozen or so girls plainly dressed and bearing on their arms a band marked WPS.

The procession disperses as the various omnibuses come rumbling along in the gloom, one group going up Piccadilly, another to Paddington, another to some other part of darkest London. These are the women police sergeants and the new recruits who are being enrolled daily.

"I think you had better go with Sergeant P to Leicester Square," said the Superintendent when I told her I wanted to join a policewoman who was patrolling the streets. So, with Sergeant P and two tall young recruits, I started out from the headquarters. Sergeant P's hair is turning grey, but her eyes are childlike in their clear blueness. They are keen eyes, too, and they look unflinchingly at life in Leicester Square – and unflinchingly into the eyes of those poor girls who only come out into the streets at night and walk up and down, up and down, watching, waiting, ready to seize opportunity, quick to evade detection.

WIT AGAINST WIT

There are young girls of seventeen and women over thirty. Some are well-dressed, some much over-dressed, some poorly clad, yet with pitiful efforts at coquetry in their gay hats and the vivid flowers which fasten the little fur pieces round their necks.

It is woman's wit against woman's wit in Leicester Square now. There is the pale, shadowy little street-walker and the resolute little sergeant. Let a gay young soldier or a rollicking sailor boy speak to one of the shadows, and the sergeant is there, motionless, but sternly chaperoning – and over and over again the soldier and sailor walk away. The presence of that other woman is more than they can face.

"Don't these women ever resent your presence here? Don't they ever insult you?" I asked.

"No," said the little sergeant cheerfully. "Some of them tell us we have ruined their chances on this beat, but I know most all of them now and they know me. I have got work for several of them who used to come, and they are doing well, I'm glad to say. And there are others I have taken to the Church Army shelter, when they had not the price of a night's lodgings, and others I have taken home when they were intoxicated and helpless. Many of them have children, you know, and I go to see them occasionally. Oh, we are on good terms, though we do not speak to each other here at night."

THE NURSES

"Those who wear nurses' uniform are the worst of all," said the sergeant, and she pointed out two tall, handsome girls in dark blue capes and floating veils. "Those are two well-known women in Leicester Square, but when they speak to a young officer he takes them for two pretty nurses out for a lark. It is such a shocking thing that nurses are not registered and that many of the women of the street can masquerade in a costume which should be respected."

It was a kaleidoscopic four hours from eight to twelve. Never did the sergeant rest or pause except when she stood by some girl who was talking to a soldier until he or she walked away, or when she spoke quietly to some boy, warning him as he hesitated as to whether or not he should follow one of the pathetic painted phantoms in the square.

Now we paced Leicester Square, now Piccadilly Circus; now we walked through the tube station, now lingered outside it. Now we watched a restaurant, from which came loud laughter; now we went up a gloomy side street where the houses seemed to send forth from their darkened windows an atmosphere of evil. Several of these houses where young soldiers and sailors were drugged and robbed, have been closed, thanks to the watchfulness of the policewomen, but there are still streets which could be cleaned up to the advantage of London.

M.R.

This was the publicity stunt of which Mr Mead probably took advantage, for the Home Office and police were furious. Messages flew back and forth demanding reports and explanations from Vine Street Police Station. Their faces were particularly red since, in common with the rest of the Metropolitan Police, they had just submitted numbers and reports of activities of WPS and women patrols in their area and had said that there were in fact no members of the former working in the West End. They had noted that six women patrols occupied themselves "watching the action of street-walking women", but that is all.

Two days after the publication of the article, the Superintendent was prevailed upon to submit a more thorough report, and this one said that for some time about six women had been seen nightly, some in uniform and some in private attire, but wearing detachable badges. He did not know under what authority they acted since they had never approached police for assistance or to tell them what they were doing.

He strenuously disagreed with many of the claims of the article, particularly that of closing houses in side streets. These people, he declared, were taking on themselves credit which was due entirely to the efforts of police. Indeed, he was of the opinion that to some extent the women patrols (he still had not got it right) had driven many of the prostitutes from the main streets into back streets so that they now covered a wider area, which aggravated the evil. He concluded that, while undoubtedly there was some truth in policewomen's statements about their work, the article was a great exaggeration of the actual state of affairs and was a fair example of "a journalist with a vivid imagination out for copy".[8] Nothing is new.

The Commissioner and the Home Office were, of course, in no doubt who the women were, and the episode can have done them little good in these quarters, especially since the police were under such pressure to do something about 'the state of the streets'.

When WPS funds were at their lowest, a fairy godmother appeared on the scene. Commandant Damer Dawson later referred to her as "a munificent donor" but never named her. She did explain, however, that the woman had lost her sons in the war and, feeling that they would have approved of women police, had they lived, she turned over to the WPS 'the fortune' the sons would have inherited. It must have been a great deal of money for they quickly took on new staff and moved to bigger and better premises at St Stephen's House, Westminster. Very soon the Ministry of Munitions was wanting many more women police and so was easily persuaded to forgo the previous agreement and start paying them while training.

In 1917 the WPS entered into a new contract with the Ministry, this time allowing the women twenty-five shillings a week while training and £2 once trained, and a grant of £750 a year for the organization. The thing was growing fast. On 27th January the *Daily Telegraph* reported "animated scenes" at the new headquarters when they were besieged in a response to an appeal for a further three hundred policewomen. Applicants numbered many hundreds, said the paper, and among them "could be discerned people of all classes, and all seemed imbued with the desire to do some kind of patriotic work".

But they were much in the news. The *Ladies' Pictorial* did a double-page spread of before and after the women received their uniforms, and, in an interview with the *Daily News*, Damer Dawson was quoted as saying that their work was essentially preventative and protective: "The girls are young, high spirited and careless. Fortunately for them, in many cases, they have little imagination, and the sense of danger is an unknown quantity: but in some cases their love of fun and mischief leads them to run serious risks, both to themselves and co-workers."

Five separate police authorities were working at Gretna: Dumfries, Cumberland, the Factory, Carlisle and the WPS, and the two different law systems of England and Scotland were involved. Naturally this caused problems, and in February 1917 an acting HM Inspector of Constabulary was sent up to inspect and report on possible ways of improving co-ordination. On his return his warmest words were for the "excellent work" of the WPS in the factory, hostel township and nearby Carlisle. He felt their numbers should be much strengthened.[9]

Conditions obviously improved for munitions women police, for among the WPS literature is a leaflet on 'The Day's Work of the Policewoman' at Gretna. After describing a day's working programme, starting at 6 am, it finishes: "4 pm. She catches her train back to Barracks, where she finds the Barrack Sergeant and Staff waiting to welcome her and after a good meal she is free to spend her evening dancing, singing, playing with the orchestra, cricketing, playing tennis or having a quiet evening by the fire in the Recreation Room, or at the Policewoman's Club, to which she may invite her friends."[10]

But working conditions were still tough. Even *John Bull*, which had made it plain it did not think much of women police, especially on the streets, made noises about the hardships they suffered: "We hear of women walking as many as seventeen miles in the course of a single night patrol."[11] If that were true, it would be at Gretna, or perhaps Queensferry or Pembrey in Wales, but the smaller places had their hardships as well, as described by a Constable G.L. King, probably writing from a factory at Erith in Kent.

We of this unit are very happy in our work, although we have practically no comfort. The weather has been bitterly cold, and from seven in the morning until six in the afternoon we have had nowhere to go to get warm. The little place we call 'Office' is only heated by one tiny lamp, and in the bad weather the snow comes through the cracks in the roof and sides of the hut, and we have to wear our heavy coats and hats all day long, and we still shiver. Though the cold has been so intense, we are kept warm, however, by the thought that we are working for our King and Country.[12]

The above is quoted by Mary Allen in *The Pioneer Policewoman*. She was less vocal about the appalling conditions of the women factory workers who laboured extremely long hours for often less than half the money allowed their fellow male workers. Indeed, she happily describes tackling the problem of "habitual loitering": "The policewomen found girls hiding away in all sorts of strange places or trying to escape from the shops on all manner of pretexts." The TNT in those shops caused eczema, and its fumes turned the skins of the fillers a bright mustard yellow, or "deep golden", as Mary Allen had it. According to an indignant Sylvia Pankhurst, in aircraft factories it was common for some six out of thirty women to be lying ill outside the workshops due to noxious fumes from the varnish used on the wings.[13] Apart from "watching for signs", Mary Allen merely mentions: "Few could work for any length of time without ill effects." But this did not stop her and Damer Dawson visiting prisons to persuade the offenders, many of them prostitutes, to go straight when they came out of prison by coming to work in the factories for their King and Country.

Nor does she mention the occasional, very natural disagreement among her "wonderful" policewomen. On 14th September 1917 *The Times* reported, tongue in cheek:

WOMEN CONSTABLES AT VARIANCE
In a Government munitions factory yesterday a difference of opinion arose between a woman constable and her inspector. In her anger the constable, a powerfully-built woman, suddenly caught up the inspector in her arms and threw her into an adjacent stream, which contained more mud than water. When extricated, the inspector was uninjured. Officers of the regular police staff escorted the woman constable from the factory.

But they mostly got on very well with each other and with the male police. At Queensferry the men donated a generous £125 from their sports fund to help with the baby home which the WPS had set up in Kent. They hoped at the same time, their Chief Constable remarked, that it would tend to show the very excellent feeling which had at all times prevailed between the women police and their male colleagues.

With so much volatile material around, the factories were dangerous places, especially during air raids. Inspector Guthrie, in charge of the women police at Pembrey, claimed that she had personally coped with three explosions and that her landlady had twice been informed that she had been blown to bits. The *Police Chronicle*, in an item entitled 'Cool-headed Women Police', described how Woman Sergeant Williams and Woman Constable Rainbird, at some danger to themselves, had saved a fireman who had been overcome by fumes from a burst shell. The women, they reported, received hearty congratulations on their bravery and promptness from the management of the (Halifax) National Filling Factory.

During air-raids 'operatives' were cleared from the workshops, which were then guarded by police, male and female, and firemen. In another issue, the *Police Chronicle* expressed some wonderment at the coolness of the women under fire: "Subjected to any such horrible danger before the war, one would have expected to find the women concerned all huddled together, crouching in corners, or in a half-fainting condition!"[14] Instead they chatted and drank tea in their little wooden huts, now and then quietly slipping away to visit their, often powder-keg, points. Even Sub-Commandant Allen was surprised at how the, now tin-hatted, ladies kept their nerve, pointing out that they had had no opportunity to grow fearless before the war since a certain degree of timidity had been considered ladylike.

As the munitions work grew and grew, the council of three spent more and more time organizing and inspecting factories and camps. For the latter purpose they acquired four spanking new motor-cycles, three with sidecars. (At this time Superintendents in the Metropolitan Police still inspected their stations in horse and trap.)[15] To complete the upward trend of their fortunes, the Chief Constable of Reading, who had refused to sign women patrol cards unless he could add a disclaiming rider, requested two WPS trained policewomen. The National Council of Women (ex-NUWW) was undeterred and claimed that the appointment was due to the good work of their patrols,[16] which it possibly was, but this counter-claiming the same success was to become a pattern.

Many other towns, cities and boroughs were approaching the WPS for information about their training, and some followed up with requests for policewomen. Nottingham asked for eight, and an officer, to patrol the neighbourhood of Mansfield and the surrounding camps, and Oxford took on one constable. "A town in Northumberland" wanted one on the cheap, twenty-five shillings a week, but got short shrift from Damer Dawson, who assured them that they could not expect an educated woman to accept that amount.[17]

Folkestone proved "the most unsatisfactory from every point of view". The woman taken on there, Sub-Inspector Fife, was, the WPS claimed, expected to clear up, in a few months, conditions which had, through municipal mismanagement, grown up over many years. This was after Fife had received her notice. She had received no support from the Town Council or the Chief Constable, Damer Dawson continued in the WPS Report for 1916-17; indeed, if the Archbishop of Canterbury and one or two other influential people had not asked her to stay longer, she would have left earlier.

It was not really surprising that Fife had received little support. She had, in fact, been wished on the Watch Committee and the Chief Constable by the aforesaid "influential people"; Damer Dawson's home was at the nearby Lympne. The nub of the trouble was, once again, prostitutes and the authorities' treatment of them. Folkestone had a huge army camp, mainly for Colonial troops, and prostitutes were attracted there from London; soon they had a "serious outbreak of VD". Particularly stringent DORA regulations were brought into force[18] by which it was possible for any girl or woman with one conviction for prostitution to be summarily ejected from the town. The authorities did not realize, complained Damer Dawson, that all this did was to throw back onto London hundreds of young girls, most of whom were ashamed to go home. Nevertheless, Sub-Inspector Fife had done good work in persuading many of them to leave before being ejected or, if she failed to do this, warning the London WPS when they would be arriving.

7

"Pluck and Determination"

Police Constable 360 Silverson was quietly patrolling Hyde Park one spring evening in 1917. With him were the two women patrols, Mrs Annie Morgan-Scott and Mrs Bagster, veteran of the original gross indecency case which had appeared before Mr Mead the year before. A current instruction from Scotland Yard had, in fact, pointed out that the PC should not accompany the women but "keep near them and be prepared to act if necessary".[1] Miss Peto declares that precise arrangements for such escorts varied. In the streets, for instance, the constable followed the patrols "and was there more for their protection than anything else", but in Hyde Park they walked just ahead, "and if it became necessary to caution and move on a man and woman, this was done by the male officer, while, whenever desirable, the women patrols interrogated and advised the woman or girl". If they had to arrest a couple, the PC did this, then took control of the man while the women patrols followed with the woman.[2]

Whether PC Silverson was ahead in the proscribed manner is not clear, but we do know that the peace was soon disturbed by a man behaving "in an apparently indecent manner", whatever that is. The constable spoke to him, but the man, whose name was Kung, did not appreciate his interest and immediately became abusive and struck him, making arrest inevitable. But it was not to be an easy arrest. Kung had a friend nearby, "another alien named Badertscher", who promptly "sprang forward" and grabbed PC Silverson from behind. In the ensuing struggle the constable was knocked to the ground.

Suddenly this was all too much for Mrs Bagster. She seized Badertscher, also from behind, pulled him away from the PC and, as the report on the incident stated, "held him firmly". Mrs Morgan-Scott then weighed in, grabbing Kung and holding him until Silverson could resume the perpendicular. The culprits were then marched to the station, charged and later fined.

The Commissioner wrote a thank-you letter to Mrs Carden: "Both ladies acted with the greatest pluck and determination, disregarding the danger of themselves being assaulted by the two foreigners, one of whom was using his walking-stick as a weapon."[3]

Three weeks after this incident it was agreed by all parties that, henceforth, the women could be employed singly with a constable in Hyde Park. Presumably one woman was felt to be enough protection for the PC.

The women patrols of the NCW (both Special and Voluntary, the Special still being under the basic control of the NCW) had started 1917 well. On 24th February a report on the "rampant prostitution" in Horseferry Road appeared in *The Times*. The area was, it claimed, a hotbed of immorality "undisguised and unchecked". The Australian Military Headquarters and a club for overseas forces were in this vicinity and, *The Times* felt, it was distressing to see the number of young girls between fifteen and eighteen who haunted the streets nearby and "thrust themselves on men who, it must be confessed, are not always displeased by their attentions". (That was quite an admission from the male-dominated Press in those days.) It was no use warning the girls, the report went on; though women patrols did their best, they had no power, so that many of the offending girls did not "escape the fate which their wanton conduct invites". What was needed, *The Times* decided, was women police – with the same powers as men.

Immediately Lady Codrington, Chairman of the London Patrols Committee, sprang to the defence of Scotland Yard. It was not true to say that the women patrols were voluntary and had no powers, she wrote; Special Patrols were employed by the Commissioner in that very area (put there, in fact, only a few weeks earlier),[4] and their work had been of the greatest value. The police themselves testified to the fact that, owing to their assistance, a largely increased number of convictions had been obtained. What was needed was huts for women workers in which to while away the time, similar to those which proliferated for servicemen, and more Special Patrols.[5]

When Mr Ferens, long-standing supporter of women police, asked in the House if women police were going to be appointed to cope with this prostitution scandal, the Home Secretary was able to say no, since such work required a long experience of police duties and considerable physical strength, but that the Commissioner was employing some women patrols for certain auxiliary work connected with these matters and spoke very highly of them. Once again the women patrols had enabled the police and Home Office to look as though they were doing something, in marked contrast to the impression the WPS had conveyed a couple of months before with their Leicester Square publicity. The NCW were rewarded with a grant of £400 a year, on condition they provided extra patrols when needed, and the appointment of more Special Patrols, two in Leicester Square, two on Hampstead Heath and two, encroaching on WPS territory, as munitions women police at the Woolwich Arsenal.[6] And they were about to make a move which would strengthen their position even more: the employment of Mrs Stanley.

SOFIA STANLEY

Mrs Stanley, who had been a patrol leader at Portsmouth, was appointed Supervisor of the Special Patrols in March 1917, her title being specially approved, Mrs Carden told the Commissioner, as not being a police title. When she took over, there were thirty-seven Special Patrols in central London and twenty-nine in the suburbs, most of them working one or two nights a week. Under the new supervisor the numbers and time worked increased rapidly. By the end of the year central London sported fifty-five, all of them full time.[7]

Mrs Stanley was a charming and clever woman who obviously had some knowledge of human nature. When writing to the Inspector in charge of Kennington Road Police Station, she casually suggested that her patrols there should work a seven-hour, rather than a four-hour, day, "in order to bring them into conformity with the hours of duty performed by patrols in other parts of London".

The officers in charge of the station which covered the notorious Horseferry Road themselves asked for some alteration in the hours of their Special Patrols. Could they come on duty a little later, they asked the Commissioner, so that they worked until 11.30 pm or midnight, "as a certain amount of indecency takes place after 11 pm".[8] Of course Sofia Stanley's light hand could have been behind that one as well, since, by all accounts, men found her hard to resist. But as well as charm and sex appeal she had common sense – enough to know when not to push or over-exaggerate conditions so as to get more women employed.

The Commissioner had been receiving continuous complaints about indecency on Blackheath and asked Mrs Stanley to organize a special investigation there. She detailed Mrs Bagster and Mrs Kate Summerton who, by then, must have been experts on detecting indecency, to patrol there for seven days. Soon Mrs Stanley was reporting to Sir Edward that, having patrolled there herself for two nights, she agreed with their conclusion that there was nothing happening which would indicate the possibility of effective work being done by women patrols attached to the police.[9]

At the AGM of the National Council of Women in October 1917, Mrs Stanley generously paid "warm tribute" to the kindness and courtesy of the whole Metropolitan Police Force. The progress of the clubs was also much discussed at this meeting, and a Miss Bondfield admitted that she had faced a great deal of opposition when trying to open mixed clubs in London, but she had persevered and been successful. They were not matrimonial agencies, she added coyly, but they did give Cupid a chance. NCW delegates felt that, generally, Bible Classes were a good thing, but it was decided that in mixed clubs the impetus for these should come from the members, since one member reported that in her mixed club the men and girls had "taken to tittering". One girls-only club had even acquired a bathing hut from which swimming lessons were given.

Lady Codrington mentioned that women patrols had recently added to their duties supervision of tube stations during air raids.[10] Mary Allen also tells how whole families streamed from the slums and poorer districts into the underground stations. It was obviously a much less orderly procedure than in the Second World War, for often it caused such havoc, she claims, that surrounding streets had to be roped off and closed to the public. The police, she felt, coped with this admirably. The London contingent of the WPS lent a hand and, like the women patrols, did duty at railway stations where growing drunkenness and even shell shock were among the big problems. In *The Pioneer Policewoman* Mary Allen gives two graphic accounts:

A boy among the first leave draft from the front, his nerves still at breaking point, discovered at the station that he had lost the train ticket to his home, or thought he had. It was the last straw. Flinging his kit down, he whipped out a razor. The policewoman closed with him and, after a desperate struggle, managed to knock the razor from his hand, and to persuade him to go with her to the Rest Room. There, after swallowing a hot drink, he instantly fell asleep, and slept for hours. During this interval she was able to find his address and telegraph to his people, so that when he awoke, comparatively quiet and in his right mind, she could conduct him to his train for the North, and was informed later of his safe arrival.

Another returning soldier was so disordered that while he was going down the stairs into the tube station, becoming suddenly aware of the crowd of people coming up, he looked haggardly about, and evidently mistaking the hollow space below for the trenches, and the ascending crowd for Germans, fixed his bayonet and charged. But for the women constable on duty at the turn of the staircase, who was quick enough to divine his trouble and, hanging on to him with all her strength, to prevent his forward advance, he would have wounded many and caused a dangerous panic.

Mary Allen also describes how, as the war dragged on, the police would call on them to handle drunken servicemen, since members of the public were becoming increasingly protective towards them and would even attack a policeman who tried to arrest one. In consequence, policemen would look the other way and be grateful to any WPS who did pick them up (sometimes in their sidecars!) and take them to the YMCA shelter. Miss Allen, you will have noticed, is a little given to dramatization, but the more down-to-earth Dorothy Peto also tells of sobering-up duties in her memoirs:

I used to get out with the Special Patrols most often on a tour of night duty in and around a railway station (they patrolled without any PC here since it was private property); and of those nights I still have vivid memories, particularly of those at Euston. In those days there were several public houses near the entrance in Euston Road, much frequented by street women on the look-out for service men on their way to catch a night train to the North. If one such man could be enticed into a public house, the woman plied him with drink and relieved him of his cash, after which he emerged drunk and sometimes penniless. The special patrols developed their own technique. When they saw a soldier or sailor being picked up by such a woman, or staggering drunkenly out of licensed premises, they got him away and, if reasonably sober, saw him into the railway station and into safe company. If he was too far gone for this, they led him instead to the gate of the central enclosure in Euston Square, within which the YMCA ran a Service Canteen. Having rung the bell for the man on the gate, we pushed our charge inside as soon as it opened and then went back to the beat.

Within the station itself, a women's organization ran another canteen for service men and women, and welcomed the co-operation of the patrols in dealing with customers either obstreperous or collapsed. It has to be remembered that most service men — or women — were generally tired enough to knock under to a comparatively small amount of drink, taken in all probability on an empty stomach. ... Patrols became skilled in 'sobering up' their patients by means of cups of black coffee laced with bicarbonate of soda which, after making them violently sick, left them sober enough to be entrained in due course.

Apart from their unofficial patrolling and training in London, the WPS had managed to get themselves employed in certain boroughs on a semi-official basis. Their greatest success was with Mrs Hampton at Richmond. She was first employed there when the local branch of the Women's Local Government Association held a public meeting to raise funds to support her in May 1915. She became involved in assisting women at Richmond Magistrates and Petty Sessional Courts, where, she reported, she was often the only woman present apart from the female prisoner. Soon her supporting fund ran out, but a member of the CLAC offered to pay her wage for the duration, and later the Commissioner was persuaded to pay her thirty shillings a week, making her the only member of the WPS employed by the Metropolitan Police.[11] As well as advising and helping women prisoners, Mrs Hampton stayed with them until a matron was available and advised women who came to court with various problems – taking summonses out against neighbours or needing help with increasingly unruly children due to the men being away.

All this court work prevented her from patrolling as much as she would have wished, but, she insisted, she was given plenty of outside work by the police: enquiries after missing girls, visiting etc. One of her visits was paid to a woman who appears to have been playing out a pathetic lie – as Sub-Inspector Hampton wrote in the WPS Report for 1916-17:

A soldier in France applied to come home on leave to arrange matters with his wife, who was in great trouble. She wrote alleging that she had been criminally assaulted by an unknown soldier while in a lonely part. He had made her unconscious, and she had a child coming in consequence. The military authorities communicated with the police asking them to verify the wife's statement. For this the police had to obtain a detailed written statement of all that had happened from the woman herself, and I was sent with the police officer to do this. In these cases it is most important that a woman should take these statements, for it is almost impossible for a respectable woman to give all the intimate details necessary to a man.

We are not enlightened as to what conclusion Mrs Hampton came about the alleged rape but one hopes she believed her. Another of her cases illustrates some of the side effects of the anti-German propaganda:

A man and his daughter applied to the magistrates for protection against a neighbour's servant, who insulted them by calling them Germans, etc. They were genuinely frightened of being thought German (they were Jews, and a son-in-law a Russian Jew). As the abuse took place in the neighbour's garden, a summons could not be granted, and I was asked by the magistrate if I could do anything. Both parties were interviewed and everything arranged satisfactorily.

The WPS employed in the Paddington area specialized in dealing with children. When they began working there, in May 1916, once again with the support of the WLGA, they were shown a good deal of hostility, but, they claimed, once they made the nature of their mission understood (the help and protection of children – but not forgetting the befriending of young women and girls to prevent their getting into trouble) things improved.

They saw children across the roads at home-time, prevented their hanging onto the backs of cars and trams and kept watch on a certain dangerous canal and licensed premises. Of the latter they reported that mothers often hurried out of public houses and took their children away when they saw 'the lady police' come on duty. Watch was also kept on the sale of unsealed bottles and jugs of alcohol to under-age children.[12]

Like the women patrols, they were concerned about the abuse of child labour. Inspector Harburn, their child expert, reported that the enforcement of the 1908 Children Act was almost impossible in wartime conditions. In one London borough she did special investigations and found no bye-laws regulating the employment of children under fourteen. Employers greatly preferred child labour to that of old people, which was often the only alternative at the time. Ten- and eleven-year-olds, Mary Allen wrote in *The Pioneer Policewoman*, were working an appalling number of hours and falling asleep over their desks from sheer exhaustion. The WPS called on parents and headmasters, trying to get them to keep a better eye on the children. Another task they set themselves was shepherding "whole armies" of children across dangerous streets and into shelters during daylight air-raids.[13]

On 10th December 1916 'M.R.' struck again. Although not named, Paddington is probably the venue of this item in the *Weekly Dispatch*:

THE BOGEY-WOMAN

Girl In Blue Of Whom Bad Boys Go In Awe

The policewoman has become a sort of mother of the mean streets, where unkempt and uncared-for youngsters spend much of their time. Her duty it is to look after their welfare and behaviour day after day, in wet weather and in fine. It is not particularly exhilarating or exciting war work, but it is none the less necessary, and the women chosen for duty among the children are carefully selected. They are those who have a love for little children and an understanding of the difficulties of tired, over-worked mothers.

"Don't you get tired of the work?" I asked the children's sergeant, who took me on her rounds the other day, and she laughed at the very idea.

She had spent her morning in court, but at twelve she led me to a school in one of the most crowded parts of London. Out of the school doors poured hundreds of boys and girls like a troop of little wild things. They were dirty and ragged, but they shouted and danced and ran into the middle of the road — unless they caught the policewoman's eye; they then became models of deportment.

A THING TO CONJURE WITH

It is quite evident that in the family circles in that neighbourhood a mention of the policewoman is a thing to conjure with. Yet she is such a pleasant, cheerful, kind "bogey-woman" that the smallest tiny-tot places his hand in hers and smiles up at her as she leads him safely across the road.

The London child of four is a model of self-reliance. He brings himself to school and takes himself home, but the policewoman sees him across the road nowadays, and she sees that no larger boys tease him or take his apple or his penny. Those larger boys are the difficulty today. They need the paternal authority, and the dinner hour must be a trial for the harassed mother if she chances to be there, and generally she is not, since she is off at work — or elsewhere — leaving a slice of bread and some cold carrots for her offspring's midday meal.

When the children are safely out of school, the children's sergeant patrols the neighbouring streets crowded with women gossiping and children playing games or eating bits of bread on the steps of the little houses, each of which shelters several families. She stops fights in their infancy, checks boys who wish to turn handsprings in front of carts, picks up the small girls who fall down, speaks a kindly word to the weeping child who has a grief she cannot express but which is noisily poignant, and keeps an eagle eye unhooded for the would-be truant.

And her reward is the confidence of those forlorn little mites who grasp her hand with their small grimy fingers, and the bright, grateful smile of those tired, bedraggled women the little ones call mother.

M.R.

8

Attitudes

Nina Boyle was also holding hands – those of wounded Serbian soldiers in Macedonia. In December 1916 she had left London as part of a small reinforcement sent out to strengthen the Wounded Allies Relief Committee's hospital at Vodena. She had gone, she made clear in a message to her friends, not because she was fired with patriotism, which was quite as well served in working for her fellow-countrywomen, but because she was becoming stale and "falling into a groove". She felt she lacked initiative and fresh ideas. "Also, this great war is the biggest thing the world has yet known; and I think it becomes me, who talk politics and find fault with politicians, to see something of it for myself at first hand, and not be dependent on other people's impressions. I feel sure I shall get a better perspective and sense of proportion as the result."

In fact she was a rather restless person who liked change and new challenges. Her short sojourn (six months) did not prove exciting. As she later commented, it merely proved how true was the saying, "The nearer the Front the further from the War!" At first this highly intelligent woman spent her time patching and darning linen, but soon the authorities went to the other extreme and gave her charge of the whole hospital as Night Sister – a task she accomplished, she declared happily, without killing anyone. Naturally she seized the opportunity to take a close look at the conditions of Serbian women, which she found good.[1]

Since the split between her and Damer Dawson, the Women Police Volunteers had continued to function, though in a much less ambitious fashion. They still had a separate branch flourishing in Brighton but, in April 1915, admitted they had not been able to count on the goodwill of the local police.[2] That was an understatement. The month before, the local women patrols had been "officially recognized" by the Chief Constable at a ceremony in the town hall. Shortly afterwards *The Times* reported that the Brighton suffragists

"who have been parading the town as Women Police Volunteers" had
been warned by the Chief Constable to desist.[3]

After Margaret Damer Dawson had departed, the declared strategy
of the WPV was to train women for duty in every Metropolitan Police
and Assize Court, and there is evidence that they had at least started
on this project.[4] *The Times* of 1st March 1915 states that when a
certain woman complained of persistent violence from her husband,
the magistrate told her that, if she wanted to set up a case against him,
she must first leave him then apply for a summons of separation. "As
the applicant did not seem to understand the position," *The Times*
went on, "Mr Fordham, observing a member of the Women Police
Volunteers in court, asked her to see the applicant and assist her."
But, after that, there is scant mention of the WPV, apart from an
editorial comment in *The Vote* of 4th February 1916 which stated that
the present object of the corps was to secure posts as police station
gaolers for trained women who had mastered the duties necessary for
such positions. However, the tone of this comment indicates that the
WPV were really fading out, and little was heard of them after that,
apart from in police reports regarding the three organizations, and
these references are vague, giving the impression that the police still
did not always know one organization from the other and merely
presumed that the WPV were still functioning. There is also a
suspicion that the police did not want to lose the tie-up between
anarchical suffragism and the WPS and so kept resurrecting Nina
Boyle's involvement.[5]

Nina Boyle continued to write for *The Vote*, give speeches and
assist in the Women's Freedom League's many other projects: aiding
Belgian refugees, sending parcels to prisoners of war, running cheap
restaurants for the poor and a settlement at Nine Elms where children
could get penny dinners or be put up while their mothers were ill or
confined. They also opened a non-alcoholic pub, where cheap meals
and drinks could be enjoyed by both sexes, as well as games and
concerts.[6] The purpose of the Women's Suffrage National Aid Corps
was to help women and children, but they always stressed that their
main aim was "to secure the Parliamentary vote for women", and
they never stopped agitating for this.

Although much of the work of the WPS and women patrols did
develop in the manner Nina Boyle had feared (even the friendly
Weekly Dispatch launched an attack on them for being Mrs
Grundys)[7], that was not the whole story. They were making their
protective presence felt in many courts. The WPS reports cite several

cases of assisting battered wives, and they were winning some recognition for the validity of this role, even among men. The Mayor of Brighton especially requested that their newly approved women patrols attend court whenever a female or child defendant appeared.[8] The WPS Baby Home is an indication that they looked reality in the eye. It specialized in looking after babies; illegitimate, orphaned or whose mothers could not look after them for some reason, who were ineligible for other homes. Regular subscriptions from members of the WPS, topped up by donations Damer Dawson raised in her speeches, largely financed the operation. Indeed she found people much more willing to subscribe to the home than to the upkeep of the WPS.

There is no doubt they were Mrs Grundys, but there is also evidence that they were starting to rebel against the one-sidedness of the way in which matters of public sexual morality were handled. On 6th June 1917 Mr G.A. Goodwin of the National Council for Combating Venereal disease was quoted in the *Yorkshire Post* as saying that the women police could be a great help in VD prevention, but that he knew women police in one city had determined never to put a woman in dock for indecency unless they got the man also, and they were relying on the honour of soldier boys in the street to help arrest male offenders.

The WPS Report for 1916-17 cites a case "typical of the impossibility under the present state of the law of obtaining any correction or punishment for men who persistently insult women". They claimed that one man, unsteady on his legs, had accosted eight girls, all of whom had resented his indecent and insulting gestures and behaviour, but, when the WPS sergeant had finally prevailed upon a PC to arrest the man, he would do so only for drunkenness and not for insulting behaviour (there was not, and is not, a specific charge applicable to men who solicit women). The man was found not guilty, after pleading that illness rather than drunkenness had made him unsteady. Of course it is impossible to judge the rights and wrongs of this case, but it does illustrate the growing resistance to the double standard.

Notwithstanding this new awareness, however, the same yearly report printed a list of purposes for which Constable Smith of Grantham granted interviews to members of the public, and among these, without comment, were the following: "Husbands placing their wives under observation during their absence. Husbands enquiring into the reported misconduct of their wives."

It is hard to ascertain the real attitudes of police to these female interlopers. At the time both organizations had the good sense publicly to thank the police for their help and acceptance. Margaret Damer Dawson, in one of her lighter moments, even went so far as to say they had been welcomed with open arms, though, at another time, she admitted that when she first went to see the Commissioner he had laughed and said they would only go and get themselves knocked on the head. However, even this remark was made to assure people how much the attitude had now changed and how they were "now absolutely upheld by Sir Edward Henry". Mary Allen later claimed that they were initially not wanted in most provincial towns and that they continuously had to prove themselves before police chiefs were converted.[9]

Attitudes of the public gradually changed as the war dragged on. On 1st May 1915 the *Sussex Daily News* had printed this ambiguous item:

London has not yet grown accustomed to its policewomen. I saw one today at the corner of Whitehall, and she appeared very conscious of the attention she was attracting. There is nothing very distinctive about the neat blue costume that the women wear, and their hats rather suggest that they have just returned from a morning ride in the Row. It is only when you notice the WP on their shoulders that you recognize the work on which they are occupied. Physically the women are not of the type you would expect, and they seem little fitted to face the hurly-burly of a street row. Most of them are slight and fragile in build, and their hands are of the small, delicate type generally associated with the artistic temperament. If the women police act with tact and discretion, there is useful work for them to do in the West End of London, but the average Cockney seems at present to resent their presence in the streets. The suffragettes are to blame for this in large measure, for in the public mind the "Copperettes", as the girls are called, have come to be associated, quite erroneously no doubt, with the women who used to break windows, and shout, "Votes for women" in Parliament Square.

By 1917, when Sergeant Lovell of Birkenhead (one of the places "making its own experiments with women police") marched her new policewomen out of the town hall one snowy morning, she found the public "charming": "There was no jesting, and we were taken quite seriously, as I hoped we should be. I must say the women looked the part. They were all under thirty years of age, healthy and of good physique."[10]

People were, of course becoming used to seeing women do all kinds of strange things from station mastering to farm work. One Bristol clergyman thought up yet another, rather bizarre, way for women to do their bit when he launched the 'League for the Marrying of Wounded Heroes'. "Maybe," he wrote, "many noble-minded patriotic women will gladly give their lives and strength to ameliorate the condition of such men, and that in the highest and best way, a consecrated marriage." He did, however, have the grace to admit that these same women might come a little unstuck when they tried to support their heroes. "Of course," he went on, "if men were as just as they might be, there would be no economic difficulty, for women who are doing men's work, and doing it like men, would receive equal wages."[11] In fact, in a south coast town, when a woman attempted to support her already-acquired and wounded husband, by driving a taxi, she was soon opposed by local drivers and refused a licence.[12]

9

Training and Testing

MISS PETO

Dorothy Olivia Georgiana Peto, who joined the women patrols of the NUWW at Bath in the early months of the war, was a country girl. As she remarks in her memoirs:

I well remember starting out for my first tour of street duty, an umbrella hooked over one arm, and my skirt held up behind me – for the skirts, in those days, came almost down to the ground, and the hills of Bath were steep. Town life was new to me. As we passed through the darkened streets (all lamps have been broken by the special constables on the day that War was declared, for lack of any means of turning them off at source) I felt – nay, I hoped – that each group of persons whom we passed might turn out to be plotting some nefarious deed! In one of the poorer streets down by the river, we came on a long, low van like a baker's cart with doors at the back; whereupon I ingenuously remarked, "How late the beagles are out tonight", only to learn from my convulsed companion that the vehicle in question was an undertaker's van delivering a coffin for an impending funeral!

Shortly after this, Flora Joseph became organizer for Somerset, and Miss Peto, on the strength of some clerical experience for the St John's Ambulance Association, was taken on as her secretary. Flora Joseph felt that patrol leaders needed proper training and began discussion on the subject with the Bristol Women Patrols Committee, meanwhile packing off Dorothy Peto to Southampton to broaden her experience even more. Soon the Bristol committee informed the central committee that they wished to open a training school for both women patrols and women police. They received London's blessing on the condition that the two bodies be kept 'distinct'. It was not to be presumed that women patrols served under women police – this was just after the women patrols at Hull had been handed over to the WPS. Patrol committees in the south of England were encouraged to send their patrol leaders for short courses, while longer training was available for women who wished to secure appointments to police forces.

Flora Joseph became chairman of the training school sub-committee. Mrs Gent combined the leadership of the Bristol patrols with the post of schools' director, and Dorothy Peto was appointed her assistant. Both Mrs Joseph and Mrs Gent had nursing experience. Flora Joseph had founded the Somerset Nursing Association, and Mrs Gent had worked as a health visitor. The convenient tie-up with the Bristol patrols meant that the school's students could gain practical experience by going out with one of their 'registered patrols' on the streets of Bristol, then still a busy port.

A couple of Damer Dawson's friends, Lady Thring and Lady Waldegrove, asked her to co-operate with the Bristol Training School (BTS), and, though she really preferred to keep all training centred on London, she consented and joined the BTS committee.[1] Mrs Joseph, Miss Peto and Mrs Gent made their trip to London to observe WPS training in mid-1915, but a year later co-operation was at an end. According to Margaret Damer Dawson, the BTS women could not take the discipline her organization demanded, especially since that discipline applied to the officers as well as to the ranks. What is more, their motive in asking for co-operation had really been to obtain a closer look at the WPS training on which they then based their own courses.

Miss Peto claims that the split came after the BTS discovered that Damer Dawson expected all the women supplied by her, or them, to remain members of her own organization and subject to her ultimate control (she was always accused of this, though she denied it), while they felt the women should integrate totally with the force to which they were sent. However, despite the rift, the BTS supplied Damer Dawson with thirteen trained munitions policewomen, though she did find it necessary to give them two further weeks' training after they had been handed over.

BTS candidates were expected to possess a good, normal physique, be rather large, rather benign and convey the impression that they saw good in people they met rather than evil. Their timetable included the currently popular Swedish drill and ju-jitsu, and lectures ranged from first aid to sex biology. The demand, they claimed, always exceeded the supply. This was probably because candidates were expected to keep themselves while training and pay 'working expenses', though there were one or two bursaries from private donors. Among the regular students was yet another variation on the women police/patrols theme: the Somerset Super Patrols. Invented by Mrs Joseph, they received the school's full police training and wore a police type uniform but were not officially appointed or sworn, merely 'sanctioned' by the authorities in Mare, Taunton and Clevedon. They were, however, known as "the Lady Police" in these areas, a BTS report points out.

In 1917 Mrs Gent's husband, who was in Holy Orders, transferred to another living, and Miss Peto took over as director of the school. By the end of that year they had trained Damer Dawson's thirteen munitions women police and one for the Admiralty, four patrol leaders, two policewomen for Bath and two for Coventry and five Super Patrols for Somerset.

While preparing the BTS course, Miss Peto had also spent some time in Liverpool, which was not only extremely tough but had been the venue of some interesting police experiments in social work. The city had the highest crime rate in the country, due largely, according to Sir Leonard Dunning, Chief Constable there from 1902-11, to poverty and juvenile crime which, he believed, were naturally intertwined. As he later told the Baird Committee:

> I went to Liverpool in 1895 and one of the first things that struck me as a stranger to Liverpool ... was the enormous number of ragged, bare-footed children in the streets ... begging under the pretence of selling newspapers, matches and so on. The first step to deal with at all events one part of that was the establishment of the police-aided Clothing Association which was initiated in 1895 by the then Lord Mayor of Liverpool, Alderman Watts ... The principle is this. The Society lends clothes to children. It does not give them; it lends them. It lends the clothes to those children who come under the notice of police, who pick them up as being ill-clad. After enquiry which satisfies the police that it is not the fault of the parents, but that the parents are not in a position to give the children clothing, they recommend that the child should be clothed, and the child is clothed. The clothing remains the property of the Society, and I must say that the police had most loyal support from the pawnbrokers, who utterly refused to take the clothing in pawn, which was, therefore, left to the children and not disposed of, as it would have been if it had been given to the parents of the children.

An average of two thousand children a year were thus clothed. "That took away the hardship which no doubt would have been the result of any drastic measures for driving those children off the streets, where no doubt they did fill their poor little stomachs by what they got by begging or selling matches or newspapers."

Three years later the corporation had taken over the licensing of children trading in the streets, not because they approved of it but to gain some control over the child. No child was licensed until the parents had been seen and urged to try to find other employment for their offspring. If they could not, the child was licensed and could apply for clothing, not as charity but from the rates. The children would then pay for it at sixpence a week, the money being collected by the police.

In his experience, Dunning insisted, eighty per cent of money was repaid, thereby teaching the children to keep their promises. But, more important, the police (one inspector, two sergeants and fifteen constables employed full time in plain clothes) could keep in touch with the children. They could help protect them, influence them and so prevent so much juvenile crime. They had not employed women in this experiment, merely because no one had suggested that police work could be done by women. Young girls had, in fact, been largely left out of this experiment due to the dangers to male police dealing with them, but, if they had had women police, they could have extended their brief to include sexual morality, as there was no doubt as much preventative work needed to be done in that direction as there was in the case of boys' criminal activities. However, he felt women could also influence young boys quite strongly.

Dunning's most embarrassing moment as a young policeman had been taking a sex statement from a pregnant girl under sixteen, so, soon after his appointment as Chief Constable of Liverpool, he had tried to find a woman to do the job. He had not succeeded in finding the right type, he claimed, until 1910, when he appointed Mrs Hughes.

The BTS adopted an extract from Dunning's handbook for the Liverpool Police as their school motto:

Anything which helps the very poor, and so relieves them from the temptation to crime; and anything which helps to take the children of the criminal classes away from evil surroundings and companions and, while there is yet time, implants in them instincts of honesty and virtue, is true police work; and a policeman should throw himself, heart and soul, into such work as readily as he does into the ordinary work of preventing and detecting crime.

MABEL COWLIN

In July 1914, just before the war started, a member of the Liverpool Select Vestry (a board of representatives of ratepayers) proposed a resolution that women police should be engaged to "discharge refined duties". The seconder, a Mr T.W. White, spoke strongly of the "miserable reptiles who infest the streets of Liverpool to the danger of women and girls", but another member protested against the appointment of more officials and suggested the formation of voluntary bands of male and female workers. This counter-motion was passed by eleven votes to nine.[2] Thus a Women's Patrol Committee was inaugurated early in the war, and in January 1915 Mabel Cowlin, a trained social worker, became organizer. (Dunning was by now an Inspector of Constabulary.) Liverpool's usual problems of poverty and density of population, and all the usual difficulties of a big port, were exacerbated by heavier than normal transatlantic traffic – due to its geographical position Liverpool was considered fairly immune to enemy attack. Later vast numbers of US military personnel disembarked there and set up camp nearby, which did not help matters much.

Mabel Cowlin thought that the patrols could gain valuable experience by seeing conditions of life very different from those of their own homes.[3] They certainly must have been that. As Miss Peto wrote in her memoirs:

> Patrol duty in the Liverpool streets certainly called for both courage and initiative. The dockside alleys, where children might be found accosting seamen on behalf of their mothers; Pitt Street, with a Chinese population at the city end and a West Indian and African population at the other, punctuated by seamen's dosshouses and dubious cafés. Scotland Road, with its Irish and Italian residents ready to boil over at the least provocation. These, with Lime Street and its environs, offered a wide and varied field of work, and of invaluable experience.

Scotland Road offered the patrols the experience of being hounded out, followed by a mob and pelted with missiles when they first ventured down there. Undaunted they returned "without distinctive dress or badges" and talked to women on their doorsteps and called on local organizations to explain themselves and their work. Then they were accepted.

Inevitably much of the work was the rescue of young women, though more the ones on the edge of real tough prostitution than flighty young things found elsewhere. In Mabel Cowlin's own words:

The patrols were given powers to inspect lodging houses frequented by common prostitutes and were enabled to take younger ones away and do really constructive work in re-establishing them. In this they were helped by the older women living on their earnings in the streets: for example, one of them brought a young girl to the office and begged the patrols to save her from the life she herself found so difficult to leave.[4]

They had in fact been given considerable power — 'to take the younger ones away'; she doesn't say what happened if they didn't want to go.

Miss Peto found that the real centre of the work was Mabel Cowlin's weekly case-meeting:

There, every person or situation dealt with on the beat was examined — their background, their individual needs and the possibilities of helping them; whilst with her trained perception and deep concern for the individual, Cowlin led the patrol concerned to seek and find the best solution. In the years between the two World Wars I met both policewomen and social workers who told me that they owed their whole conception of constructive work to Mabel Cowlin's teaching; and I know how much I learned myself whenever I had an opportunity of sitting in at one of her case-meetings in the Liverpool Patrol Office.

Work was done with children too, especially standing by them in court. The patrols also set up a hostel for runaway girls at Knotty Ash and opened one of the first mixed clubs, with music, dancing and games. The club was run by two committees, one of local girls and one of servicemen. In 1917 the Liverpool Women's Patrol Committee decided to open its own training school, which then became federated with the BTS.

In January 1917 Margaret Damer Dawson wrote to the Home Secretary, Sir George Cave, pressing the matter of official status for policewomen and requesting an interview for herself and Mary Allen. She received a cool reply and a refusal "due to other engagements", but the pair were seen by Sir Leonard Dunning. He found Mary Allen much the stronger of the two, though I doubt if this was true. I would guess that she was merely more superficially pushy because less sensitive. One needs to study any close relationship for quite a time before one can really deduce where the real strength lies.

The truth is [he wrote in his report], that Miss Damer Dawson cannot get rid of her ideas of the Women Police Service as an independent body and does not realize that the real thing to be aimed at is the employment of women by police authorities as an integral part of the police force, in which case the Chief Constable will be able to find plenty of work for them without coming across any of the difficulties which she sets out. But as a matter of fact most of her difficulties are imaginary.

Conversely he concluded that he saw no reason why women should not be given the powers and privileges of a constable, indeed he had always been in favour of women police, but thought that the advantages of doing so were not so great as would justify the introduction of what would no doubt be a highly controversial question which sounds more like a politician talking than a policeman.

Sir George Cave agreed that there was not much advantage in having women sworn in and was not sure that any step need be taken at the present moment but warned that the question should be under consideration, as a decision would have to be made sooner or later. Personally he did not feel that women were, in fact, suitable for police work but admitted that they were "peculiarly well-qualified for certain special work".[5]

The WPS leaders were not the only such visitors to the Home Office that year. Peto and Flora Joseph used the influence of a mutual friend to win an interview with Sir Edward Troup, the Under-Secretary of State for the Home Office. Swearing-in was the subject they chiefly wished to raise, wrote the friend, "which is, I suppose, no matter of pressing demand for an interview. But I think they also want patting on the back and to feel the Home Office knows all about them. Sir L. Dunning seems to think they are worthy people."

The BTS duo obviously made a much better impression than did the WPS women. "I saw these two very sensible ladies," Troup reported. They told him that the demand for their policewomen was much greater than that which they could supply, and this was due to the poor pay offered by police forces and the lack of pension. Most of the women were middle class, they advised him, and would like to make it a permanent profession. Strangely enough, they do not appear to have pressed much for power of arrest but rather concentrated on assuring the Home Office that when they had handed the women over to their force they made no further attempt to control or supervise them in any way.[6] Perhaps, somehow, they had heard a whisper that that was one of the main objections and fears of the men.

During these war years, every now and then another force would recruit women police without recourse to women patrols, the WPV, the WPS or either of the training schools. Birmingham City appointed two uniformed women (largely as a result of WPS propaganda, their yearly report claimed) solely for rescue work, and Lancashire began using women on detective work. Some fell quickly by the wayside; Sergeant Lovell of Birkenhead, who started so promisingly that snowy morning, resigned a few months later, saying she was ineffective due to lack of power of arrest.[7] Bristol took on three women "for inquiry work", but not from the BTS. However, others in Bristol began to utilize their facilities: the large recruitment centre for the QMAAC sent a group of women to train as military patrols, the equivalent of the male military police. "Non-attested as usual" is Peto's dry aside in her memoirs. Later the WRAF sent, in all, forty-eight recruits and an officer.

The chief obstacle to women being given full powers were the police acts which specified "fit men" but, as Dorothy Peto points out, where there was a will, there was a way — as one Chief Constable proved to both their and his satisfaction:

In 1918 Major Stanley Clarke, Chief Constable of Gloucestershire, paid us a visit at the Bristol School and asked us to supply him with two trained women, to whom he intended to give full powers and status by the simple procedure of first swearing them in under the Special Constables Act of 1831 (which relates to the appointment of fit *persons*, not of fit *men*), after which he would appoint them as full members of his Regular Force.

The BTS gladly gave him Constables Gale and Rowe. " ... On their appointment, Major Stanley Clarke not only swore them in according to plan but gave them the fullest possible scope by posting them to centrally placed Stations, supplying them with motor-cycles and giving orders that they were to be sent for in every case occurring within a certain radius when either a woman or child was concerned."

10

The Battle for London ...

One autumn day in 1917 a large crowd gathered around Mr Hollingsworth who was speaking in Hyde Park. But he was so ill-placed, and the crowd so large, that the adjacent footpaths became completely blocked. PC 706 A. Cleary asked Hollingsworth to move. He not only refused but resisted the inevitable arrest that such a refusal demanded. A struggle ensued. "A large number of people attempted a rescue," a subsequent report stated – a rescue of Hollingsworth that is – and the constable was "badly hustled". In fact two women in the crowd seized the constable from the rear and tried to pull him away from the speaker but, just as PC Cleary was becoming exhausted, Woman Patrol No. 1957 Baldwin saw what was happening and snapped into action.

Forcing her way through the now five-hundred-strong crowd, she dragged the two women from the constable's back and, at his request and with the help of a private person, took them into custody. " ... But for the timely assistance of Mrs Baldwin, who was not on duty at the time, the Constable might have been seriously injured, besides which the prisoner would probably have escaped," said a thank-you letter. "Mrs Baldwin's prompt and courageous action on this occasion, taken as it was, at considerable personal risk, is much appreciated by the Commissioner ..."[1] That was twice in six months they had come to the rescue of his policemen; he could hardly refuse the Special Patrols' plea for winter coats now.

As the October nights began to get chillier, Mrs Stanley had discovered that most of her full-time Special Patrols were "quite unsuitably clad" and, furthermore, not in a position to provide themselves with adequate clothing. Only two or three weeks earlier, at the NCW Annual General Meeting, Mrs Creighton had pointed out that the policewomen of the future were likely to be taken from the class of women who were forced to earn their living by the work and not so much the educated, who now took smaller pay for the sake of helping people. These new women would need equal pay, but they could not expect to be paid more than male constables so that, of necessity, the policewomen of the future would be the women who could live off the pay offered.[2] To make sense of this, one has to be aware of the current widely-held opinion that 'ladies' needed much more to keep body and soul together than 'women', who could manage quite happily on less. Obviously the 'lady' had higher expectations and standards to keep up. The Special Patrols were already having difficulty in persuading well-to-do women to work full time, and, as is obvious by the overcoat saga, they were now having to take on the less prosperous.

Mrs Stanley shopped around the large firms for suitable winter coats at a reasonable cost and came to rest at Harrods which, she found, would supply a garment of "excellent value, being of heavy winter serge lined with flannel at a contract price of £2.14s each". She arranged for these coats, thirty-seven of them, to be charged to her own account, then had the patrols pay her by weekly instalments of 2/6d. But even this was, she insisted, a serious drain on the limited means of the patrols. Could the authorities not see their way to a grant?

Mrs Carden passed on the request to Sir Edward Henry, assuring him that she had seen the coats and that they were not only good value for money but such that any lady might wear. Sir Edward wrote to the Home Secretary, marking the letter "Pressing", saying that he thought it a most reasonable request. Could he grant them £4 a head which would cover the cost of the coat plus sixpence a week boot allowance?[3]

They received their allowance, and, very soon, Mrs Stanley was given a raise. The work of the Special Patrols had increased a great deal since she started in March, Mrs Carden had explained. Not only that, her husband was permanently retired due to poor health and needed a resident trained nurse to look after him. Also Mrs Stanley was out such a great deal that she had been obliged to engage a housekeeper, which was extra expense. Despite some Home Office objections, "What about the £400 grant we give the NCW?", Mrs Stanley received her increase after the Commissioner had pleaded that he did not want to lose her since she was exceptionally well qualified for her post.[4]

In the spring of 1918 Sir Edward told the Home Secretary that he thought, in view of the constant pressure of a large section of public opinion, that the Special Patrols should be regarded as permanent in some form or other. He suggested therefore that they "settle its extent and conditions more definitely". He was suggesting nothing so outrageous as giving them power or uniforms or even the title of women police, merely fixing an authorized strength of thirty and so doing away with the onus of the NCW to provide extra free patrols when necessary, so that they could then reduce their grant to £300. Discipline, he felt, could still be left largely in the hands of the NCW, but the question of pensions would sooner or later arise in such a permanently employed body of women. "This would obviously involve some further contribution from the Police Fund."

The Receiver of the Metropolitan Police reacted strongly to this last suggestion. It would be a mistake, he insisted, to bring this little experimental force, which was only in its infancy and was not directly under the Commissioner's control, within the provisions of the Metropolitan Police Staff Superannuation Acts. The Home Office also saw the danger of creeping involvement. The Assistant Secretary, Harry Butler Simpson, supported the Receiver and commented that the women were engaged on work which was not police work in the ordinary sense but philanthropic work. He was in no doubt that there was a growing body of public opinion which favoured the expenditure of public money on promoting morality, at least sexual morality, but he doubted whether the auditors would see it that way. In fact he felt the work would be better carried out if it were not paid for at all, since it called for individual zeal and devotion, and too much official interference might stifle enthusiasm.[5]

The pension idea was duly quashed, but the public popularity of the patrols and women police was growing. Newspapers gave glowing accounts of their work, often aided and abetted, if not instigated, by the women themselves. Letters of support continued to plague the Commissioner and Home Secretary, most often from WPS admirers, and there was even some encouragement from inside the force.

In May 1918 a Croydon Chief Inspector sent a *crie de cœur* for at least four women patrols on full-time duty in addition to the two who already patrolled nightly from seven to 11 pm. Croydon's problem was four thousand women factory workers at a nearby aircraft factory, who kept bumping into "a large number of soldiers" who were training locally, not to mention perambulating patients from half a dozen military hospitals in the vicinity. Resultant 'behaviour' was giving cause for complaints.

"The women patrols deal with these cases (laying about in a

suggestive manner) very well," the Chief Inspector declared, and it was not necessary for them to have an accompanying PC, they could patrol in pairs. In fact so anxious was he that he had all the details already worked out, from the issue of beat cards to the precise hours and areas to be patrolled. When, a few months later, they tried to cut down on part-time volunteers in the area, the Commissioner received an outraged letter from the Mayor of Croydon and Chief Magistrate commenting sourly that what suited central London did not necessarily suit Croydon and that the patrols should be extended, not cut back.[6]

Even Joseph Chamberlain, then a member of Lloyd George's War Cabinet, asked the Home Secretary if he would consider using women police to a greater extent in the precincts of railway stations. They would not, he suggested, arouse the same degree of resentment as the employment of male police. He was under the impression, he told the Home Secretary, that women patrols, either police or volunteers, had been used for this purpose in the United States of America with conspicuous success.[7]

In March 1918 Sir Edward Henry asked Mrs Stanley to supply him with regular monthly reports on the work of her patrols. She produced an efficient area-by-area assessment, e.g.:

Report of work of Women Patrols 26th May to 30th June

Hyde Park	Three women patrols on duty daily 4 pm to 11 pm.
A DIV	During the month nine arrests were made for indecent behaviour, all of which were convicted. A large number of couples were spoken to and warned for unseemly behaviour.
Rochester	Two patrols (working without a constable) on duty daily 4 pm to 11 pm.
Row	Patrols took two young girls to Supervisor's Office to get work.
A DIV	Patrols broke up forty-six groups of soldiers and girls loitering. Several boys were stopped from begging from soldiers. PC asked patrols to help in moving women and children away from SA (Salvation Army) shelter where a number of men were billeted belonging to Jewish Legion from America, the crowd were begging for food. A complaint was made about girls being introduced to soldiers at the 'Albert Tavern', Victoria St. Patrols are

investigating this. PC asked patrol to take a lost child to police station they eventually found out his home and took him there.

As well as liberally sprinkling her reports with "a PC requested", Mrs Stanley did a little more judicious plugging for her ladies with regard to public attitude to them:

> Hyde Park   During these two days they spoke to forty-one couples for lying in suggestive attitudes. No one resented the action of the Patrols, and in every case complied with their directions.

Mrs Stanley's reports also began to feature the WPS, though not in the same "caused no resentment" light:

> Strand   On 24th inst. the Patrols were stopped by a working-class man with a respectable working woman, who accused them angrily of having interfered with the woman, who he said was his wife. Patrols assured him they had never seen or spoken to this woman, and on further enquiry found that the persons he wished to complain of were an 'Inspector' and a 'Sergeant' of the 'Women Police Service' who had apparently cautioned the woman a few days before when (she stated) she was waiting for her husband. After a little conversation the couple shook hands with the Patrols and parted on friendly terms.

According to Mary Allen, the Strand at that time was "the devil's playground". Another "unpleasant scene" with an Inspector of the WPS took place there when, Mrs Stanley reports, the Inspector berated the patrols for assisting police to arrest a woman for soliciting but not arresting some men they were with. "Patrols made no attempt to argue the point," she wrote, "but left the 'Inspector' talking angrily to some of her companions."[8] The Inspector could have been Harburn, who was now in charge of training some of which went on in this area.

In April 1918 the Commissioner, finding himself beset with complaints about "conditions in Woolwich", asked Mrs Stanley to look at the area again. She was able to inform him that two of her experienced workers were already involved in a month's investigation of the Woolwich area, on behalf of the Ministry of Labour. Her brief was chiefly to report on the incidence of drinking among women and girls, but she would be only too pleased, she assured Sir Edward, to extend their enquiries to accommodate his needs.

The report of the patrols turned out to be calm and quite objective. They had, they declared, found a complete absence of brawling and excitement. Cases of drunkenness were extremely few, and the people were very good-tempered, taking the crushing and waiting to get served quite cheerfully, and there was little spilling of liquor. They put this down mainly to dilution though the restricted hours (12-12.30 and 6.30-9.30 during the week, 7pm to 9pm on Sundays) must have played a considerable part.

Many smartly-dressed girls drifted from bar to bar or pub to pub, the report went on, but they were little the worse for this form of amusement. However, they warned, should drink return to its old pre-war strength and the hours be de-restricted, the dangers of this habit would soon become evident. In fact the number of women in the pubs was startling even by today's standards, though most of them were, of course, from the Woolwich Arsenal. For example, in three pubs in one square 188 women and 120 girls were counted between the hours of 8.30 and 9.30 pm one Saturday evening.

"A good deal of drinking can be put down to war conditions," they reported. " 'Four years ago I couldn't have believed I'd be doing this,' said a well-dressed woman in the crush at Plaisted's, then with a laugh – 'Well! it's war time.' Other women are anxious and lonely, an old Irishwoman said, 'You see my dear it's cold and wet, my landlady is hard and won't give me a fire. I'm that worried about my poor boy in France, and it's warm and comfortable here, it's poor stuff this beer they give us now but a poor soul must have something.' " Under DORA, 'treating' – buying a drink for someone else – could be an offence in military and munitions areas, but one, they found, which was hard to detect.

Mrs Stanley's accompanying report was also quite cool and objective. Her two patrols had been living, for the entire period, in one of the poorer streets, she assured Sir Edward. They had mixed freely with the working classes at all hours of the day and night. The senior member of the team (Lenny Smith, an artist and the first trainee at the BTS in August 1915)[9] had done similar work in Bristol, Portsmouth and Taunton, and found the behaviour of the people of Woolwich compared very favourably with these places. "In fact she assures me that she was impressed with the extremely good conduct of the town as a whole." They had seen girls laughing and talking with soldiers but "doing no harm" and showing singularly little inclination to pair off and go to secluded places. On Sundays laughing, noisy crowds filled Beresford Square, but she saw nothing that implicated the necessity of police or patrol interference. As for the low-class prostitutes, the police were doing the best they could for these, and she did not think women patrols could do more under existing conditions.

The report even gave the Commissioner the opportunity to bask in some reflected glory when Lord d'Abernon of the Central Control Board (Liquor Traffic) wrote to him saying how valuable was the information the patrols had gleaned, particularly as regards dilution, and how impressed he was by the common-sense views taken by the writers.[10]

All in all, the first half of 1918 was reputation-enhancing for Mrs Stanley and her charges, and more evidence of the growing acceptance of them is shown by the final, casual note at the end of her August report to the Commissioner: "On 29th August fifteen patrols each did a tour of four hours duty at the Zoological Gdns: to assist during Metropolitan Police Fête."

During the summer of 1918, Home Office and Ministry of Munitions officials began to discuss the feasibility of appointing Home-Office-controlled women police patrols. Subsequently a committee was set up to consider the proposition. Among those interviewed were Margaret Damer Dawson and Mary Allen (jointly), Mrs Carden and Mrs Creighton (jointly) and Mrs Stanley. Their evidence was illuminating. After saying that they thoroughly approved of the idea, Mrs Carden and Mrs Creighton weighed in with some strong anti-WPS propaganda. The fundamental difference between the two organizations, they informed the committee, was that the NCW thought that, on the whole, the police were good and carried out their duties well, whereas the WPS sought to reform them and wanted power of arrest for their body as a whole. They, the NCW, wanted it for only certain cases and to be exercised by tried and experienced patrols. Many members of the WPS had found they so disliked the aims of their own body that they had left and joined the Women Patrols of the NCW – in fact six had. Not only that: the WPS started the BTS but had now parted from them. This last information, seemingly given to make the WPS appear able to get on with nobody, was, of course, false. It was a vicious attack, but, to be charitable, it may be that the persons who wrote the report misunderstood what they were told or put a wrong emphasis on it. (It was not verbatim).

Mrs Creighton did add that the WPS had worked amiably with their women patrols in many areas – Hull, for instance.

Mrs Stanley declared that any opposition from the London police to her Special Patrols had ceased. The women were welcome everywhere and received full support from the men. Even training, she felt, was better done in the company of male police rather than with the voluntary patrols, since the work was quite different. Startlingly, she considered the power of arrest "quite unnecessary for patrols in general", since they could always call on a policeman. She went further and (against the quietly stated aims of the NCW) said that the work was better done by patrols, in co-operation with the police, than by policewomen.

Considering their reputation for being aggressive, and the way they had been presented by the others, the evidence of the WPS leaders seems remarkably reasonable and without malice. As the report said:

> They welcomed the scheme. The present unsatisfactory conditions of opposing Associations could not continue. While very proud of their own share in the matter and anxious to maintain their own Associations, they would, in the national interest, be quite satisfied to merge themselves in a Home Office Corps and be taken over, because they recognize that this would be of public advantage, but nothing less than a Home Office Corps, officially recognized, would compensate them for all they would give up in sinking their individual positions and the position secured by the Women's Police Service.

No nasty remarks about their rivals were reported. To be fair, the committee was organized by the Ministry of Munitions, and, by now, they had some firm friends there who may have defused their replies for them. Damer Dawson seems to have had a remarkable ability to generate loyalty as well as alienation. The committee recommended that Women Police Patrols should be formed. Their headquarters should be in London, and they should be officered by women to whom they were answerable for general discipline, but their work should be directed by the Chief Constables or Commissioner.

In July 1918 the Home Office received a prestigious deputation calling for women police to be appointed. On it were high-ranking representatives of the Church and armed services of the Dominions, USA and Great Britain. They were met by Sir George Cave and most of the important Home Office officials. None of this deputation was in the least interested in the appointment of women police on behalf of women; what they were after was protection for men. It was shocking, they thought, that the fine young men, who came from the Dominions and elsewhere for military service, should be exposed to temptations if they could be avoided. The Dominions felt very sorely on the subject and were not satisfied that the question had been dealt with as vigorously as it ought to have been. Women were best suited to deal with problems of their own sex; they were the best deterrent against the existence of disorderly houses and had proved exceedingly effective in dealing with soliciting. The influence of women with girls was enormous, and their influence over men not less extraordinary, especially when the women were of the right class.

In replying, Sir George assured them that he recognized the weight of the deputation, and their arguments. He too deplored the state of the streets, but what was really needed were stiffer penalties. He did appreciate what women had done, and women were, in fact, even being employed with great effect in munitions factories where some of them had even been sworn in* though it was doubtful whether this could be done legally. They could alter this by legislation, but they must proceed cautiously. There were practical difficulties, such as women trying to arrest violent criminals.

A minute on the file relating to this deputation, by Assistant Secretary, Home Office, Harry Butler Simpson, reads:

I venture to suggest that the appt. of some energetic but discreet lady to an *official* position in the Metropolitan Police – say as an additional Asst. Commr. or some purely honorary post – would put you in a better position to urge the more backward of the county and borough authorities to appoint policewomen. The deputation was mainly interested in London, and it appeared that their views would be met by some visible recognition of the police work and semi-police work done by women, which besides emphasizing its importance at the present time might also lead to its further development. At all events a lady of practical experience of the London streets might be of great assistance to the Commr. in dealing with this subject – of which we are likely to hear more.

The report on this deputation coincided with the presentation of the

---

* This remark was particularly ironic since, when it had been reported that sixteen women had been sworn in as Special Constables at Waltham Abbey, the Commissioner had complained to Winston Churchill, the Minister of Munitions, that it was "an embarrassing and most undesirable happening". Churchill had apologized, saying that the factory had done it without his knowledge and would be instructed that it had no legal sanction.

Ministry of Munitions' sub-committee report on women police patrols. Soon the Ministry began worrying the Home Office, wanting to know how the matter stood. They were told that the Commissioner had not yet seen the papers; he was on holiday, and they must not expect to hear anything until he had returned. On 30th August Harry Butler Simpson sent the papers to Scotland Yard, insisting they must do something *speedily*. He did realize, though, that the Commissioner was unlikely to have much time to give this question at the moment.[11] That was an understatement. Marching down Whitehall, possibly at that very minute, were columns of London's striking policemen. By the evening of that day the Home Secretary, Sir Edward Troup and Sir Edward Henry were all hurrying back from their holidays, but the strike was now virtually total and the City of London Police had joined in. Sir Edward Henry arrived back from Ireland the following morning; by evening he was no longer Commissioner of the Metropolitan Police.

Sir Edward had been Commissioner since 1903 and before that had been Inspector General of the Bengal Police. Credited with introducing the fingerprint system to New Scotland Yard, according to Mary Allen, his knowledge of police matters could not have been surpassed. In appearance, she noted, he was tall, dignified and well-built and had dark piercing eyes and the look of a diplomat. That was part of the trouble. According to T.A. Critchley in his *History of the Police in England and Wales*, Henry was a patriarchal ex-Indian civil servant who administered the force on pro-consular lines. Police pay was extremely low and had failed to rise with the cost of living, but the ageing Sir Edward, Critchley feels, was unable to understand their demands or why they wanted a union to represent them. To be fair, he had made efforts on their behalf, but the government had chosen to ignore them. Now they made him scapegoat.

He had obviously impressed the ladies. Mary Allen much regretted the strike which occurred "on one of his rare holidays" and his subsequent 'resignation'. "He was very kind to us," Damer Dawson later declared, and the Central Women's Patrol Committee sent him a letter of thanks for being such a good friend.[12]

The new Commissioner, the bluff, tough soldier General Sir Nevil Macready, whom Churchill had sent to Tonypandy to quell the miners' riots in 1910, had supplied troops to protect London during "the critical forty-eight hours" of the strike, then succeeded to the Commissionership "against his inclinations".[13] He claims to have been appalled by the lack of communication between the hierarchy at the

Yard and the ranks, and decided that much of this was due to useless Chief Constables (in whose appointment only influence and never talent were considered – none was a policeman), fiddling uselessly with papers at the Yard. He immediately split the policing area into four and sent a Chief Constable out to look after each. Since he only had three chief constables, he appointed another, this time a policeman. He saw no reason why this rank should not be attainable by a policeman, though he realized that anything above that needed wider experience than a policeman in London could acquire. He also gave his superintendents motor cars, instead of ponies and traps, and 'invented' women police.[14]

11

... London Capitulates

On 3rd October 1918 the *Daily Mail* reported:

A force of women police is to be created for London, officially recognized, under the control of the Commissioner of Metropolitan Police, and subject to the same discipline as the men. This is another 'break through' by women of that long line of positions that were assumed only to be fitting for men.

Women are likely to be firm and efficient constables ... Our urban life will be cleaner by the presence of the woman constable.

In the woman constable's dealing with the venal minor male offender against the law, she is likely to be less lenient than the policeman, and to be less inclined to 'look the other way'. Man is apt to be merciful with man – and woman. Woman is not to be cajoled. When a woman has a sense of duty, she is inflexible. There is some amusement in the prospect that those who hear the chimes o'midnight will have to be wary of women police. These would be ill days for Sir John Falstaff.

It is interesting to note that, according to one of the earliest women recruits to the new force, much of the male constable's mercy and flexibility, especially with prostitutes, was in direct proportion to the bribe he could extract.

The Commissioner refused to be pinned down as to where these new women were to come from. He had a great objection to the amateur in any form, he told the *Daily Mail* on the following day, and for this reason women without any voluntary experience might prove more use to them, but he was not going to say definitely.

A month and a half later details were announced. The complement was to be 112; Mrs Stanley was to be Superintendent and had a place on the selection board, as did Mrs Carden, who was ultimately to become its Chairman.[1] The WPS hierarchy was ignored. It was a shock and bitter blow, Mary Allen reports.[2]

It is difficult to understand why it was such a shock, but of course we can read what the Home Office and Scotland Yard thought of them; obviously they had no real idea. Perhaps it is not so surprising. Sir Edward Henry had always been charming to them, and, though they were distressed by Sir Nevil Macready's apparent ignorance of their history,[3] they had no idea that he thought their views 'extreme'.[4]

They put down some of their failure to the Commissioner's ignorance of them, and Mary Allen later salvaged more of their pride by declaring that they had really won anyway, since the easy acceptance of the others was due mainly to the work of the pioneer policewomen (them). However, a few pages earlier, in the same book, *The Pioneer Policewoman*, she claims that the move really "savoured of a setback" since the terms accepted were so poor. They certainly were. Pay was meagre; policewomen were not pensionable; their employment contracts were on a yearly experimental basis, and they were not to be called women police ("I object to the name,"[5] said Sir Nevil) but Metropolitan Women Police Patrols. Worst of all, they were to be neither sworn in nor given power of arrest. As a Home Office minute pointed out, the only difference between them and the Special Patrols was that the latter were employed through an outside body, the NCW, and now the Commissioner was to employ them direct,[6] and they were to be uniformed.

While waiting for the hoped-for call, Margaret Damer Dawson did a strange thing. Although obviously on tenterhooks as to whether the Commissioner was going to include them (letters to a friend and benefactor, Lady Norman, showed concern and uncharacteristic unsureness as to how far the WPS should push themselves or whether it would be wiser to go quietly about their business),[7] when interviewed by a magazine, *Christian Commonwealth*, on 16th October, she said things she must have known would not please Sir Nevil. As the interviewer reported:

"I suppose you want to know what I think of all this correspondence on 'The state of London Streets'," she said quickly. "It's all so one-sided, so unjust to women. They talk as if men were innocent angels, helpless in the hands of wicked women ... many of them have worked for the starvation wages women used to get, and they have found a way of earning as many pounds in a night as they used to earn shillings in a week. If there were no demand there would be no supply." She went on to rail about poor social conditions, which, she insisted, were to blame for most evils. Then she got back to the burning question. "It is strange that nearly all those who have taken part in the discussion, whether they defend the character of London or not, are agreed as to the general responsibility of women for all wrong doings. That equality of men and women which has made so much headway in the world of labour is unknown here. In the realm of morals we have not advanced beyond Adam who was tempted by Eve."

It has been suggested that Margaret Damer Dawson was merely a prurient snob and moralizer, but, clearly, this is not the case. Nonetheless, she had chosen, in her almost beguilingly indiscreet way, quite the wrong time to make this known, particularly since Sir Nevil had made no secret of the fact that he wanted one of the main duties of the new corps to be prostitute control. Women would be more discreet and thorough than men, "in whom it is difficult to eradicate the sex instinct, unless they are religious fanatics, the worst type to deal with that form of vice".[8] It is doubly ironic to think that Damer Dawson may have lost this particular battle for the very same reason as Nina Boyle lost hers: the determined defence of her own sex and, especially, prostitutes.

However, the WPS were not quite as "completely ignored" as Mary Allen later made out.[9] The first batch of twenty-five women recruited were ex-Special Patrols, but many of the second were from the WPS, and Sir Nevil had asked Miss Damer Dawson to give him the names of some officers she thought might be suitable for work at Scotland Yard, making it plain, however, that they would have to work under the already-appointed Superintendent Stanley. Nonetheless, she had acquiesced.[10] But, in the event, Mrs Elinor Robertson, who had worked as a senior officer in the Women's Forage Corps (RASC) during the war, was appointed Mrs Stanley's assistant.[11] No other senior women were appointed at that time.

On a dreary afternoon at the end of November 1918 I found myself with twenty-four other young women sitting on a window-seat in one of the long corridors that run the whole length of Scotland Yard. Since early morning, fog had threatened to envelop London: now, by late afternoon, it had carried out its threat. It swirled eerily along the dimly-lit corridor, forming fantastic shapes and pictures. From out of this gloom every now and then the figure of a man would appear, glancing with curiosity at us, then fading away into the distant murk of some office where doubtless he was indignantly telling his colleagues of the strange phenomena he had just seen. Women – and women who were to become policewomen.

So wrote Lilian Wyles in her book *A Woman at Scotland Yard*. Before applying to join the Metropolitan Women Police Patrols, she had served several months as a Special Patrol at Woolwich Arsenal. After a long wait in the foggy corridor, she was called in to be interviewed.

"Miss Wyles," called the voice of the sergeant on duty outside the library door, and shaking off my reflective mood, I walked into the long, high-ceilinged room. It was dimly lit, and the fog added to the dimness. At the table sat the members of the Selection Board. The Chairman was Sub-Divisional Inspector Duncan of 'A' Division. He was known to be a staunch supporter of the women patrols and had experience of their work, for several women had been stationed at Hyde Park Police Station of which the Inspector was in charge. Mrs Stanley sat with Mr Duncan, and her confident smile inspired courage and stilled the nervous flutter of the butterflies that are always so busy within one at a time like this. There was another lady present, who said nothing at all and whose name I have forgotten. I forget too, what questions I was asked by the members of the Board. I know that they were few but to the point. I was in and out of the room in less than ten minutes, yet I felt, when I rejoined the waiting women in the corridor, that I was on the brink of something new – something that would be for me my life's work, a career. I was right; about half an hour later I walked out of Scotland Yard into Whitehall. The fog was so thick that traffic was almost at a standstill. Big Ben struck six o'clock in muffled clangs. Despite the depression of the night, the damp and the fog, I was jubilant, for I had just become a policewoman.

As it turned out, her acceptance was as fateful for Mrs Stanley as it was for her. Had Mrs Stanley known how it would change her life, she might not have smiled so confidently or been so encouraging.

"There were a lot of 'ladies' amongst them," recalls Beatrice Wills of her fellow-recruits at that time. Lilian Wyles certainly gave the impression that she was hovering on that status, having been, by her own account, educated in a private school, finished in Paris, brought up in comfortable surroundings, sheltered from unpleasantness and with always sufficient money for her "not extravagant needs". She could never, she says, have lived on the wage offered. But it was handy pocket-money.

Bertha Alice Clayden, another of the early acceptances, had been a member of the WPS and seen service as a munitions policewoman at Pembrey in Wales.[12] However, she had one asset that many special patrols could not match: a solidly police family. Her father and two brothers were all inspectors in the Police.[13]

"We want only those suitable in every way," a 'lady official' at Scotland Yard explained to the *Daily News* of 21st March 1919. "It is not enough that a girl has been a conductress and longs for an open-air life." Beatrice Wakefield's (now Wills) friend and colleague at the Portsmouth dockyard where they were working though she was suitable in every way, showed her the newspaper carrying the Metropolitan Police advertisement and encouraged her to apply.

Beatrice, a tall and handsome thirty-year-old Cornishwoman, was from a working-class family and had never been to London before. When she was called for an interview, her mother accompanied her, just in case. "I thought I'd dress neat," Beatrice recalls, "in a blue costume and a small, matching hat." Obviously the strategy worked, for Beatrice became one of the fifty accepted out of five thousand 'outside applicants'.

On 23rd December Sir Nevil issued a Police Order officially inaugurating the Metropolitan Women Police Patrols, and on the first Monday after Christmas the initial twenty-five recruits entered training school at Beak Street in Soho. Two weeks later they transferred to Peel House, which had been occupied by the military during the war. They were given instruction in police duty, education, first aid and foot drill, which took place at Wellington Barracks under a sergeant with a very loud voice and attracted crowds who stayed to watch the women's attempts at marching. "I do not see brothels mentioned," complained Sir Nevil Macready when shown the proposed instruction schedule. "They should know what constitutes a brothel – and that suspected houses should be reported."[14]

At this stage they had no uniforms, as fresh supplies of police uniform cloth were not yet available, but, according to the *Daily News*, they were quartered "in comfort" in a police section-house. Comfort is not what Beatrice remembers. "It was very primitive," she says, "floors were bare boards, the only furniture in my room was a little dressing-table and a small let-down shelf, and my pillow was like iron. For tablecloths we used sheets."

When the first batch left training school to go on the streets (still minus uniforms) in February 1919, three of them were made sergeants straight away: Grace Russell, Patty Alliot, who had been in charge of the women patrols at Woolwich, and Lilian Wyles. London was divided into three, and they each got a third. Lilian Wyles was given the whole of central London and the East End – "a part of London full of Jews and foreigners of all sorts and conditions", she found. Her first five underlings were, she recalls, well built, well covered, a trifle severe of expression and wearing an "I'll stand no nonsense" air. "They were already proved workers, having served with the women patrols for more years than I had months. I can truly say they seemed pleased, and said so, that I was to be their sergeant."

But some people were far from pleased by the new women police patrols – their male colleagues in particular. Probably the women's leaders had previously fibbed a little when describing their complete acceptance by the men, but, in any case, it had been war time then: everyone had been pulling together, and there were not sufficient men to go round. And they had not been made official. Now there was a dramatic change of attitude. "To a man," claims Lilian Wyles, "they deprecated this utterly foolish experiment." Once on the streets, the women were treated with extreme hostility and insults from the male police, who constantly told them to get back to their washtubs. Beatrice Wills feels that much of this was due largely to the fact that the men did not like the women seeing the wholesale bribery that went on. She recollects that even if a policeman did speak to a policewoman, it was not a pleasant experience, since all they talked about was prostitutes.

Commissioner Macready, after reading an article in 'the Magazine', "crabbing women police", made a heavy-handed attempt to breach the gap by exhorting his men, in one of his "I'm-not-the-tyrant-you-think-I-am" speeches, to give the women a chance. After all, he had invented them, and there was "a certain class of social disability" he felt they could tackle. It was not quite the thing for full-blown constables to go stirring up ladies and gentlemen lying about in parks, but the women could do it. Give it a try, he concluded, "see if it turns out to be a farce."[15]

The first public appearance of the uniformed women police patrols was in May 1919 at a memorial service in Westminster Abbey for Metropolitan Police officers who had fallen in the war. The new uniforms, worn by the six women selected for duty, had been made by Harrods. They were composed of high-necked tunics, similar to those of the men, and long skirts. Underneath the skirts were tough serge breeches, and on their feet hard and heavy knee-length boots of solid, unpolishable leather. Lilian Wyles discovered later that they were old land-army issue which had been considered too heavy even for that work. The whole of what she termed "this unspeakable apparel" was topped off with a heavy but shallow helmet. Miss Peto claims that this uniform had been designed by Mrs Stanley on the pattern of the men's. This simple matter of just what the uniform consisted of and how it had been arrived at was the subject of a court case.

The job of presenting Lilian Wyles spick and span for this occasion was taken over by the head porter in the Wyles family's block of flats. Being an ex-guardsman, he managed to get a mirror-like glow on the two-inch-wide leather belt, but the boots, after hours of labour, defeated him. Looking as shiny as possible, WPS 23 Wyles had a nerve-wracking journey to the Yard by public transport, having rejected her father's offer to take her there by car. Once there, further trials awaited her.

The walk from Scotland Yard across to the Abbey was another ordeal; the windows and bridges of that vast police headquarters were crowded with curious officers, typists and officials of all sorts. Press photographers lurked in the streets ready to snap their cameras, and one or two enterprising reporters even approached Mrs Stanley asking for an interview as we were crossing Parliament Square. At last we were safely inside the Abbey, seated, I felt, far too prominently. Presently, HM Queen Alexandra, accompanied by HRH Princess Victoria, took their seats in the stall almost opposite to us, and the service began. From time to time I took surreptitious peeps at the Queen and Princess, and found they also were interested in us. To see six women clothed almost exactly as men police officers, except for trousers, must have been something of a surprise to these royal ladies, even accustomed as they were to meeting the unusual.

Beatrice Wakefield found the attitude of the public a mixture of curiosity and aggression: "They felt we were putting the rates up. When we travelled on the underground, men would drop their newspapers and stare at us quite openly. We were taught just to stare back. Once one shouted at me, '*That's* where our money goes!', and a member of the public reported one of us for powdering her nose in Trafalgar Square. We weren't supposed to wear make-up."

As though not handicapped enough by lack of power, public and police attention and aggression, yet another difficulty was put in their way. Mrs Stanley insisted that they change their division every month, which, Wyles claimed, irritated sub-divisional inspectors, who were just getting to know and trust a woman when she was moved.

They had to exercise a lot of pressure to get any work at all to do, but, gradually, the men soon became adept at passing on their least favourite jobs, such as the escorting to the station of lost children and dogs and the fetching of the barrow for the conveyance of drunks. Very slowly, and in pockets, they managed to acquire some other duties, escorting women prisoners and juveniles, observations requiring the presence of women, and hospital observations on female attempted suicides. Another factor in the strong resistance to their being used on observations and escorts was that the policemen often took their wives or girlfriends along on these duties and were paid the extra allowance for them. But mainly, and inevitably, they dealt with prostitutes and girls on the road to prostitution.

They claim to have saved many girls from their café-owner protectors in the East End by dint of long observation, persistent inspection and just making a nuisance of themselves. As a by-product they earned some reluctant approbation from their CID colleagues who had been 'unable' to check the procuration going on wholesale under their noses. "We used to turf the girls out of the restaurants in Chinatown," says Beatrice, "the owners didn't like it but didn't say anything, just bowed very low with their hands held together under their chins."

However, their colleagues could not prevent their getting involved in incidents when they were out patrolling. In one day, as a new recruit, Beatrice recollects, she dealt with an attempted suicide by a man who had cut his throat and escorted to hospital a woman who had "gone off her head". On another occasion she came across a drunken old lady tottering up and down Vauxhall Bridge Road amusing a large crowd with her gait: teetering, legs straddled far apart. "We took her to Chelsea Hospital on the handcart. I carried the lantern. She was so drunk that people thought she was dead and one man took off his hat. I got the giggles." On arrival at hospital, they found the reason for her odd gait – sixty pounds of gold in a bag slung round her waist and under her skirt. She was an extremely successful beggar who blackened her face and hands to make herself look very poor. The hospital knew her well; every now and then she would go on an almighty binge and land up there, and get cleaned up.

Eventually the policy of moving the women so frequently ceased, due to her own insistence, Lilian Wyles relates, but describes how Mrs Stanley blamed her when one of the women became engaged to a policeman on her division. "Had I kept my women on the move," argued Mrs Stanley, "this could not have happened." As more sergeants were appointed, they were given smaller areas in which to operate, and Wyles soon had sixteen women in her care, covering Vine Street, Marlborough Street, Bow Street and Tottenham Court Road. Most of their work comprised of dealing with hardened prostitutes who were by no means willing to be saved, so there was not much opportunity for rescue work. There was, she claimed, a good deal of trafficking in young girls, but they could do little about it apart from persuade the constables to charge the girls with insulting behaviour. This had the effect of getting the girls away from the influence of the madames but carried no stigma, and they usually went straight after that. The big difficulty, they found, was to track down a constable, then talk him into doing the arresting.

Lack of power was proving irksome, but policewomen were learning to use what is in any case the police officer's main power, the common law powers of any citizen in cases of larceny. Miss Wyles declared that she had no trouble in executing this power, especially since there was always a member of the public who would step in and help.[16]

12

After the Armistice

After the Armistice, Commandant Damer Dawson tried to keep the best of the demobilizing munitions women police together and get Chief Constables to take them on. By 1920 she had thus settled forty-seven women in twenty places from Bolton to Chipping Norton. Seventeen of these had power of arrest, and, she claimed, there were now towns where, whenever women were arrested, it was done by women police. Moreover, before the war ended, she had found that there were encouraging demands for their policewomen, even, as she so tactlessly put it, from towns hitherto recorded as asleep and old-fashioned, such as Colchester and Tunbridge Wells.[1]

Captain Henderson, Chief Constable of Reading, and one of their first customers, particularly liked WPS-trained women. He declared himself "well satisfied" with the recruits they had given him, which, on the face of it, was a little surprising since he admitted that:

The first two had to leave for family reasons – one was an executrix under her father's Will, which related to an enormous sum of money. Of the next two, one of them absolutely broke down and is now, unfortunately, in an asylum. The other had to leave because they had always worked together, and one of them would not work with anyone else. The two I have got now [in 1920] have been about three years, I think, in the Women Police Service. They were in munition works. Then they were employed at the Beaver Hut,[2] where, I think, they gained an enormous amount of experience. That is why I am so glad I have got them.

But, he admitted, he had had the last two only six weeks up to then and they were the first 'wage-earners' he had had as opposed to women with private means. He expressed some concern that the supply of "good calibre women" might be running out. Macready, too, complained that they were not attracting the class of women they wanted, due to low pay and lack of prospects. However Reading's women police were better off than many. They received the same pay as the men – the new rate since the strike of seventy shillings (plus uniform allowance). The Chief Constable was ambivalent about power of arrest: while not wanting any of his women "knocking about", he did appreciate it would be useful occasionally. For example: "There was a woman I had great difficulty in getting hold of, and the most extraordinary thing was that none of the men constables seemed to come across her, but the women police, who had not the power of arrest, came across her two or three times." He found no friction between the sexes in his force. In fact the men often approached their female colleagues and suggested they keep an eye on a particular woman who was "making a fool of herself". Despite his pro-woman police stance, he was quite adamant about one thing; women could never be put in a position where they could give orders to men.

Mrs Hampton, the only member of the WPS to be employed by the Metropolitan Police was (according to Lady Nott Bower, a poor law guardian at Richmond and a long-standing patron of theirs) very shabbily treated after Mrs Stanley came to power. She told the 1920 Committee on the Employment of Women on Police Duties (the Baird Committee) that Sir Nevil Macready had removed Mrs Hampton "without any substantial reason". It was a great grievance in Richmond as they valued her services exceedingly, and she was speaking not just for herself but for the magistrates and local police. One of the committee members, Sir Francis Blake MP, probed further:

1406. Was it in consequence of her training? Where was she trained? She was one of the Women Police Service. She was told last summer that although she was engaged by the Metropolitan Police and paid by them during the last three years, they did not propose to have anyone who was not in their own service. She got leave and went through their training and passed very satisfactorily. She passed all the tests and had high testimonials, but at the end of the training was told that they did not propose to re-engage her. Then she made some enquiries and the reason given to Mrs Hampton was that they did not think that Richmond required the full-time services of a sergeant.
1407. Did she hold the rank of sergeant?
Yes. Ever since she left they have had a sergeant and three other women working there, Richmond felt very dissatisfied and very much aggrieved at losing her. Her work was marvellous. The vicar of Richmond went up and had an interview with Mrs Stanley and enquired the reason

why Mrs Hampton was got rid of. He was told it was because she was a Christian Scientist and, therefore, would not take women and children for medical treatment. The vicar did not know about that. He came back and we were able to prove that it was quite untrue. Mrs Hampton had taken cases for treatment in connection with rescue work, and in a number of cases it was her influence which persuaded girls to stay under treatment, and only her influence. After that we got a lady to visit Sir Nevil Macready. He said it was not because Mrs Hampton was a Christian Scientist. We had therefore two official answers, neither of which was correct. The third answer was that Mrs Hampton had criticized her superior officers. I can say quite confidently that that was as untrue as the other two reasons. She never criticizes anybody, and she herself is prepared to give an absolute denial to that. The people she worked under during her training have expressed their gratitude to her for her excessive loyalty. She was going through her training at the time of the strike. I think we can only conclude that it was because a member of the Women Police Service was not desired. I have seen reports of the male police in Richmond with regard to her; they were absolutely enthusiastic over the work she did.

1408. She seems to have been somewhat hardly treated?

She was hardly treated. I must tell you another thing. Mrs Stanley sent her orders that, if she wished to go through her training, she must give up her position as Probation Officer. She did so with regret. She saw Mrs Stanley and said it was with regret she was giving it up.

1409. She was doing good work as a Probation Officer?

Yes. Her influence with women and girls was very good. Mrs Stanley now denies that she told her that. She said she only wanted to say that she was to give it up temporarily. We have Mrs Stanley's letters and they do not agree with that statement.

After that Sir Francis carefully changed the subject, but later on Lady Nott Bower referred back to it when asked what type of women she thought should be selected as women police? Those they had in Richmond in place of Mrs Hampton seemed to be quite a different type of woman, she said; in fact people had come up to her and said, "What funny policewomen you are getting in Richmond now." It transpired that they had neither the education nor the personality of Mrs Hampton. Who could have had?

Lancashire had taken on two of the Gretna policewomen but found that they had to be re-trained since they had learned nothing. In fact Chief Constable Lane of Lancashire was using women police in a quite revolutionary manner — as detectives. Not only did they deal with "every crime that came in", even murder, but they made their own enquiries and reports. Moreover, they had the same training, pay[3] and conditions as the men, and the title 'detective constable'. Lane had begun by employing female clerks, then, as they showed aptitude, he had "put them on the detective side". They had been particularly helpful, he said, in a murder case where a girl gave one of them "information about her health which she might not have given to a man". This information (he does not disclose what it was) turned out to be a vital clue. The women were not put in charge of cases; even the advanced Lane realized that it was not possible to risk the situation developing where a woman might give orders to a man. But they worked with the men and were not resented. In fact he did not know what he would do without them now. However, the present-day survivors of those early women detectives recall that their work was largely clerical and secretarial with the occasional indecency statement, pickpocket observation at markets and races, and decoy duty during spates of sexual attacks.

And they were not quite as unresented as the Chief Constable imagined – for good reason. A couple of weeks after his evidence at Baird, *The Police Review and Parade Gossip* received a letter complaining about the Lancashire women detectives. The writer, who signed himself "Clogs and Shawl", pointed out that police*men* had to have at least five years' service and pass an exam before they were "promoted to CID work".

Rather surprisingly, Margaret Damer Dawson did not generally approve of women being used as detectives. As a rule they were unfitted for the work, she felt, and, in her experience, did not like it either. "A woman is all right," she declared, "when she can be straightforward, but not otherwise." This despite the fact that the WPS had had "one wonderful detective" who had been seconded to Special Intelligence during the war.[4]

Chief Constable Lane did not like women wearing uniform without legal status and powers to back it up. He was not, in fact, very much in favour of their wearing uniform at all. However, if they were to be used in this manner, he thought they should be equal in every respect with the exception of length of service. Women should work twenty-six rather than thirty years, since they went off quicker than men. Unlike Macready, he did not approve the idea of women police having power of arrest mainly to deal with prostitutes. In his opinion, if they were to get rough handling, this was where it was likely to come from, as prostitutes were often "horrid, low-class" types of women, who were very violent.

As far as work content is concerned, probably the 'most equal' policewoman in the British Isles at that time was BTS-trained Mildred White of Salisbury City Force. She had been thrust upon a very unwilling Chief Constable by his Watch Committee, who, in turn, had been pressured by a highly influential women's patrol committee (built up due to the large local military presence). But the Chief Constable was an unusual man. Rather than try to spike her chances, he chose to make sure that she was properly trained, to give her every chance of success. Possibly the minuteness of the force (twenty-three in all, including himself and Policewoman White, though the complement was thirty) made it imperative that there were no passengers.

Her duties, with the exception of traffic control, were the same as the men's, and she was frequently left in sole charge of the police station. Her hours were the same or often longer than theirs, if there was a woman prisoner to look after, and she had power of arrest which she had executed three times, twice with women deserters and once in a case of petty larceny.

Constable White was not, however, grovellingly grateful for these concessions – quite the contrary. She had had a tough time in a previous appointment in Bath when she arrived, unwanted, at Salisbury. These experiences must have toughened her, for she appears to have been frightened of nobody. Though her pay was the same as a man's, and she agreed that it was surprising that such a small force had a policewoman when much larger ones had none, she still felt they were getting a cheap police officer since she received neither pension nor rent allowance. When the Chairman of the Baird Committee asked her why she thought this was, she replied, "By reason of sex, that is all, I think. I do not know whether I am supposed to live in a tent." What is more, she pointed out, working as she did in a small city meant she had no prospects. Why should that be, asked the Chairman. If there was only one woman, she could not have the rank of sergeant; it would not have any meaning, she replied. Which indicates that even this outspoken lady did not contemplate the possibility of a woman giving a man orders. How about transferring to a larger force with more women in it, when she wanted promotion, the Chairman persisted. Constable White did not think much of that idea. She believed in getting to know the people in your city and staying there. "It is my ambition," she announced, "to stay in Salisbury ten or fifteen years." The men of Salisbury City had been very nice to her, and, as for the Chief Constable, he was now "quite ready to say he was wrong". The Chairman assured her that the Chief Constable had, in fact, written to the committee saying that the experiment was entirely satisfactory. "Yes," she said, "I think he really means that now. But he was very unwilling."

Scotland had been tardy in the employment of women police, though not as tardy as Wales, which had none. Mr Walter Hogg, Senior Clerk to the Scottish Office, told the Baird Committee that as only thirteen women had been appointed as 'police auxiliaries' in Scotland, ten in Glasgow, two in Edinburgh and one in Ayr, in contrast to four hundred in England, and this had been done only recently, they were not in a position to offer any conclusive evidence. They did think that since the new act women could be sworn in, but the question was, was it expedient to do so, considering their lack of physical strength? There were some duties they could perform, but they could not possibly be paid the same as men since they would not be taking the same risks. They should, however, be pensionable.

Mr David Buchan Morris, the Town Clerk of Stirling, represented the views of Scotland's Royal Burghs (towns and cities), which were that most of them neither needed nor wanted women police. In answer to a circular sent to them in April 1919, only seven had indicated approval. These were Glasgow, Dundee, Edinburgh, Aberdeen, Ayr, Dunfermline and Rothesay. The rest were either "indifferent or unfavourable", Mr Buchan told the enquiry. Several felt that policewomen were all right for other burghs but not for them, as they were too small, had no facilities etc. Others were curtly dismissive of the idea. Since the time of asking, Aberdeen had changed its mind and was now against, and Dunfermline was now divided, especially since the Chief Constable was entirely against "this innovation". That left five.

Mr Buchan bravely declared that he felt most of them had not given the matter proper consideration. What they needed was more information and a lead which, he felt, this enquiry and consequent publicity might provide. Where he would like to see women police was in holiday resorts and garrison towns, where they could do morals patrols for the protection of the young soldier.

The person who spoke for the Scottish counties, Captain Charles Balfour, was brief and to the point. The counties did not need them and did not want them, and, besides, there was no room for them at any county headquarters.

In mitigation the Senior Clerk, Scottish Office, pointed out that until recently Scotland could not claim for more grant aid for women police since they received a set amount from the government. It soon became evident though that even the Glasgow ten were largely a fiction, possibly a last-minute gesture so as to have something to tell the committee. Their appointment, HM Inspector of Constabularies for Scotland admitted, had finally been approved "only the other day", and to date only three had been taken on "as an experiment". Their training had not even begun. The two claimed for Edinburgh were also admitted to be "really probationers". In fact they were really still employed by the National Vigilance Association, as the committee was to learn, and had not yet even become probationers.

Glasgow and Dundee already had what were largely sex-statement-takers like Miss MacDougal of the Metropolitan Police. HM Inspector of Constabulary for Scotland, Lieut. Col. Ferguson, made much of these, and later they were called to give evidence themselves. He also made much of the fact that Miss Miller, Glasgow's statement-taker, had said she would rather not have a power of arrest, but when this lady came to speak for herself, she made it plain that, although she did not want the power, since she rarely came in contact with offenders, merely victims, she did feel it was advisable for women police generally.

The Chief Constable of Glasgow grudgingly admitted that there were some jobs on which women police could be employed, mostly the type of thing Miss Miller did, and he intended to give her one of his three new women as an assistant. The reason he still had only three women was because it was so difficult to find the right type. In fact Miss Miller had already told the committee that the reason he could not get the right type was that the pay offered (thirty-five shillings a week plus twelve shillings war bonus) was so low.

Dundee's statement-taker, Mrs Jean Forsyth Wright, was probably Scotland's closest approximation to a policewoman yet employed. The main part of her work was taking sex statements but, since sex crimes were not nearly so common in Dundee as Glasgow, she had time to spare so also did court duty, patrolled "areas where girls might be found" and was invited to accompany the men on investigations where they thought a woman might be needed. Indeed, the men had been very generous and helpful to her, she told the committee, and had always been prepared to utilize her services. Sometimes she wore uniform and sometimes not, but she too was for power of arrest, if only for the confidence it would inspire. She stuck to this opinion throughout a long cross-questioning and despite the Chairman's warning that she might thus be foregoing the protection her sex afforded her.

The power of arrest question came up again immediately the Chief Constable of Edinburgh, Mr Roderick Ross, began his evidence. His hasty answer betrayed his true attitude, however. They should not be given power of arrest until the movement had received a thorough trial, he said, and even then it should be left to the discretion of the Chief Constable. It would be very serious to give power of arrest to a lady who was not acquainted with the Acts of Parliament. When Major Baird pointed out that the same would surely apply to a man, he replied;

A policeman very rarely arrests any citizen unless he is accompanied by a practical policeman. For a period of three, four or six months it is very rarely that a policeman, with us at any rate, is allowed to get out on his own; so that he always has the benefit of a practical, trained man beside him.

2337. Would that be a difficulty in the case of a woman?

You only have two to begin with, and they could not be split all over the city; at least, I should only have two.

2338. Why should not a woman have a man with her?

You mean that a constable could be detailed to do duty with these women?

2339. In the same way as a constable would be detailed to do duty along with a new constable.

He was trapped and had to admit that it was 'a possibility'.

Edinburgh's Town Clerk and Treasurer were obviously feeling a bit touchy about outside interference, especially in relation to the purse. After saying they must stress that they had not committed themselves to the view that women police were required, but they realized they would have to put it to the test, the Treasurer addressed the committee;

... If you come to the conclusion that there should be women police, it would be better from our point of view if you authorized and did not order.

You need not be afraid of that; we have no power to order. With regard to the police, we have just experienced the Order in the matter of pay, and it is being followed up by the other services demanding the same pay as the police. Immediately the other services get the same pay as the police, the police will want more ... We are rather tired of getting instructions, and we think we can manage if you only authorize.

Is it not the point rather that even with regard to the pay of the police it was a recommendation?

It was a recommendation with an indication that you will not get the grant unless you pay it.

That is the worst that can happen; but you cannot get an order.

The only little variation that we did want to make was turned down, and the indication was: if you will not do this thing you cannot have the grant.

That was very like a pistol?

[Town Clerk] A big gun.

Another of Scotland's representatives was Miss Edith Tancred, an ex-house-mistress of a well-known girls' school[5] and currently Director of the Scottish Training School for Policewomen. Her school, which was based in Glasgow, had grown, like Bristol and Liverpool's, with which it was federated, out of the local women patrols. Indeed, before opening, Miss Tancred had studied and patrolled with Miss Peto and Mrs Stanley but had found that she had to unlearn a great deal of this since Scottish customs and laws were so different. She realized that they were latecomers in the field, having only just got off the ground by autumn 1918, but this had its advantages. The Scots had taken to heart the experiences of England. They would rather have no policewomen than start with bad conditions and get into the chaotic state of the English movement. However, she had soon realized that 'no policewomen' is exactly what they would have unless, like Peto, she put propaganda first. Up to now they had trained only three women, two of whom had worked for the National Vigilance Association in Edinburgh and a third whom she hoped would soon be appointed as Edinburgh's first policewoman. They had also trained twelve patrols for the WRAF before embarking on her fight for more openings and better pay and conditions. Unfortunately, her efforts had not prevented Glasgow's offering poor pay, no powers and no pensions, or, as she said on another occasion, less than "the Corporation cleaners".[6] And at Ayr the policewoman did not even have a room in which to conduct her interviews with women and girls and had to use her own bed-sitter. Since many of them were "the very lowest of the low" and often diseased to boot, the policewoman was always getting notice to quit from her landlady.

Miss Tancred did not think much of Glasgow's selection ideas either. The duties indicated a woman of education and qualifications, whereas the selection process required only elementary education. For example, applicants had only to be able to do the first three rules of simple arithmetic without help.

13

Baird: "This Extraordinary Quest"

"Here you have a woman sent out on this extraordinary quest at night time in company with a man, both of them being sufficiently youthful for the ordinary human passions to be in full play, and they were sent out together to observe the disgusting indecency that unfortunately takes place in the park."

Mr Mead was describing the exploits of the Special Patrols to the 1920 Baird Committee.

There was this quaint distinction: a woman was not allowed to go with a single man, but the arrangement always was that her companion must be a married man. It seemed to me a most anomalous thing, because the single man might be a model of moral purity, whereas the married man might be a libertine. But it points to the fact that the authorities had some ground for apprehension with regard to the extraordinary relations that were established between these persons.

Frederick Mead had only just started his long and indignant evidence, which was to go on and on, since he seemed determined to leave nothing out. The Committee on the Employment of Women on Police Duties, known as the Baird Committee after its Chairman, Major Sir John Baird, had been set up after further pressure from the various church and women's organizations, when they had failed to get women included in the 1919 Desborough Committee on Police Conditions, itself set up largely as the result of the 1918 police strike. Then the Parliamentary Under Secretary at the Home Office, Major Baird, had vaguely promised them a committee of their own instead. With the passing of the Sex Disqualification Removal Act, which allowed women to become civil servants, jury members and Members of Parliament, Miss Peto enquired of the Home Secretary whether this did not also allow them to become fully-attested police officers?

Home Office officials disagreed among themselves on this question.

Harry Butler Simpson, an Assistant Secretary, thought the new act made no difference, but Sir Edward Troup thought it did. Nonetheless, he felt that the practical difficulties remained and suggested a *small* committee to consider them.[1] Miss Peto, who had decided to put everything else aside at the moment to concentrate on propaganda, kept up her harassment and, finally, on 24th September 1920, the Baird Committee interviewed the first of the forty-seven witnesses called.

"I hope," Macready had written to the Home Secretary, "if you have a Committee on Women Police, that Miss Damer Dawson or any of her other satellites will not be included thereon, otherwise there will be considerable trouble over here."[2] They weren't sitting on the committee but were, naturally, called as witnesses, as were many of our characters. The Committee was comprised of five men, headed by Major Baird, and two women: Dame Helen Gwynne-Vaughan, Controller in Chief of the Women's Auxiliary Air Force, and Lady (Nancy) Astor, the first woman MP.

On Day One, Harry Butler Simpson gave the committee the definition of a policeman, his history and a run-down of the statutes on which his powers were based. Then he argued that a constable was effective largely because of the prestige which his behaviour had gained him and a very handy weapon which he had to assist him, but, not least, to his superior physical strength – superior that is, to the average law-breaker, who was not likely to know about the constable's special powers of arrest and be influenced by them; thus it was pointless giving these powers to women. Dame Helen enquired whether it was not possible to supplement the woman's physical powers with a handy weapon also, but received the prim reply, "I would hope that women should be so employed that they would not have to come into actual personal conflict with malefactors."

On the second day it was the turn of Sir Leonard Dunning. He came out very strongly in favour of women police, particularly with regard to juvenile crime and probation work, which he felt was a police function, though he knew the Home Office did not agree with him. He told of his experiences in Liverpool and reiterated his belief that high crime figures and widespread poverty go hand in hand. Women should also be employed in courts whenever a woman appeared there, he insisted, and they could be used in investigating the activities of fortune-tellers (in fact civilian women usually were) and in much other detection work.

It was immaterial, he felt, that existing women police had stemmed largely from the activities of the feminist movement and told the committee that he would have no prejudice against women trained by the BTS or WPS. He would, in fact, regard them as having learned part of their job but would also make sure that they knew the job according to his ideas before allowing them loose on the streets. As he had said before, they all had exaggerated ideas of the power of police, especially since DORA had been so sweeping. He had, he felt, persuaded Miss Peto of the error of this opinion but he did not think he had ever convinced Miss Damer Dawson: "So many of these women think that that is the principal way the men do their duties — by continually arresting people. The first thing you have to teach a police recruit that that is the thing he has to try and avoid."

When a member of the committee, Sir Francis Blake, suggested that there had been much more work done in this area in America, Sir Leonard told him: "It is rather difficult to judge as to that. Americans start a thing like this and in six months they proclaim it a roaring success. It is, therefore, very difficult to measure the value of any information you get from America ... The rapidity with which they arrive at that decision makes one get a bad opinion about the value of it."

His personal opinions on what the conditions of employment for women police should be were most enlightened. He saw no reason why they shouldn't get equal pay, pensions and conditions. He even thought it quite acceptable that a woman should give orders to a man. Woman might lack a man's strength, but they would necessarily be of a higher education and class, so this would justify such equality. His liberality, however, stopped just short of power of arrest. It was immaterial whether they had it, he felt; after all citizen's powers were almost equal to those of a constable. The biggest difficulty was going to be stopping them arresting everybody anyway. But, in general, his evidence, gave great support to women police. "I am rather disappointed," he told the committee, "that Liverpool has only got two policewomen. I think that if I were still there they would have more." Small wonder Miss Peto called him "our good friend".

Next in the line of witnesses came the representatives of the Metropolitan Police: the Commissioner, Chief Constable Olive, Superintendent Billings and Mrs Stanley. Macready supported the women in their quest for power of arrest but thought it should be a limited power to operate only over women and children under sixteen. Despite what had been said, he felt that women would exercise such a power with discretion — that is, if they were properly selected, like his.

If he received permission to give them the power, it was his intention, he assured the committee, to hand over the control of prostitution entirely to women.

Then the Commissioner launched forth on his burning problem, the WPS. Just before the committee had began sitting, his patience, goaded by Mrs Stanley, had finally given out, and he had sent the Women Police Service chiefs a letter threatening legal action if their officers did not cease masquerading "in a uniform which can reasonably be mistaken for that of a Metropolitan Police Woman".[3] He was on tricky ground here since his women, not being attested, were not really policewomen. Before sending off the letter he had consulted with solicitors to ascertain whether they could claim that Metropolitan Women Police Patrols wore "police uniforms". He was given the go-ahead on the grounds that, as the women were employed by the Metropolitan Police, they could be so called.[4] The letter mortified and horrified the WPS, but it did not stop them.

To back up his case Macready had brought with him papers on two 'cases' which showed the confusion the WPS caused. In one instance a couple had written to him from Scotland enquiring whether the man appearing in a newspaper photograph with the WPS might be their missing son? The Commissioner produced the offending photograph which, he declared, was not only not of his women police patrols as this couple supposed but of the WPS and a woman dressed in man's clothing. (I came across a picture of them 'arresting' a rather odd-looking 'man'.) The WPS later vehemently denied his accusation, saying that the young man in the photograph was "a respected member of a well-known company" but did not, however, name him.[5]

Macready chose this moment to reveal why he had not made use of the WPS hierarchy when forming his own force. On enquiry, he said, he had discovered that the moving spirits had been militant suffragettes. Now his average policeman was very conservative, and it was going to be difficult enough to get this thing going without taking on women who might have been in court for assaulting police. His predecessor had not seen eye to eye with the Women Police Service, he went on, which wasn't surprising since these women wanted to purify the male police and show them how to do the work. In his letter to the Bridgeman Committee in 1924, he was to be more explicit. Though he did not name the WPS particularly, he declared that one of the main difficulties had been to acquire the "right stamp of person". "The main point was to eliminate any women of extreme views – the vinegary spinster or blighted middle-aged fanatic." However, he told the Baird Committee, the WPS were dying down now, fortunately, though there were still some about, and he would wait until they reported before he took any further action.

The very vague Chief Constable Olive, Macready's appointee from the ranks, and Superintendent Billings, not surprisingly supported their Commissioner in his plea for a limited power of arrest for the women. It would prove particularly useful in indecency cases in the parks, they thought. Billings, whose Division covered Hyde Park, spoke well of the Women Police Patrols, saying he felt their scope of duties should be gradually expanded. He also felt that something should be done to make it illegal to wear police badges and uniform if one were not a police officer.

Mrs Stanley was the last witness on the afternoon of Thursday 26th February 1920. She weighed in straight away against 'unofficial bodies'. In her experience, she said, the training given by amateur women and patrol societies was practically useless and, in many cases, a distinct disadvantage, as many of the women themselves had pointed out to her. It is pertinent that she included women patrols in this attack. She had, in fact, been highly instrumental in the disbandment of the London Voluntary Patrols in July 1919. Macready had asked her to look into their work, and she had duly reported "great friction" between the local London committee and the central Women's Patrol Committee controlled by Mrs Carden. She had gathered from the latter that she would not be sorry to see the London patrols wound up, providing that it was officially stated that the Metropolitan Women Police Patrols were the outcome of the work organized by Mrs Carden at the beginning of the war. The NCW had always aimed at the appointment of women police, Mrs Stanley told him, and now their object had been achieved. The Commissioner duly wrote to Mrs Carden, thanking her for her work and crediting the NCW with being responsible for forming the body from which the official women police had sprung. He felt now, however, that their work had come to an end since they were merely duplicating his women's duties.

Mrs Carden's reply and a subsequent letter very much regretted his decision to sign no more cards for them, and this regret sounded fairly genuine, so it is possible that Mrs Stanley had either got the wrong idea or was deliberately clearing the field. Of course, in professing profound regret, Mrs Carden may just have been boxing clever herself. She thanked Macready for giving them due credit and asked his permission to quote him to the Press, adding that perhaps the best bit of work she (Mrs Carden) had done was to secure the services of Mrs Stanley.[6]

In her evidence to the Baird Committee Mrs Stanley went along with the Commissioner's scheme for limited power of arrest which, she considered, would be especially useful in dealing with prostitutes. She did not want full powers. "You could not," she said, "expect a woman to arrest a burglar." Dame Helen brought up her weapons question. Did the women have anything resembling a truncheon. No, said Mrs Stanley, they had no weapon of any sort. Would they be given one if they had power of arrest, Dame Helen persisted. Mrs Stanley did not think so; it would be a danger rather than an assistance since it might be snatched from their hands and used against them.[7]

When reporting on the attitudes of the male police towards her charges, Mrs Stanley revealed that she was either completely out of touch with the treatment her women were receiving or she felt it politic to lie. There had been no friction whatsoever, she declared. The women had received the greatest possible assistance. She even saw fit to reiterate the statement and assured the committee that there had not been a single case of friction of any sort. According to both Lilian Wyles, in her later book, and Beatrice Wills, whom I interviewed recently, the 'friction' had been both extreme and continuous. But, Beatrice recalls, Mrs Stanley was a remote figure who did not trouble to get to know her women or behave in a friendly fashion towards them herself.

14

Baird: "A most Ludicrous State of Things"

Margaret Damer Dawson had some disturbing news for Commissioner Macready, who had been woefully misinformed that the Women Police Service were "fading out". They had, she chose this moment to reveal, sufficient funds, courtesy of the munificent donor, to equip a small standing army of policewomen. In fact the donor was anxious that their service should continue until it was taken over by the state.

After reading out Macready's threatening letter to her on the uniform question, the Commandant informed the committee of her reply. She had acknowledged, she said, that there were anomalies in her position but had pointed out that the WPS had had the uniform first, and, moreover, it had been approved by Sir Edward Henry. She had asked the Commissioner to wait until after this committee had sat before taking any further action. He had done so, but she had heard nothing further from him.

The members of the committee probed deeply about the relationship she maintained with her women once they had been handed over. Did she not usurp the authority of the Chief Constable? As always she adamantly refuted the charge. She contacted the women, she told them, only through the Chief Constable, and this happened rarely, perhaps when one of them had an interesting case, the details of which might be useful in their training.

However, Damer Dawson did restate her conviction that women police should be an entirely separate, state-controlled force and not operate under individual police authorities. Their work was different from the men's, she insisted, and, if this were done, all comparisons about pay, physical strength, hours women were capable of working etc, would cease.

How much control they attempted to retain over the women they trained was a question pressed home with the BTS witnesses as well.

Miss Peto took the opportunity to put in a plea for a woman assistant to the HM Inspector of Constabulary who could keep in touch with the scattered women police and help to co-ordinate their work and pass on useful knowledge. Dunning, who was recalled to have this suggestion put to him, said he could not see any necessity for it. He did not anticipate any disciplinary problems; he was very impressed with the women so far employed, and there was no need to be anxious about their doing their duty or behaving properly. He did concede, however, that a person of their own sex might occasionally be useful in obtaining some information. For instance, on one occasion when he was making an inspection of a force where there were women, his wife was with him, so he asked her to talk to them and find out anything he could not. She did discover one small matter of detail about their uniform "which perhaps they did not like to mention to me". So although women might be needed occasionally in this respect, Chief Constables, who were usually married men, could always do it through their wives. Also, he pointed out, their powers over constabularies were really quite limited and ill-defined. Chief Constables might listen to their advice, but they did not have to take it.

Establishing what kind of work the women could do better than men, and thereby justifying their employment (something never required in reverse), was one of the main aims of the enquiry. Lady Nott Bower felt that the custody of women should always be in the hands of women and revealed that this was still not the case despite continuous protestations to the contrary.

If you go to the average Police Court, they say: "Of course we have a woman for the cells at night." When you come to investigate, you very often find it is the wife of the sergeant who may be called upon, but she is also often the woman who cleans the Court and cells in the day. In other words she is a woman who has done her day's work before she goes to bed for the night. She can be called upon in case of emergency, but the policemen are left to judge what would constitute an emergency in such a case. My point is that if there is a woman in the cells there should be a woman in attendance. The poorer women feel so intensely that it is such a dreadful thing that at any moment if there is any noise heard a man may look in upon them; but you find that very usual. It is left to the man in charge to decide as to the emergency. Their only idea of an emergency is either that the woman is very ill or very violent.

She also put in a plea for women's privacy in common lodging-houses which, in the provinces, were inspected by police. She felt that only women police should visit women's lodging-houses, for the simple reason:

> They must pay surprise visits, and they must pay them at the most crowded hours in the evening. The common lodging-house is the last refuge of the respectable woman who wants to keep off the streets – the woman who is perhaps in desperate poverty and almost being driven to supplement her earnings. She very often has only the clothes she stands up in. The only opportunity she has of getting a job is to keep herself clean and to wash her clothes, and she takes them off at night for that purpose. A man may come in and find the woman with hardly any clothes on at all. They are in their underclothes, perhaps with just a petticoat on, washing their chemise or gown. It is a very hard thing for women who are trying to keep themselves respectable to have two men entitled to run in on them any time.

Enquiries with regard to suspected abortions, especially the examination of bedclothes and underwear, was another area in which she felt women should operate.

Male police frequently claimed that women did not mind, indeed there was a certain type of woman who preferred, giving sex statements to a man. "I have not heard of her!" was Lady Nott Bower's response to this suggestion. Edith Tancred was even more succinct. "That is nonsense."

Mrs A.C. Gotto, General Secretary of the National Council for Combating Venereal Disease, gave trenchant reasons as to why her body supported the establishment of women police with full powers. Their presence on the streets, as had been shown at Hull and Grantham, reduced the likelihood of adolescents being exposed to VD. Nonetheless they saw grave dangers in their "degenerating into *police des moers*" (morals police), therefore their duties should not be restricted to sexual offences. Mrs Gotto also pointed out that the male police were constantly being asked by men where they could go for VD treatment but that women had no one to ask and would be too shy to ask a man. She did not go as far as Lady Nott Bower, who claimed that policemen had sex, indeed positive orgies, with prostitutes, but she did make a pertinent point that the laws pertaining to procuration were "extremely laxly administered", and as for abortion: "All of us who are in close touch with social work know the activities of the abortionists – a number of women in the less reputable parts of town who are practising abortion. The whole of womanhood of that part of the town know who are the people to go to. Men police would never reach them."

It was, of course, back to the original polemic. Many men insisted that women police were unnecessary, they could do the job perfectly well, while women who knew the actual conditions thought that female interests were merely being ignored. Women were not protected; nor was their modesty and sensitivity, which society insisted they demonstrate in other spheres, considered.

Though Chief Constable Lane of Lancashire spoke up for his women detectives, Sir Ernley Blackwell, Assistant Under Secretary of State for the Home Office, was dead against women detectives. He simply thought the work too dangerous: "Detective work is by far the most dangerous work of the lot. In the work of the ordinary detective there are very few crimes that do not involve considerable danger, culminating with the arrest of the criminals. There is always the off-chance that the man is armed. He is quite likely to be armed, and if he is not, there is always the possibility that he will resist by violence."

Lieut. Col. the Hon. G.A. Anson, Chief Constable of Staffordshire, who was being interviewed with Mr Lane, particularly felt that women would be unable to handle crowds, at least their kind of crowds. When the chairman mentioned that some of the women witnesses had told them that a woman going into a crowd had a wonderful influence and sometimes induced civilians to help them, Lane put in, "That is in London is it not?" The chairman agreed. It is so different with us, Anson told him, "I am afraid that in some parts of my district the men would interfere. In some districts the women are just as rough as the men." Lane agreed: "You cannot compare London people with these pit-brow lasses and colliery women."

Work with children featured very little in the arguments for and against women police in those days — possibly because there were few laws in operation relating particularly to them and their protection. Those who brought the subject up most strongly at Baird were Dunning, with his Liverpool experiences in mind, and Mr William Clark Hall, a magistrate in the East End courts. Mr Hall had done a great deal of work with juveniles, and he argued that women should be employed on this work, not, strangely enough, because they would be any better at it than men but because he thought it might systemize procedures.

... The police vary extraordinarily in their interest in children and their method of dealing with them. I am struck by the fact that so many cases against children are brought by particular officers. That seems to show that the police are not at all systematic in the matter. Some police officers will think it always desirable if they find a child committing larceny, for instance, to arrest him and take him into the station. Others rather shirk the trouble, or they consider, perhaps, it is better not to arrest them but simply go to the parents and tell them about it or to warn the child. My own view is that in all cases where a child has committed an offence he is the better for being brought before a police court, not the worse. I do not think I have ever known a case where I can honestly say I think a child has suffered from being brought before a police court, and I think, therefore, if there were women police it might help to systemize the matter more. They would take a greater interest in the particular child, and one would get more children brought before the court instead of their being dealt with in other ways, which, personally, I think is a mistake.

That is another argument which is still raging.

Hall also wanted women police to deal with prostitutes and, in common with some of the other witnesses, indicated a great deal of concern as to how they were at present being dealt with by police. It puzzled him, he said, why only certain brothels were prosecuted and not others and would feel a good deal happier about the whole business if women police were involved, as they would be "more impartial". He did, however, agree that women should not get mixed up in probation work. The two functions were not compatible.

The question of selecting the right type of recruit also exercised the committee a great deal, class and education taking, as usual, prime place. Macready announced that he wanted "all sorts" but that he must have a proportion of "in an unprovocative sense, ladies" whom he could put into evening dress "with some diamonds or whatever they wear" and some women "at the other end of the scale". When Lord Cottesloe enquired just how low on that scale he had gone, Macready replied, "We have a certain number of constables' wives whom, I fancy, are about the domestic servant class. Then we have got a number of bus conductresses; I hardly know to what class they belong. Those I think are about the limit." They both agreed that the advantage of this type was that they would understand the life and habits of the class with whom they would have to deal.

Even down-to-earth and sensible Dunning felt that women police should be recruited from a higher social class than policemen since their influence was going to come "from their characters". Mrs Stanley merely required that her recruits have a fair degree of education, because of the amount of report-writing required of them. Edith Tancred felt that class was unimportant but that the first women employed should have a higher standard of education than the men because they were likely to become officers later. Professional or semi-professional women or just women who had had some kind of training, be it in teaching, nursing or dressmaking, were favoured by Margaret Damer Dawson and Mary Allen. Of their munitions women police, 669 had had training of some kind, and 411 were of private means, they told the committee. But most important to them was experience of human nature.

The argument that a woman could not do the job due to lack of physical strength did not confine itself to her ability, or otherwise, to exercise power of arrest. Fears that she could not were, after all, reasonable and rational and still not completely assuaged; but could she stand on her feet for eight hours or even work for long periods at all, not to mention endure the rigours of being out of doors in all weathers, the committee wanted to know. Considering the incredibly long hours of sweated labour that women had endured and still were enduring, this was almost a sick question – a point not lost on a nurse, Olga Nethersole, who represented the People's League of Health: "We have done a great many more hours than that during the war – twelve and thirteen hours – and the nurses in the hospitals before the war did thirteen and fourteen hours regularly at a sweated wage." Superintendent Billings of the Metropolitan Police saw no problem. In his experience a woman's power of endurance seemed almost equal to a man's. And there was an unintentionally amusing exchange with Damer Dawson on the subject when she was asked if she had had any cases of breakdown from nervous or other causes. She replied in the affirmative, adding that they generally arose from varicose veins, but on the whole they had a very clean bill of health. Strangely enough, it was Mrs Stanley who stood out against her women doing the same hours as men because she did not think they were up to it.

Medical evidence was called in the shape of Dr Letitia Fairfield CBE, Woman Medical Director, Royal Air Force. Like Superintendent Billings, she saw no problem whatsoever in women doing eight hours at a stretch but made the telling point that 'ladies' who had been well fed and not pushed into factories at fourteen would undoubtedly have better reserves of endurance and last better in the long run. She readily agreed that height and physique must give a tremendous advantage in a physical contest; therefore the recruits should be as tall and strong as possible. When asked if their life expectancy would be reduced by their exposure to the elements,* she replied that it should, in fact, be an unusually healthy occupation for a woman – much better than industry.

A note of farce began to creep into the proceedings when Dr Fairfield was asked whether she could say anything about hammer toes? Was there any difference between the sexes there? She replied that the surgery book said that they were more common in men but added dryly that she doubted whether anyone had compared them.

Miss Peto revealed that one of the reasons the BTS did not supply Bristol with women was because the pay they offered (thirty-seven shillings a week) was so low, and another that they demanded a height of five feet eight inches or over. While she felt that women police should be not less than five feet four inches, lest they could not be seen on the street, she found five feet eight inches too high. If one insisted on it, one might lose many of the right type of women. Another drawback of Bristol was that they employed women under twenty-five years of age, which she thought too young. Twenty-seven was her minimum, for the sensible reason that "the very moment they are sent into a force ... they are put onto really responsible duties such as no raw recruit among the men would be given." There was no opportunity for them to gain experience and grow into the job, and in many cases they were giving no training, so they needed to be older to start with.

Nonetheless, Mrs Florence Young operated her patrols quite happily in Bristol and claimed that they were on excellent terms with both male and female police there. They made sure, she said, that they never did anything of which the police would disapprove and handed on certain cases to them. When asked whether she thought women could cope with the physical difficulties of power of arrest, she said that in five years on the streets she had never met anything too bad to tackle, and besides, there was always one's whistle and probably a constable nearby. A member of the committee, Mr Ben Spoor OBE MP, asked;

616. You would rely also on the use of ju-jitsu, I understand?
Yes, I could easily get a man down and sit on him.
617. If nobody came along for a considerable time, you might have to sit there a long time?

*In the list of reasons for men's sickness, 'Diseases of Exposure' were listed – rheumatism, catarrh, bronchitis and tonsillitis, and, on the last reckoning of these, in 1907, there had been 4,068 of these cases.

Yes; I think one could do so and still keep him in agony.

Whether married women should be allowed to join or remain in the police was a matter which, oddly enough, greatly exercised the representatives of the newly-formed Police Federation for England and Wales. Their motives are a little obscure but appear to be straightforward male chauvinism. Married women had their obligations to think of, insisted Sergeant James of Gloucestershire, who felt very strongly. "One of our judges said yesterday that there are certain responsibilities upon a woman when she becomes married, and that one of them is the propagation of children. Therefore from a country policeman's point of view, I do not think women when they are married should be employed, otherwise there is the risk of causing our nation to remain a C3 nation." To back up their opinions, they pointed out that married women would compete with single women, which was unfair since the latter had no husband to support them. Even the largely pro-women police Inspector Chapman of the Metropolitan Police endorsed this sudden concern for the single woman applicant and insisted that women police should resign on marriage, though they could be let back in as widows – providing that they had no small children to support. Who else was going to support these children while they were so kindly protecting them from the horrors of a working mother, they omitted to mention.

But generally speaking they felt there was a place for women police and that they should be sworn in and given power of arrest and a reasonable wage – four-fifths of the men's. They did not, however, like the way they were organized in London at present – that is, under the control of a woman of little police experience who could send them wherever she thought fit. Women police should be assigned to a division under a male superintendent but operate as a separate, specialist branch, as did the CID. This would obviate the chance of their ever being in a position to give orders to a man, which would be keenly resented.

Sergeant James of Gloucestershire felt that there was really little need for women in the country forces. It was all very well, he explained, for big cities and industrial centres, but in scattered villages on top of the Cotswold Hills the women would be idling their time away. As for using them in night clubs, they did not have them in Gloucestershire and knew little about such things, and if they wanted a woman for escort duty they always used their wives.

When questioned further on power of arrest, the men from the

Police Federation said they thought considerable discretion should be used. Inspector Chapman felt that, for instance, if the women police saw two big, buxom women fighting, it would not be policy for them to interfere. Later on he must have remembered the stalwart Mrs Bagster, Mrs Baldwin and Mrs Morgan-Scott, for he added: "I think we should get some women in the force big and strong enough to go in when there are two men fighting. I have seen a woman do that, especially when the policeman has been hit and knocked down." All of them agreed that it was just not fair, and far too difficult, for women to carry on in the fashion they had been, with no power of arrest. But their main message was that they should not be thought of as part of the force's normal strength and thus be in a position to displace men. That could not be stated too plainly, they advised. The success of the whole operation finally depended on "a spirit of co-operation and feeling of unity", so any regulations should be drafted so as to avoid "causes of friction and petty jealousy". They did not say on whose part.

As I have pointed out, it is probable that Mrs Stanley saw fit to fib about the attitude of male police, and Lilian Wyles certainly did. It is not possible that she did not know what was going on. In her book she repeatedly emphasizes the "petty spite" and "hostility and insults" which the women had to put up with in the early days. But at Baird, when she was asked if the women police should be run as a separate organization or whether this would make for jealousy, she plumped for working with the men. They were not jealous as things were. Lord Cottesloe responded: "1150. Relations are quite friendly and they are glad of your help, I have no doubt?" But she could not bring herself to go quite that far. "I think they are. They are quite nice — all of them — to us." she answered lamely.

Next to Mr Mead, the strongest opposition to the appointment of women came from the Scottish Police Federation: policewomen, they said, were just not necessary at this point. The representatives were obviously put out that they could not make as good a showing as the England and Wales contingent, who had produced an impressive many-paged manifesto covering every point, and complained that they had had little notice. It had been decided to include Scotland in the enquiry only three weeks earlier.

Detective Sergeant Webster of the Edinburgh City Police assured the committee that the Scottish police had no difficulty performing their duties without women and were of the opinion that women could not possibly give taxpayers the same satisfaction as men. They would not even be of any use handling prostitutes, as they would have to have two policemen as attendants on every policewoman. Dame Helen asked, what about ju-jitsu? and received the cutting reply, "That would not obviate public disorder. I do not know that an exhibition of ju-jitsu in the streets is quite what one wants."

It was soon clear, however, that arrest was tricky for male police also in Scotland, as Webster explained: "I do not know whether it is that the police are respected more or not in England, but they have more powers. One officer can arrest you in London and take you before a magistrate and you are convicted on his evidence. That is not so in Scotland." This awareness that a second witness was necessary probably made Scottish people feel more independent, Webster felt. They were certainly more apt to turn against the police and assault them than they were in England. As for the likelihood of a woman's getting help from the public, he had often asked members of the public for help and they had turned their backs on him. His summing up was not encouraging: "What I have got from all over Scotland is that no difficulty has ever arisen. It is not that the Scottish police are antagonistic to the employment of women, but any thinking man who knows anything about police work does not want to see a woman touching it at all. It is not a thing for women."

The evidence of Constable Anderson of Lanarkshire shed a slightly different light on this 'no necessity' theme. As in England, policewomen were thought not necessary mainly by the people who did not suffer from their absence and so truly believed what they were saying. No females were ever sent on escorts with female prisoners in his constabulary — a 'premier county' as regards numbers of police — even if they were going as far as London. To realize the full import of this, one must realize that prisoners being escorted were not even allowed to go to the toilet alone. "Indecent behaviour", he revealed, was never complained of, and if they heard of it at all it was through gossip in a round-about way. The assaulted woman would rather keep it to herself. When taking sex statements from the few who did complain, he had found that, "If she is a woman of decent repute, she is reluctant to tell you the true facts, and sometimes you are not in a position to ask her." He agreed that the employment of women police for this purpose might "help bring the facts out more clearly". Constable Anderson had also circularized all the counties and found that "away north they do not seem to think there is any use for policewomen at all". They might be useful in indecencies, "but they say they very seldom have these crimes up there".

Lieut. Robert Sweeney of Glasgow City Police was the least anti-women police of the Scottish Federation group and obviously embarrassed by the low wages offered to women in his force. He lost no time in declaring their wages "ridiculous" and saying he felt they should have at least three-quarters that of the men and equal status. Besides, sex-statement-taking women could be employed on the supervision and visitation of picture-houses, he said. Apparently picture-houses were pretty active places in Glasgow at that time. As he explained:

It is well known that picture-houses are common places of assignation. Twenty-five years ago soliciting in the street was very common in Glasgow, but that soliciting does not take place there now by what is known as the 'swell prostitute'. It is nearly all done in the lounges of picture-houses. I must say that is common.
2670. What advantage has a woman over a man in dealing with that kind of case?
I have been sent for before now by the manager of a picture-house to take a seat in plain clothes. The mere presence of a police officer there has cleared the place out in a few minutes.
2671. Would a woman do that better than a man?
A woman might go forward and speak in a friendly way to a young girl who is inclined to go astray, whereas if a police officer went forward, even if he were in plain clothes, it would cause a scene and would cause people to look. If a woman did it, it would cause no scene at all.

Webster had been derisive about women making arrests and mentioned "some case" he heard of in which one of the Edinburgh, 'policewomen' got her face slapped – which was just an example. Sweeney, while agreeing on the difficulties, mentioned a lady tramcar conductor he had seen run after a man who had stolen another man's gold watch and hold him until the police came. She was not a big girl, but she was smart and active, and it showed what could be done by a woman. The Scottish Police Federation agreed with their English counterparts that a woman should leave when she got married. As Sweeney explained: "A man joins the police for a career, but a woman only joins until she gets a husband." The Lieutenant's summing up was not so anti as that of Webster, but it was rather lame and patronizing: "Of course, we are living in a progressive age, and there is always something new developing. I think females ought to have one or two of their own sex to look after them."

Mr Mead was of the opinion that women police should have power of arrest. If there were to be policewomen, they should be either constables or not constables. He much preferred, of course, that they did not have them. He thought that women's demand for equality was rather selective:

> I do not find there is agitation for women to be seamen; I do not find there is agitation for women to go into stokeholds of ships and stoke the fires going through the Red Sea, for example. So it seems to me that is the distinction. Men would hate to see women doing hard, laborious work. That is something which has distinguished Englishmen from persons in foreign countries. We go abroad and we are shocked to see women engaged in very heavy agricultural work. Women are not fitted to lug heavy weights about or lift heavy weights, and they do not do it, and they do not ask for it.

He also objected to this "bi-sexual employment" bringing men and women into close relations unnecessarily. He went bitterly through every stage of his clashes with the women patrols and Women Police Service, insisting that there had been no need for women to get involved in the Hyde Park indecencies in the first place, especially indecency between males. The police dealt with them perfectly adequately, and there was no difficulty in getting convictions. He did not, he assured the committee, doubt the intelligence of the women. Those who had come before him were persons of education – he might almost have said refinement though he may have been mistaken about that, and they had given their evidence very clearly and well. But there was nothing they could do that a man could not, and they had not the physical ability to arrest people. Were they going to have truncheons or rely on their hatpins?

Having treated the committee to a long harangue on all the incidents, he came to "the present system":

> My acquaintance with that was made merely as a man in the street. In several parts of London I saw two women dressed as police constables, with a much nearer approach than I had ever seen before. There was no distinction at all in the dress except in the matter of the nether garments. They were strolling along the street, followed at a distance of about fifty yards by a constable. It seemed to me a most ludicrous state of things.

He had been under the impression that this Hyde Park practice was to be stopped because the Home Secretary or someone responsible thought it repugnant to any person of average decent ideas, but only a fortnight earlier a case had been brought before a colleague of such indecency between two men "that I could not possibly describe it here". And as for the argument that by staying in court during such cases they were gaining experience, what sort of experience was a policewoman to gain from listening to the abominable arcana of abominable crimes? Would anybody in his senses allow children to be put in the hands of abnormal women of this sort? It was Sir Francis Blake MP who put what must qualify as the most unnecessary question of the enquiry when he asked Mr Frederick Mead, "I take it you are dead against women being constables at all, are you not?" The answer was in the affirmative.

Of all the learned and experienced witnesses at Baird, the person who made the point which was at the kernel of the whole argument, and which was really irrefutable, was Olga Nethersole of the People's League of Health. In general her evidence tended to the abstract and airy-fairy, and she spoke romantically of a woman's presence always ennobling a scene and of her being the natural protector of the race, but her main argument, which she hung on to and kept returning to despite being told to stick to practicalities, was that the human race was made up of two sexes, therefore anybody policing it should be also, or there would be no justice – a simple principle which is now accepted as true for minority groups as well.

The last witness, Mrs Carden, was heard on 30th March 1920, and the report was presented to Parliament on 5th August, but the gist of it was leaked to a correspondent of the *Glasgow Herald* on 7th July. "I have discovered the delinquent. Nothing can be done," wrote Major Baird in answer to a Home Office complaint. Fortunately, Troup thought there was not much harm done.[1]

The gist was that the committee recommended the employment of women police. They acknowledged that there might not be the work in the country areas, but there was an urgent need in thickly populated areas, "where offences against laws relating to women and children are not infrequent". Their employment should be left to local discretion, but, where they were employed, they should be sworn in, have power of arrest (with its limits locally defined), pension, rent aid and a wage of sixty shillings a week, rising to eighty shillings after ten years. Age of entry should be twenty-five to thirty years, but there was insufficient experience to make any definite statements about marriage. Where large numbers of women were employed, they should be organized as a separate body within the force, like the CID, and have their own officers. A Woman Assistant Inspector of Constabulary should be appointed.

The newspapers duly reported that the women police were going to be put "on an official footing" and that "London policewomen were pleasurably excited" by the prospect. Mrs Stanley, predictably, was quoted as saying that she thought power of arrest would not make a great deal of difference to their work. The *Bristol Times and Mirror* chose the sarcastic approach:

> There is a note of hesitancy in the report of Major Sir John Baird's Committee on the employment of policewomen which suggests that the male members entertained some private doubt but sat in wholesome dread of their fellow-members in petticoats, Lady Astor and Dame Helen Gwynne-Vaughan. Their report is unanimous but records wavering opinion on certain important points. They mention important and weighty evidence against policewomen, including that of the most experienced Metropolitan Magistrate, but finally decided cautiously that their employment is probably desirable for crowded urban areas on special duties connected with crimes by or against women and children. ... The question of uniform or plain clothes – fancy a police woman in plain clothes: what a contradiction in terms! – should in the committee's judgement be left to the local authorities, like that of their actual employment at all and most of the other points that present any difficulty.[2]

There was no wavering about the next action of the Home Office. They sent copies of the committee's report to the constabularies and enclosed with them circulars advising them to ignore the recommendations for better pay and power of arrest.[3]

15

Ireland: "Delicate and Dangerous Work"

Six weeks after the Baird Committee heard its last witness, Margaret Damer Dawson dropped dead of a heart attack. Her death, at the age of forty-five, was undoubtedly hastened, Mary Allen declared, by overwork and bitter disappointment that, instead of being appointed to the task of organizing a permanent body of women police, she was deliberately overlooked and ordered to cease her work. Miss Allen had been with her at the time of her short "and seemingly slight" illness and was there when she died.

On the day of the funeral, the *Daily Telegraph*, after telling of the history of the WPS and the plans of thirty uniformed policewomen to escort the coffin that day, went on to say: " ... She was singularly unassuming, and never sought distinction or advantages for herself ... she had force of character as well as tenderness and her death creates a blank that will not easily be filled." *The Times* felt her to be "A woman of naturally fastidious mind; she faced the realities of life with such courage that her work was of far more use than that of a woman of coarser fibre could have been."

The police Press was complimentary and generous too, though it concentrated on the trait which the men obviously found so disturbing and noteworthy in a woman: her indomitableness. And *The Police Review* cannot have cheered the new Commissioner, Brig. Gen. Sir William Horwood GBE KCB DSO, with its final words: "Though the guiding spirit has been removed, there is every indication that the work will survive its founder to keep green her memory."

But perhaps the finest tribute was from Mary Allen who had been "instantly nominated chief" in her place. In her book *The Pioneer Policewoman*, published four years later, she says: "She could not bear the sight of unnecessary suffering, it revolted her sense of the fitness of things." Elsewhere in the book she went into a more detailed personal description:

Blonde, blue-eyed, of a delicate complexion, Miss Damer Dawson was of a fastidious even scholarly turn of mind. She nevertheless faced each problem of life with a resolution that shrank from no revelation that could increase her knowledge or arm her experience. Danger steeled her; she was encouraged, even inspired, by difficulties. With her keen intelligence, her untiring energy, her lively wit, she made an instant impression upon those who came into personal contact with her, but it was, above all, the steady flame of her enthusiasm that kindled in the hearts of her followers a high-minded allegiance that never swerved.

Such fulsomeness might suggest a homosexual affection, particularly since the writer was, by now, grotesquely masculine in appearance. It is perfectly possible that this was so, but, of course, writing did tend more to the purple in those days. Her description of Sir Edward Henry had been equally adoring. There is no doubt, however, that she was genuinely admiring and fond of "the Chief", and, while she always played up her own part in the history and did not do justice to people such as Nina Boyle and Edith Watson, she never tried to undermine the memory of Margaret Damer Dawson.

The Chief was buried near her animal refuge home at Lympne in Kent, and Mary Allen and the other officers took over her heavy programme of public speaking. Uncharacteristically, the new chief admitted some trepidation over her abilities in this direction. She acquired the new skill only gradually and cannot have been helped by the frequent and deliberate presence of Edith Watson, who would ask questions to bring forth acknowledgement of the vital part the Women's Freedom League, Nina Boyle and Edith Watson, had played in the story. Her ploy worked, and Mary Allen was forced to admit the truth, but Edith later wrote, "I had no means of enforcing the mention in her book, and Nina never sought recognition but let the whole question go by default."[1]

In June 1920 Commandant Allen went to Scotland, interviewed several Chief Constables and opened the WPS Scottish Training School in Edinburgh. In the same month Scotland Yard passed on an emissary from the Royal Irish Constabulary, then in the thick of 'the troubles', asking for fifty trained policewomen, mainly to help with the searching of suspects. A few weeks later the first contingent of WPS, comprising a chief inspector, sergeant and seven constables, left for Dublin. They had been expected to turn up dressed as nuns or matrons but appeared in full uniform, and the welcoming sergeant was so afraid for their safety that he refused to allow them to leave his station until he had received further instructions from Dublin Castle.

Ellen Harburn, one of the first two semi-official, uniformed policewomen

Lilian Wyles who, in 1919, became one of the first official Metropolitan Women Police Patrols and was the first Metropolitan woman to join the CID

Women patrols of the National Union of Women Workers on duty at Euston Station during the First World War, giving advice and assistance to troops on leave. They became experts at sobering-up tactics

Women Police Service, 1915.
From left to right: D. Meeson Coates (Chief Inspector), Miss St John Partridge, M. Damer Dawson (Chief Officer), M.S. Allen (Chief Superintendent), B. Goldingham (Principal of Clerical Department)

Metropolitan Women Police Patrols, 1919. Some of the first members. Front left is Superintendent Stanley

Women Police Service Munitions Police. A member takes it upon herself to smarten up factory workers at Gretna who were awaiting a Royal visit. Since many of the 'munitionettes' were young the women police found themselves cast as mothers, though some workers found them over-officious

The royal party arrive to a guard of honour by other members of the women police squad under Woman Inspector Stark. Another first, they claimed, for women police

Women Police Service Munitions Police. Police on air raid duty at small arms and gunpowder factories at Enfield Lock and Waltham Abbey during the First World War

Patrols of the NUWW warning small boys outside Euston Station during the First World War; unruliness due to lack of male control at home was the main problem then

Members of the Lancashire Constabulary, Preston, 1922. Though the Chief Constable, Sir Phillip Lane (centre), was not in favour of uniformed women police he pioneered their use in detective work. Alongside him here, far left to right: Policewoman Parker, Woman Inspector Charlotte Storey, Assistant Chief Constable W. Trubshaw, Woman Inspector Lilian Naylor (reputed to have been active in 'special' anti-IRA work), Superintendent Gregson and Woman Sergeant Jackson. Behind them are twelve PWs (Policewomen) and four SPWs (Specials)

Members of the Women Police Service, probably in Paddington in 1918

Some things don't change much! A post-Second World War Metropolitan Woman Police Constable

Transport not provided.
WPC Lodge, Forest Division,
Gloucestershire Constabulary, with
her own motorcycle, an AJS 350cc,
in 1928. When riding it on duty she
was allowed 1½d a mile in expenses

Getting motorized.
Commandant Margaret Damer
Dawson comforts a rescued child
whilst Sub Commandant Mary
Allen drives them to safety. By 1918
the Women Police Service were
equipped with four motorcycles
(three with side-cars) which appear
to have been largely for the use
of the senior officers, mainly for
inspection purposes

Just practising. A Metropolitan WPC demonstrating self-defence on a male colleague

Jubilee, 1935. The redoubtable Mabel Read of Hove receives her Jubilee Medal

Specialist branches open up for women. Here, a Metropolitan WPC escorts the Guards to Buckingham Palace

One of the first two
Metropolitan women
dog-handlers with her
drug-detecting golden
Labrador

Pauline Clare, who
in 1995 became the
UK's first female chief
constable when she
was appointed to lead
Lancashire Constabulary

Chief Superintendent
Shirley Becke in friendly
conference with Yard
colleagues. Becke,
who became the first
woman to attain the
rank of Commander,
guided the Metropolitan
Women Police towards
integration

The women felt they would be in greater danger if they dressed as nuns, and eventually, a compromise was reached. They would wear uniform on duty but travel in plain clothes, since the trains were often held up and boarded by Sinn Feiners if it became known that police were travelling on them. Chief Inspector Campbell's diary tells of their first hours in Dublin:

19th June – About midnight I was startled by the loud explosions of bursting bombs. The policewomen joined me in my room, and from the window we saw a great fire burning, and heard shouting and the exchange of shots. Towards three o'clock the flames died down, and searchlights played over the town. On the following morning, to our surprise, no mention of the occurrence was made by anyone at the hotel. We were made to realize forcibly that we were in the war zone. Two days later the young waiter who served us at table was shot dead on the doorstep of the hotel.

The WPS were soon dispersed about the country and accompanied male police and soldiers on often long and hazardous journeys to make raids or erect road blocks, where women might need to be searched or escorted. The WPS Report 1920-21 states:

Those to whom the idea of women helping in this particular work is repugnant have the satisfaction of knowing that it was carried out with the utmost consideration, and frequently the women cadets were met by women with exclamations of gratitude, that it was women – not men – who had come to search them. One illustration may help to make this clear. A certain cottage was under suspicion, and an order was given to search it; the woman living there had only a few hours previously given birth to a child, and when policewomen entered the cottage they were received with the exclamation, "Thank God it's you and not the men!" To those who take the opposite view, the following extract from *Blackwood's Magazine* will give some idea of the value of the women's service: 'Soon after the battle of Glenmuck the belles of the district received the shock of their lives when shopping in a town some miles away with these young men (members of the IRA). About noon four Crossley loads of cadets suddenly dashed into the town, with two women searchers dressed in dark blue uniforms, and that day the first real haul of revolvers and automatics was made. As usual the men passed the arms to the girls directly they saw the Auxiliaries arrive, but this time no notice was taken of the men; while the girls, who on former occasions had stood jeering at the cadets, found themselves quickly rounded up, the women searchers did the rest. After this the moral effect of the women searchers was so great that not a girl in the district dare carry arms or dispatches.

The first batch of policewomen was soon joined by another inspector, two sub-inspectors, a sergeant and a stream of constables. Inspector Walton records a typical day on duty:

5th April — Started out about 10 am on a fifty-mile expedition. Three lorries full of military and RIC. My colleague and I sat on the front seat by the driver; on our left was an officer with a loaded revolver. The armed men were seated back to back in the rear of the lorry. At one point we left lorries in the road and, led by the CO, crossed fields, mud, water, hedges and stone walls. It was a beautiful but wild spot. From the point of view of the women police, it was good to be formed up and marched with the men. We kept up well and climbed stone walls without demur. Several farmsteads were raised and searched. All returned safely at 6.30 pm.

While not averse from trying to starve the police by refusing to serve them food (during a boycott by intimidated shopkeepers) and pelting their lorries with stones, the Irish nonetheless impressed the women "with their sweet voices and kind gentle manners". On one occasion an Irish girl, seeing two policewomen sheltering from a downpour in a doorway, came out and offered them sheets of brown paper to put under their coats. In *Lady in Blue*, Mary Allen, who visited her troops in the field, wrote:

Actually, the revolutionaries, bloodthirsty and cruel as many of them undoubtedly were, treated policewomen with true Irish chivalry and good-humour throughout the whole of our service there. The much-maligned Black-and-Tans did the same. ... One of the most amazing things to us was the Irish sense of humour, rising triumphant above chagrin, pain and disappointment. We saw Sinn Feiners who would joke, pass a death sentence on a captive, receive a fatal wound and joke again, all in the same breath.

Meanwhile, back in London, newspaper placards were carrying the slogan, "WOMEN POLICE SUED BY THE COMMISSIONER!" General Horwood had taken action and sued the leading members of the WPS for wearing uniform resembling that of the Metropolitan Police and the Metropolitan Women Police Patrols. To add an irony, Macready was now GOC in Ireland, and part of his job was to co-ordinate the work of police and military there.

The case was heard during March and April 1921 at Westminster Police Court, before Mr Cecil Chapman who, as it happens, had been a supporter of the WPS for years. He and his wife (a member of the

WFL) were listed as patrons in WPS annual reports, and he is thanked for his lectures to them. Commissioner Horwood, a military man brought in by Macready who subsequently used his strong influence also to obtain the commissionership for him,[2] had been a prime instigator in the original moves against the WPS.[3] He was now called to give evidence and, according to Mary Allen, displayed a woeful ignorance about them and even admitted he had not read 'the blue book' (Baird). Mrs Stanley told the court of the confusion between the two bodies which the uniform caused, and Lilian Wyles was made to stand adjacent to Mary Allen so as to demonstrate similarities in attire.[4]

In court, and prepared to come forward in their defence, were the Bishop of Kensington, Olga Nethersole and Lady Nott Bower, but they were not needed. Commandant Allen eventually offered to change the uniform by adding scarlet shoulder straps, altering the cap badge and dropping the word police from their title and replacing it with "auxiliary". This was accepted, and, after praise from the learned magistrate for their work, and a token fine, the case ended. Subsequently, Mary Allen claimed, greater prestige ensued, and she and her team were invited to speak all over the country. Nor did it halt her "activities", as the Metropolitan Police called them. In court she had announced that the WPS had long since ceased to do any police duties in London, merely administration in connection with their duties elsewhere; however Lilian Wyles said that, after the "somewhat supine" court case, they continued to function energetically in and around the Piccadilly district.

Soon, with the signing of the peace treaty, the Women's Auxiliary Service was no longer needed in Ireland. James P. Foley, representing the RIC, wrote to Mary Allen saying how struck he had been with their culture and courtesy and enclosing a resolution passed by the men in which they said of their now redundant helpers:

> They came over to assist us in very delicate and dangerous work. This they did in a most commendable manner, and in very trying circumstances, often, if not always, handicapped by reason of their sex. They shared our hardships and our dangers; this being so, we now ask the government to suitably compensate them. We submit that these ladies be liberally treated upon the cessation of their duties in Ireland.

Of course they were nothing of the kind, their usefulness being at an end, but within a year "the lady searchers" were once again needed, this time in the new Northern Ireland. In June 1922 Mary Allen was invited to meet the Ulster Government and, as a result, sent twenty women to Belfast.

Sir Leonard Dunning was most amused: "Miss Peto," he exclaimed, "you will never get a police appointment along those lines!", and he was right. After the favourable report from the Baird Committee, the Bristol Training School had closed down and Miss Peto set about applying to "likely forces" for a job. Always she received the same answer, "No vacancies," so she went to see "our good friend" and told him of her dilemma. Sir Leonard, obviously a shrewd man, enquired as to exactly what she had been saying in her applications. She told him how she had modestly explained that though she had held a rank equal to that of police superintendent in the Bristol Training School she was perfectly willing to accept no higher rank than that of inspector. Small wonder he was amused. Just state your experience, he advised her, say nothing about rank and be prepared to take anything you are offered. As it happened, he knew that the Chief Constable of Birmingham was looking for someone for the investigation of sexual offences against women and girls. He suggested that she apply and offered to "write him a line on your behalf". Thus, in November 1920 Dorothy Peto found herself a member of the Birmingham CID, "unattested, with no specific rank and saddled with the appalling title of 'Lady Enquiry Officer'." She managed to dispose of the 'lady' during her first week by the simple expedient of substituting the word detective whenever she signed a report, and "Detective Enquiry Officer I remained throughout the four years of my service there."

Since 1917 the number of uniformed women in the Birmingham force had quickly increased from two to ten. Though they were unattested, according to Dorothy Peto they were treated in other respects as regular members of the force, trained with the men and employed on outdoor duties under Woman Sergeant Miles. However, Constable Collins had told the Baird Committee that they were employed solely on rescue work, and the evidence of the Chief Constable Charles Haughton Rafter before the Bridgeman Committee in 1924 suggests that this was still largely the case. Miss Peto received the normal probationer's course, then a CID course, both while being on call day and night for the purpose of sex-statement taking and attending medical examinations on the victims of sexual assaults.

At first she was guided by a Divisional Detective Inspector who stood over her and prompted the questions she should get answered. Her first opportunity to do the job unaided came when the Detective Inspector was so overcome by the smell in the victim's living-room that he escaped into the garden and left her to it. She had always had, she said, a defective sense of smell. There was poverty and unemployment (though she found the labour exchange queues useful sources for identification parades), and Birmingham people turned out to be very different from the easy-going Bristolians. But she learned to appreciate the parting "You ken com agen" from a mother in a back-to-back more, she says, than any soft-spoken insincerity. She also found mothers very relieved to see a woman arrive to take the statements of children who had been sexually assaulted, and they frequently told her that they would have complained before had they known that a 'lady police' would come. Though her male colleagues were without exception kind and helpful to her, she did regret their eagerness to disbelieve victims of sexual assault.

When not taking statements, Detective Enquiry Officer Peto traced families of servicemen killed in the war and passed on medals or pensions to which they were entitled, or loitered about in big departmental stores on the off-chance that she might catch a shoplifter. On the few occasions she succeeded, to her chagrin the case always appeared on the court list next to that of a male inspector or sergeant with whom she was working, even though she had made the arrest with her citizen's powers. The Chief Constable, kind though he was, would not budge on this point. Also, although the force boasted ten policewomen, all long-distance female escorts were still done by men. Since the women were unattested, they could not go alone, they were told, and the force could not afford to send two officers.

Within the city, it was different. Any female moved about there was always accompanied by a wardress, and no woman appeared in court without 'the court girl' being present. Outside the city, women often still braved the courts alone. The Sex Disqualification Removal Act had allowed for the introduction of women barristers (Birmingham had two, one of whom, Sybil Campbell, was to become the first woman stipendiary magistrate) and jurors, but even this could be thwarted, as Miss Peto relates:

A particularly brutal rape of a respectable girl of nineteen or twenty, who suffered not only physical injury but extreme distress, took place just outside the city boundary. Though it was, in fact, dealt with by our own force, the trial took place at the County Assizes some distance away, for which reason – since I was not myself a witness – I was not allowed to attend court with her when the case came up for trial. When the proceedings, which ended in a conviction, were over, however, I went to her home to hear how she had got on. I learned that no women police officer or matron attended her in Court; and that, although there were two women on the jury, the judge, addressing them before the case opened, told them that as there might be evidence of an unpleasant nature they could, if they wished, retire. Whereupon they both got up and left the Court. "I did think," said the poor girl, "that they might have thought what I would have to go through, all alone with men, in that court. I did wish there was just *one* woman there – I did think they might have stayed!"

16

The Geddes Axe

Lilian Wyles, when she was later writing of the events of 10th February 1922, described how a male sergeant carried into her office a large sealed envelope flagged in red 'Strictly Confidential'. She would always think that he knew the contents of the envelope since there was a look on his face "of supreme enjoyment as at some joke known only to himself", and he eyed her "with a certain amount of patronizing pity". The letter, addressed to Mrs Stanley, contained notice to disband their small force by 31st March, six weeks away.[1]

The notice was the result of the findings of the Geddes Committee on National Expenditure, which had decided that, though policewomen's pay was only ten shillings less than that of the male constable, their powers were strictly limited and their utility, from a police point of view on the evidence submitted to them, negligible. The Committee did not think, under the present circumstances, that this expenditure could be justified and recommended disbandment. There was also to be a reduction in horses and the maintenance of motor vehicles.[2]

The evidence the committee had received was solely that of the Home Office and General Horwood, the new Commissioner, who did not like women police.[3] Of course the conclusions they came to were largely true. The women were ineffective due to lack of power, and in addition they were being utilized to fill womanless gaps in courts and so on, which, on the face of it, did not look like work. The Conference of the Police Federation of Superintendents, held soon after Geddes to consider exactly where to make ordered cuts – in rent aid, boot allowance, plain clothes allowance etc – went beyond their brief and volunteered that the mounted branch should be decreased and all women holding positions as police officers be removed. That meant all over the country. Part of their justification was that, in those hard times, the women were taking men's jobs and placing their allowances in jeopardy, but in fact most of the women needed to make their own livings too, and at least a third of those in the Metropolitan Police were widows with children to support.[4]

Mrs Stanley won the concession of letting the women go as their yearly contract expired, and Horwood did plead for a gratuity for them, pointing out, quite rightly, what a difficult time they were going to have finding new jobs in the current state of the labour market. He made an extra strong plea for the "exceptional case" of Mrs Stanley, showing that her charm also worked with this Commissioner, but to no avail. The Home Office regretted that the women could only have their rateable deductions returned.

The whole execution had been carried out before any of the women really knew what was happening, probably on the premise that a *fait accompli* might stymie the opposition. But it was not going to be that easy. Quite the reverse. The women's societies acted with similar alacrity and an impressive show of solidarity, and there were now two women MPs, Lady Astor and Mrs Wintringham. The National Council of Women quickly organized a protest meeting of sixty-three societies whose numbers included Catholic, Protestant and Jewish organizations, the Discharged Prisoners' Aid Society, the National Vigilance Association, assorted suffrage organizations, the Women's Auxiliary Service and the Women's Freedom League. They passed a resolution to send a strong deputation to the Home Secretary.

From their front-line headquarters just behind Marble Arch, the Church Army sent an especially impassioned plea to *The Times* on 5th April 1922;

Sir,
Before it is too late, may the Church Army be allowed to plead for the retention of policewomen? The moral and physical evils prevented are worth infinitely more than their cost.

They are as eucalyptus in the swamps of the Roman Campagna, and, if cut down by the Geddes Axe, the country is the great loser, and thousands of poor girls will cease to be helped. Our Church Army Sisters of the Night hope the disbandment, if it must come, may only be temporary.

The Metropolitan Women Police Patrols were not about to give up easily either. They called a meeting, and four of them, Chief Inspector Robertson, Inspector Lilian Wyles, Patrol Sergeant Violet Butcher and Women Police Patrol Mary Morris, immediately signed a letter asking Mrs Stanley if she would lead a deputation to the Prime

Minister protesting that no evidence had been taken from any of them and nor had any record of their work been submitted to Geddes.

The situation in the Constabularies was somewhat different. The very rule, 'local discretion', which had so held up the progress of women police in many areas, was in some instances to prove their salvation now. An emergency conference of Chief Constables, held to consider Geddes, upheld the local discretion dictum as far as women police was concerned, and some Chief Constables stated that they would be most unwilling to dispense with their women. The Home Office agreed that it was up to them what they did but advised them that, if they did get rid of them, they would have to make other provision for custody and escort of women prisoners. A rather odd instruction this, considering that many of them merely ignored these requirements anyway. In the event, roughly half the Constabularies who had women now kept them.

Conferences were held in the Houses of Parliament by Lady Astor and Mrs Wintringham, and questions about lack of proper evidence at Geddes were asked in both chambers. With the mounting pressure the Home Secretary had no choice. "I suppose I must receive a deputation," he says wearily in a file minute. He did, and it was led by Lady Astor and was stormy. They found the Home Secretary quite unmoved by their pleas to retain at least a nucleus until better times. Their work, he insisted, was not police work, no matter how noble. They argued the 'preventive work' saved the taxpayer money in the end, that the women had limited utility through no fault of their own, that the Baird recommendation that they be given power of arrest had not been adopted;* and that all women were behind this: they wanted protection for their daughters. It was even hinted that they would show their displeasure at the polls, but the Home Secretary stood firm.

Afterwards, Lady Astor publicly declared herself very much dissatisfied and added that the matter was not going to stop there. The Home Secretary had been unsympathetic and unimaginative, said another member of the deputation; what was more, they felt he had made up his mind without taking evidence on the other side. The newspaper reports were largely sympathetic, and the *Manchester*

---

*There had been two deputations pressing for the implementation of Baird. One by Baird Committee members on 17th December 1920 and one led by the Federated Training Schools on which Mrs Carden, Mrs Young of Bristol, Mabel Cowlin, Eleanor Rathbone and Edith Tancred were present, on 25th February 1921.

Guardian published a long and very sharp piece from a woman correspondent who stated that the total disbandment of the women police would amount to "a provocative flouting of the organized women of this country".[5]

The Women's Freedom League even issued a pamphlet which said, quite blandly, "As early as 1914 two uniformed policewomen were appointed in a semi-official capacity to Grantham" and went on to agree that Sir Nevil Macready's suggestion that women police take over all dealing with prostitutes would be an economy![6] Who was being expedient now? Miss Peto recalls of that time:

> I think that only those who knew Lady Astor in those early days of her Parliamentary career can fully realize her impact on the male solidarity of the Lower House as she rose, on 8th of March 1922, to open the debate on which hung the future of women police. Fair and graceful, in the plain black dress with its light lace collar, so carefully designed for her new role, fearless in attack and swift in retort, she gave a factual account of the preventative work achieved by the Metropolitan Women Police Patrols on behalf of thousands of young girls whom they found on the brink of disaster; winding up with a brilliant defence of the right of policewomen to recognition as forming an essential part of the British Police Service. Mrs Wintringham and Sir Arthur Steel-Maitland followed her in support – and the Home Office gave in!

No, they did not. Miss Peto, normally so honest, has, like Lilian Wyles, acquired a convenient attack of amnesia concerning what happened next, though doubtless for more noble reasons. The Home Office did give in, eventually, but only after the most extraordinary sequence of events had taken place.

That particular debate (actually on the 28th – the Lords debated it on the 8th) achieved no stay of execution, and disbandment commenced two days later. The conferences, protests and questions in the Houses continued through to June, and finally Mrs Wintringham wangled another debate on a pretext. By then a promise that some kind of nucleus would be retained had been made, but the Home Secretary had not specified how many and for what, and refused to be pinned down.

Mrs Stanley's second, Chief Inspector Robertson, had by now been disbanded, which left the two women inspectors next in line. In fact Wyles and Dixon should also have gone by now but had received a stay of execution after a special plea by Mrs Stanley. At 11.30 am on the morning before the debate of 29th June, Inspectors Wyles and

Dixon and WPS Butcher were offered posts as sex-statement-takers, which would make, with Miss MacDougal, four so employed in the Metropolitan area. The posts were civilian. What happened next was to be much contested. In Parliament on that day of 28th June, Lady Astor asked Mr Shortt, the Home Secretary whether he would now state how many women he proposed to retain and in what capacities? He replied that he could not give a definite answer as yet, but up to the present it had been arranged that three women patrols should be retained for the purpose of taking statements from women and girls. Lady Astor then asked, was it not a fact that the three women had refused because they realized it was only camouflage? Mr Shortt did not think that was so. He understood from the Commissioner that they had, in fact, accepted. "I think you have understood incorrectly," Lady Astor retorted.

Later that day the brother of Lilian Wyles telephoned Mr Olive, Assistant Commissioner A Department, who was in over-all charge of women police patrols, and told him that his sister was upset. Mr Wyles was invited to Scotland Yard where he was interviewed; an interview with Lilian Wyles followed.

During a stormy debate the following day, Mr Shortt, who was now facing considerable opposition from all sides of the House on this question, defended himself by saying that he was honestly trying to retain a nucleus of experienced officers, and yet he was thwarted by disloyalty from them. Yesterday morning it had been all settled; yesterday morning they had agreed to do what he asked. Lady Astor interrupted to tell him this was not so; they had not agreed, merely said they would think it over. "Apparently," said Mr Shortt, "the Hon. Member for Plymouth is better informed about what goes on confidentially in Scotland Yard than I am." "I am," she snapped back. This opened the flood gates.

Mr SHORTT: I repeat that it was absolutely settled yesterday morning, and I have with me a statement which was made to the Commissioner, showing how two of them came to change their mind. They were approached, and they were told that they must refuse until after today's Debate, because to consent to help me form a nucleus would injure those of their colleagues who were not being detained.
Viscountess ASTOR: Oh, no. That is not so.
Mr WALLACE: Would it be possible to let us have the statement?
Mr SHORTT: Yes.

He then read out a statement which accused Mrs Stanley of telling

Inspector Dixon, Sergeant Butcher "and myself" not to accept the posts as it was only a ploy to give the impression that a nucleus had been retained, and the following day's debate on the subject would subsequently fall through. They should play for time until the debate was over. The writer of the statement was sure that the other two wanted the jobs, just as she did, but they were told they would be disloyal if they accepted. She had, however been told about the pending offer, by Mrs Stanley, on the 24th and felt that she had, in fact, accepted the previous morning, 28th June. The statement had been taken that day.

Dr MURRAY: Voluntarily?
Mr SHORTT: Yes.
Lord R. CECIL: May I assume that this statement will be laid on the table?
Mr SHORTT: I should not have read it unless I were prepared to do so.
Viscountess ASTOR: May we have the name?
Mr SHORTT: I was honestly trying to carry out my promise to form a nucleus. I am willing now to carry it out and to leave a sufficient body to make this nucleus. I will tell the Committee exactly what I had in mind to propose. I wanted the chief officers, and I wanted the total number of officers of the force to be twenty. I thought that that was a fair and reasonable offer to make, as a nucleus upon which a new force could be immediately built up any moment that there was financial power to do so.

This may have been true, but it is interesting that the day before he had no idea about numbers apart from the three-statement-takers. The debate went on, Mr Shortt maintaining his attitude of injured innocence. The statement appeared to have been accepted as Gospel until Lord Eustace Percy pointed out that they must reserve their judgement until they had heard both sides of the case, but at least the Home Secretary had been pinned down to twenty women, and subsequent questioning had made sure he elaborated on this until it had become an accepted fact. Mrs Wintringham tried to push for retention of the fifty-six who now remained or, at least, power of arrest for the twenty, but they had got all they were going to get.

Two weeks later Sir Arthur Steel-Maitland, who had been strongly supporting the women's case along with the two women members, asked a very pertinent question. Would the Home Secretary lay upon the Table the comments, if any, called for from Mrs Stanley upon the statement containing accusations against her? That is, the comments called for as to its accuracy or otherwise *before* the statement had been laid on the Table. Of course there were none. Mr Shortt had rushed into debate without any attempt to check its authenticity. He now admitted that Mrs Stanley had, in fact, since denied the accuracy of the statement and added that, since it had nonetheless been published, it was only right that Mrs Stanley's statement should also be published, so he was, accordingly laying it on the Table. When things get as embarrassing as this, there is a tried and true get-out, and the Home Secretary brought it into play now, saying that, as the whole matter would clearly have to form the subject of a disciplinary enquiry, he must refrain from further comment at this stage. This did not stop him from getting a roasting for submitting a statement without any attempt to check its authenticity. He defended himself by asserting that the Commissioner had obtained it, and he had had no intention of using it, but that it had been brought out owing to a statement made by the Hon. Member for Plymouth. The house still did not think this was good enough, but help was at hand.

Captain W. BENN: As the House, in coming to a decision, was greatly influenced by the statement of the Home Secretary, how is the House to set the matter right, if that turn out to be the case? [if it is inaccurate]
Sir J. BUTCHER rose –
Mr SPEAKER: We cannot debate every question ...

End of discussion. The ranks had closed. Two days later the Home Secretary ordered the Yard to start an enquiry.

On 7th July the Commissioner had an interview with the Home Secretary to discuss what they were going to do with these twenty women, and he was asked to put forward a scheme. When it was submitted, the Commissioner mentioned that he had just discovered that there was not, after all, enough statement-taking work for three more women; one more would be plenty.

The enquiry was conducted by Deputy Assistant Commissioner Laurie and Chief Constable Billings who, as a Superintendent, had given pro-women police evidence at Baird. The main areas of contention were whether the women had indeed accepted the posts, then changed their minds; whether Mrs Stanley had asked them to play for time; whether she had failed to assist Yard officials when they were searching for the women after the interview with Assistant Commissioner Olive in which they were officially offered the jobs; if she had divulged Scotland Yard business to outsiders, and whether there was any truth in the counter-claim that Wyles herself had stirred up the women to resist disbandment.

Mrs Stanley's story was that the minute she and the other women had left Mr Olive's office, after the interview regarding the jobs, Sergeant Butcher had remarked that Mr Olive had not answered one of the questions they had put to him. After trying to see him again, she had gone to the Inspector's Room where all three were talking to Miss Morris, a clerk. She told them that she had arranged with a messenger to let her know when Mr Olive would be free, and about twenty minutes later he did, and she saw Mr Olive again. However, when she had returned to her office, Dixon and Butcher were gone. She had no clear recollection of how the three were subsequently warned for a further interview with Olive. She did not know what happened to Lilian Wyles, but she was quite sure she had not spoken to her by telephoning her home as had been suggested. The rest of her evidence concerned the efforts of the clerk, Mr Abbott, to trace Lilian Wyles and how she had not been obstructive in this and how she had also told Miss Morris to warn her. Miss Morris, a friend of Lilian Wyles, denied this, and Mr Olive also denied that she had seen him only half an hour after the first occasion. It was much later, after lunch in fact.

Mrs Grace Dixon, whom Lilian Wyles later described as "a cultured, travelled gentlewoman who had been interested in social questions for some years", said that after the interview Sergeant Butcher had voiced a fear that Mr Olive might take it that, if the Commissioner agreed to the suggestions that he (Mr Olive) had made, they might think they had accepted the posts. Later Dixon said that Olive had asked if they accepted, and she had told him that they must know what the conditions were first.

WPS Butcher, whom Peto was to refer to as an outstanding officer, made it clear she had not wanted to accept because she thought it strange the offer should be made on the eve of the debate and, if she accepted and the debate had decided to retain women police, she would then have severed her connection with the force since statement-taking was a civilian job. She thought Mr Olive would send for them again, after seeing the Commissioner about terms, and when he did, they would make it clear they wanted time for consideration. This confirmed the statement of Wyles and Dixon, said the enquiry report, that time for consideration was not asked for at the first meeting. Violet Butcher also denied that she had told another patrol that she would have her revenge on Miss Wyles for her treacherous conduct if it took her to her dying day.

As well as the playing-for-time accusation against Mrs Stanley, much was made of the "sinister fact that confidential transactions of New Scotland Yard" had been divulged to outside persons, e.g. Lady Astor. In fact ex-Chief Inspector Robertson admitted that she was responsible for both these misdeeds. She had heard about the appointments from "a third party" before seeing Dixon, with whom she had discussed the idea of playing for time. Then she had seen Lady Astor on the morning of 28th June and told her that the appointments were being offered that day but that she thought they would not be accepted as the women would ask for time to consider. Her reasons for this conclusion were her conversation with Dixon and her knowledge that Sergeant Butcher would do everything "that would be of advantage to the cause" and that Inspector Wyles did not like taking statements. She had also passed on further information to Mrs Wintringham on the day of the debate.

Wyles stuck to her story and came in for a good deal of flak from the others. She was not only disloyal to Mrs Stanley, they said, but had frequently voiced the opinion that she was not fit to be Superintendent. She loved talking to policemen for long periods herself but would scold any of her women who even spoke to them; she was untruthful and secretive. Mrs Robertson maintained that Wyles had got a swelled head since being promoted and was inclined to go over her head to Mrs Stanley. Finally, Mrs Stanley asserted that she had been aware for some time that Wyles was anxious to supersede her and would not be very particular as to the means she used to obtain her ends.

Nonetheless, Billings and Laurie came to the conclusion that, although none of the women was telling the whole truth, Wyles was telling more of it than most, but they were not impressed with her evidence either. She was obviously of a rather boastful disposition and was probably as involved as the others in initially attempting to force the Government's hand. The other women were now embittered against her because she had broken away from an agreed policy and in their view secured an appointment by underhand and traitorous methods.

Mrs Stanley, they decided, had given her evidence in a direct manner, but there were grave doubts as to its reliability, and her communications with outside individuals showed a "non-wholehearted loyalty" to the police and did not inspire confidence in her. They did admit that her position had been difficult and felt some credit was due to her for the way she had handled it up to a certain point.

Mrs Robertson had frankly acknowledged her part, but they were not satisfied that she had not also taken upon her own shoulders responsibility for many things Mrs Stanley had done. As for Mrs Dixon, she was an enthusiast for her own beliefs to the point of being a fanatic.

The fact that the whole débâcle had been brought on by the machinations and duplicity of the Yard and the Home Office, and they were asking the impossible of the women – to be loyal to people out to destroy them, did not stop them adopting a high moral tone about the revelations that all the women were probably lying to some degree. The whole enquiry had, they declared, disclosed certain traits and character motifs in the women which would not otherwise have been revealed. Obviously intrigue and petty jealousy existed to a considerable degree and, since most of their statements disagreed with each other, grave doubts must be entertained of the women's reliability.

Mr Olive's evidence, that the women had agreed to accept the posts in the first interview and that Mrs Stanley had not seen him again until after lunch, must be taken with every seriousness, considering his long and tried experience in giving and taking evidence. If it were given the weight it deserved, this evidence disposed, *ipso facto*, of a great deal of contradictory assertions in the other statements. In fact Billings had got Olive's job when he had been elevated to a place among the gentlemen by Macready.

When the report of the enquiry was sent to the Home Office, it was accompanied by a covering letter adding the opinions of the writer to that of the report. Astonishingly that writer turns out to be a person directly involved – Assistant Commissioner* Olive! He was, he assured the Home Office, mainly entirely in agreement with the findings but felt that Mrs Stanley had been much more active than they had concluded. In addition it must be remembered that no witnesses had been called to support Wyles, while Mrs Stanley had asked for and got several, all but one of whom had been compulsorily retired and so had a grievance against the Home Secretary and the Commissioner. There was no reason whatsoever to doubt Wyles's

---

*Actually signed as "Acting Commissioner" – he was Deputy Commissioner normally.

statement; the others had obviously ganged up on her, though she had been looked upon with a favourable eye until she had broken away from the combine. Mrs Stanley had represented her as the incarnation of all that was deceitful, and yet she had recommended her for the post of Inspector and as one suitable for one of these posts.

The Home Secretary decided that, since they were all so morally lax, the services of all four should be dispensed with, but the Commissioner explained that Inspector Wyles had been placed on special duty as soon as she had accepted the offer and had continued to do the work ever since, and the Home Secretary therefore agreed that she should be retained "notwithstanding obvious objections". In the event only Mrs Stanley was "found redundant", as Miss Peto puts it, subsequently going out to Calcutta as an officer of the RSPCA and working closely with the police. Soon she began taking part in police investigations and raids when the detention of a young girl or child in a brothel was concerned, and in arrangements for the after-care and protection. This work, Miss Peto claims, paved the way for the employment of women police in India.

Opinion on both the leading ladies in this occurrence varied considerably, as they are wont to do. Beatrice Wakefield, who had left to get married before the Geddes Axe, remembers Mrs Stanley as an aloof figure, "hands covered in rings", who handed out their pay packets without so much as a smile or greeting, but agreed that she was very popular with the men: "We used to joke about her and the Commissioner." It appears that Mr Olive was the only one not won over. Mrs Stanley did, however, warm towards Beatrice when she was leaving – and wanted to pump her for information as to what went on on division. Miss Peto, though she does not say so in so many words, seems to have liked and admired Stanley, and Wyles herself, who keeps mentioning her in her book, admits that she radiated personality, had "allure" and used feminine wiles. She also gets in a few cracks against her, but Wyles used the technique of the extravagant compliment, alternating with the quick jabbing insult on quite a lot of people.

As for Wyles, Beatrice liked her, finding her kind and friendly. Other opinions are very assorted from a straightforward "smug" or "humbug" to "a nice woman really" or "a good guvnor". But all agree that she was rather boastful and proud. If she truly did not like taking statements, as Chief Inspector Robertson had stated, she was to do penance for many years to come, in just that occupation, she taking one half of the Metropolitan area, and Miss MacDougal the other.

The remaining women were posted to various areas "where large open spaces existed" and there was thought there might be work. They were now entirely under the control of the local Superintendents who could use them in uniform or plain clothes as they wished. There was no senior woman officer at all.

In February 1923 Sergeant Clayden, of the police family and veteran of the WPS munitions police, was promoted to Inspector and given the job of visiting the women and sorting out any particular problem they might have, but only in conjunction and consultation with the local male senior officer under whose supervision they remained. At the same time four women police patrols were made sergeants, each taking a quarter of the MPD area as their domain, and the word 'patrol' was replaced by the word 'constable' for, at long last, they had been sworn in and given power of arrest.

17

Mary Allen the Globe-trotter

In November 1922 Mrs Corbett Ashby, Secretary of the International Women's Suffrage Alliance, visited Cologne and was shocked by the rampant vice, disease and crime and the resulting deteriorating relations between the British Armies of Occupation and the local authorities and population. When she returned to England, she, as Mary Allen so modestly puts it, "drew me into consultation in my official capacity as one of the most experienced women in the social problems of Great Britain".

They decided to approach the War Office, where Mrs Corbett Ashby recommended they send a party of British women police officers to Germany. The War Office sent her back to investigate further, and she reported that the Germans were anxious to co-operate. Next, Mary Allen was sent over, having been told that if she could persuade the Cologne authorities to accept them, her women could go. While there, she met civil and military dignitaries, gave speeches to local women and inspected women's cells, a farm colony for girls, hostels and state-controlled brothels. The locals proved amicable and, on 22nd June 1923, she signed an agreement with the War Office to provide one officer and five constables for a period of six months. Five days later she returned again, by air, with Inspector Ellen Harburn, "an excellent German scholar". A few days later Sergeant Halfpenny, who had seen service in Ireland, and four constables followed them.

It was at her own suggestion, Mary Allen maintains, that a small number of well-educated German women should also be recruited to serve with them. They selected three from a recommended six experienced social workers. The German women were expected to deal with women alone or accompanied by civilians, while the British women tackled those in the company of soldiers or, sometimes, the soldiers themselves. At first, the local women were not keen on wearing uniform but soon gave way, she claims, on seeing how smart the British women looked. They were given an office at General Headquarters and another at the railway station, and Inspector Harburn was left in charge. Although it was stated at the time that the British women would have nothing to do with the 'morals police' and would concentrate on protecting the fifteen to eighteen-year-old girls, much of the work, by Mary Allen's account, sounds reminiscent of Grantham – accompanying the military on raids on 'suspected houses', patrolling the streets in pairs, day and night, examining the passes of Tommies, preventing them from entering out-of-bounds cafés with prostitutes and inspecting licensed premises. However, they did save many fifteen to eighteen-year-olds and opened a hostel where they could be temporarily accommodated and where runaway girls could stay.

They soon found themselves in the familiar role of advisers on personal problems (as most police in non-totalitarian states are). Both Tommies and prostitutes brought their worries to them – the latter, Mary Allen claims, preferring them to the German women police, who were less kind and sympathetic. Their German counterparts thought them too lenient, she says, but they were popular with the local authorities due to their impartiality. "Cases of rape and other brutalities towards the German population were swiftly and sharply punished, with the result that the general public trusted the policewoman's unbiased attitude, and voluntarily assisted them in every way possible." It needed to be unbiased considering some of the sentences which were being handed out to the Germans. A report in *The Times* of 8th December 1924 states:

Twelve years imprisonment, the heaviest sentence ever inflicted by a military court in British occupied territory, was passed on Michael Skarlet for the burglary of British Officers quarters in Cologne. Hubert Esser received four years for striking a British policewoman, and Heinrich Half, a one-legged man, six years for a violent assault on a military policeman. In each of the last two cases, one year of the sentence was remitted by the Commander in Chief.

Women police were not new to Germany. Experiments had previously been made in several cities but always in plain clothes and more on the lines of welfare workers or morals police in conjunction with the state-controlled prostitution. Mary Allen paid occasional inspection visits to the German branch of her service, and their six-month contract was repeatedly extended, until the British left. The

Army Council declared themselves deeply grateful to the women, whom they felt behaved with tact, courage, energy and common sense. More to the point, the local authorities took on the three German women for as long as they would be required, and the ties with the German women police were always to remain strong and friendly. The latter was due largely to the character of Ellen Harburn, a very sensible and fair woman. What Mary Allen omits to report in her books is that Inspector Harburn was at one point recalled from Cologne because she would not knuckle under to the unfair way she thought prostitutes were dealt with by the British and the Germans. She was very unimpressed by British high command, and men in general, and was not frightened to say so, which cannot have gone down well. However, she was good at the job as well as being a fluent German speaker. The authorities climbed down, and she returned to Germany, but she always felt that Mary Allen (whom, while admiring her in some ways, in other ways considered a silly woman) might have backed her up more.

Right from the start of the campaign for the appointment of women police in Britain, the United States had been held up as an example of progress in the field. As early as 1910 Mrs Alice Stebbin Wells had been taken on by the Los Angeles Police Department, and by 1925 women police were employed in 145 US cities, mainly in what were termed 'Women's Bureaux'. Their work had developed on lines similar to that of Great Britain and Germany, but none of them wore uniform. Both the WPS and women patrols had had a good deal of publicity in the US, and in 1918 the Deputy Commissioner of the New York Police asked the WPS for a sample uniform to take back home with him. Evidently, they were unimpressed, for their women stayed in plain clothes. In fact, when the wealthy Mrs van Winkle, Chief of Washington's Women's Bureau and President of the International Association of Policewomen, visited Britain in 1923, she is reported as saying that a woman could not do good preventative work unless she was in plain clothes. She was later to modify that opinion which was so diametrically opposed to that of the majority of British women police. Of course the difference in laws, especially those dealing with sexual morality, did account for some of the divergence.

The WAS particularly had always been convinced of the utter necessity of uniform. In *Lady in Blue* Mary Allen, as always, goes a little further and says she cannot think of anything more contemptible than for women police to masquerade in silk stockings, satin gowns and high-heeled shoes in order to entrap male and female offenders.

"If this practice became at all general," she went on, "every woman in a public place would be suspected of being what is termed in the more vulgar criminal classes 'a police nose'." Which seems to be overstating the case somewhat. Of course, she herself had the utmost aversion from dresses and an even greater aversion from Macready, who had suggested using women for these purposes. Oddly enough, though he had wanted 'ladies' for this purpose, one of the women then being used on night club and drug-trafficking observations, Lilian Dawes, was in fact, according to a colleague, "your actual good old cockney who had to have her fag and her beer".

Naturally, American women police were much called upon to justify their existence in lectures on their work up and down the country, and it is not surprising that the aggressively-uniformed Mary Allen (she seems never to have taken her uniform off, even wearing it for travelling and attending banquets in her honour) was asked to make a trip across the Atlantic – not, initially, by the US women police, though they had maintained contact with them down the years, but by the American National League of Women Voters, who wanted her to speak at their Fifth Annual Convention being held at Buffalo, New York State. Further speaking engagements made the plan "more feasible", and on 20th April 1924 Mary Allen steamed into New York aboard the *President Harding* to be greeted by Mrs Mary E. Hamilton, Chief of New York's one hundred women police. Mary's uniform, complete with peaked hat, navy blue breeches ("I haven't worn a skirt for six years," she told avid newsmen), knee-high shiny black boots and monocle, caused a sensation. It was the last mentioned item which really fascinated them: "They were quite convinced – and so was the whole of America within twenty-four hours – that it was a sign of office, like the crozier or the Black Rod! They simply refused to believe I wore it for use. To them, my uniform was incomplete without the eyeglass, and I believe they were firmly convinced that I could not make an arrest until I had screwed it into place." The last sentence is indicative of the impression the Press had sold of her as Chief of the British Women Police, one she did little to dispel. Crowds followed her around, and one young woman, she reports, even had the temerity to ask her if she ever wore pink satin. Inevitably the Press insisted that she direct New York traffic, at the corner of Lexington and Forty-Second Street. What her appearance did, of course, was to bring it to a total standstill. "Every vehicle that came in sight instantly pulled up, with a squeal of brakes, and the drivers leaned out, frankly stared at me, and began shouting to each other. They ignored the signal lights, they ignored the 'Stop!' and 'Go!' notices, they ignored my directions to move on."

During her four weeks stay she fulfilled a heavy speaking schedule and tours of inspection of reformatories, courts and police stations. At Buffalo she found some black policewomen, " ... who had been added to the white force of that city in order to deal with the large numbers of Negro delinquents. The black girl officials looked typically good-natured and eager, and I was forcibly reminded by them of the H.G. Wells' prophecy, in his novel *When the Sleeper Wakes*, of a whole world policed by coloured people, since they certainly make an excellent type of police officer."

She was most impressed by the policewomen of Detroit where, whenever possible, women and children were arrested by women police or handed over to them soon after arrest. The Chicago group, who had developed out of the suffrage movement as had the WAS, she found a more uncompromising type than she had met elsewhere but admitted they had to deal with a much rougher type of female criminal. The casualness of a Chicago gangster trial shocked her, but her most graphic and lasting memory of the whole trip was the night of the police ball. Fortunately she had tact enough to wait until her second book, published in 1935, to record her impressions of that event, at which police chiefs extricated hoards of illicit booze from suitcases which she had imagined contained their dinner-suits into which they were going to slip when the opportunity arose. Of course this was during Prohibition. Soon, wild drunkenness set in, and the policemen began dropping like flies. Mary Allen and Mrs Hamilton wisely took their leave, but later that night the dinner was raided, she claims, by New York's Anti-Vice Society who happened upon a cabaret "in which Negro girls were dancing so indecently that the affair later developed into a *cause célèbre* in New York's courts". However, very little of the truth leaked out as "political strings were pulled" and the proceedings fell through.

At her much more decorous farewell dinner, courtesy of the American National League of Women Voters, many people expressed to her the hope that on any future visit she would find American women police in uniform. At a luncheon speech soon after her return to England, she reported that in America the prettiest policewomen were used as decoys and that any unfortunate young man who addressed them was immediately arrested, which she thought was a mean trick which would never be used in Britain.

All in all, the visit seems to have been a big boost to her confidence and morale, which was just as well since it was soon to receive a blow from Dunning when she gave evidence before the 1924 Bridgeman Committee. The brief this time was to review experience gained since 1920 and to make recommendations concerning the future organization and duties of women police.

Dunning clearly disliked Mary Allen intensely and seemed to take an almost sadistic delight in tearing her evidence to pieces, in particular her list of disadvantages brought about by lack of attestation, such as not being able to carry out escorts alone or to follow through one's own cases. Sir Leonard refuted each of her five points: Bristol women carried out escorts without being attested; police*men* could not carry through their own cases – a police officer was merely a witness like everyone else. He was being deliberately perverse, for he must have known that Chief Constables did curtail women's work in this way, as Peto had experienced, because they were not attested. But the information Mary Allen had was all wrong, he declared; she did not know the inner workings of a police force, and apparently her informants were equally ignorant, he told her. The recent, over-extravagant US publicity cannot have helped, nor some remarks on the inadequacy of female chaperoning for women prisoners while in police custody which, she had pointed out, must allow for some opportunities of the wrong kind.[1]

The Police Federation of England and Wales reversed the opinions they voiced at Baird and now came out vehemently against women police, declaring them absolutely useless and asserting that it was "a man's job alone". Men could even take sex statements much better than women. They did concede that, for the men's own protection when taking statements, there was no reason why a woman should not be present. But they were referring to statements from children when they thought the mother could be allowed to stay. When Dame Helen Gwynne Vaughan pressed that a constable taking a child's statement must have someone else present, Inspector Varney of the Metropolitan Police replied that there must be a woman present or another officer. Nobody was much bothered about chaperoning a woman. (They would not be so sanguine after the Savidge Case in 1928.)

The Police Federation's opinions were shared by the Chief Constable of Brighton, who had not replaced his three women after the last of them had resigned in 1921 and now said he had no use for them. But some male supporters were in attendance; the Chief Constables of Lancashire, Birmingham and Gloucestershire. The latter, Major F.L. Stanley Clarke, brought along one of the policewomen whom Miss Peto had supplied in 1918: Miss Ethel Gale, who was, by now, a sergeant. After acquiring Gale and Rowe from the BTS, Stanley Clarke had quickly taken on nine more women, all ex-munitions police. However, these were employed as police reservists, mainly to replace men in clerical jobs and as grooms, but, in 1919, he had sworn six of them in. Geddes had put paid to most of the county's women, but Cheltenham and Gloucester refused to part with theirs and agreed to support them wholly from local funds.

"I am strongly in favour of the employment of Women Police," the Major told the Bridgeman Committee, "and consider that they are an important and necessary section of the modern Police Force." This was not rose-coloured comment for, like the Chief Constable of Reading, he had found their employment not without difficulties. Firstly, there had been very strong local antagonism, especially when he had tried to install them on the outskirts of Bristol where many poverty-stricken ratepayers felt burdened enough. "They said they were going to do all sorts of things to them but did not," he recalled. Now public opinion had been won over, but there had been other problems. Quite early on, one of the women had suffered a poisoned finger after grooming his horse. The finger had had to be amputated. Another had fallen off her bicycle while on duty and broken her ankle, and was now permanently lame. Both were receiving disability pensions and were still doing so when they died (in their eighties) during the 1960s, by which time they were getting £64 and £70 a year, respectively.[2] Nonetheless the Major wanted more women police in the towns. He even felt they would be useful in the country areas on certain occasions, such as at the big horse fair at Stow-on-the-Wold which was frequented by "a tremendous lot of riff-raff".

Chief Constable Lane of Lancashire announced that he too was more pro-women police than ever but still only as 'detectives'. He had by now instituted promotion examinations for them, which he set himself. These were centred mainly on dealings with women and children and were thus obviously far less demanding than those the men sat. Two of his women officers, Detective Inspector Lilian Naylor and Detective Constable Margaret Mackay (a police widow), also gave evidence from which it was fairly obvious that much of the women detectives' work was keeping and collating crime records, taking evidence in shorthand and typing reports. Intermittently they took sex statements, interviewed and escorted women and were employed on observations – since a man and woman had been found to be less conspicuous than men alone, Lane explained. Some of the women seemed to do more of the interesting work than others. Lilian Naylor said that she had been employed on "several murder cases" and made allusions to her "special work" for which she had been commended. Since Lane had already revealed that the women had been "invaluable" on "Sinn Fein work" this is probably what she was talking about. Her surviving colleagues recall that she was at one time seconded to the Metropolitan Police, where she is reputed to have sold matches in the street in an attempt to obtain evidence against the Sinn Fein.

The Bridgeman Committee's Report largely favoured women police, stating that the efficiency of a force was improved by their employment. But the Home Office, though recommending their appointment, was not prepared to bring any real pressure to bear and 'local discretion' remained – which meant: leaving things as they were. However, this ineffectual committee, and the support of its findings by some members of Parliament, did arouse ire in certain quarters, namely those of the newly-formed 'League of Womanhood'.

The aim of this organization, whose membership was open to both sexes, was "to put before the public the view of the modern woman who dissents from the feminist creed". Feminist societies, they claimed, in no way represented normal women. Motherhood and marriage was "the best and highest walk of life" that a woman could follow; all other occupations were second best. They announced their determination to "resolutely challenge the whole epicene creed of Feminism on every possible occasion", and Bridgeman was one. After the report was issued, the League published a pamphlet on 'The Women Police Question', of such vehemence that it might have been a feminist tract, only they were rarely so vitriolically personal in their attacks. It was written by Captain Henderson Livesey and introduced by Ashley Brown.

The gist of their arguments was familiar, and they concluded that politicians were taking the idea of women police seriously only because they were hypnotized by the idea of the woman's vote. That was probably very true. The Captain assured his readers that:

Of course, nobody worth calling a man would allow himself to be forcibly conveyed to a police station by a woman; if she attempted to use force, he would be morally bound to restrain her until the arrival of a male constable. If not, his life would probably be made miserable by the banter of his acquaintainces, and he would inevitably and properly earn the contempt of all the women who knew him or heard of his case. The many psychic hermaphrodites in our midst cannot understand the spirit which prompts this expression of opinion, but all normal men and women will appreciate it.

"Bi-sexual police officers" and "Macready's monsters" were two of the terms Captain Henderson Livesey applied to women police on behalf of his home-loving ladies, but some of his comments are interesting:

The National Council of Women cannot be accurately described as a Feminist Organization, for it numbers many desirable and normal women in its ranks, and always held aloof from the so-called 'militant' societies, that is those who believed in propaganda by brawl; it is in fact a body to which a woman may belong without losing her reputation as a normal human being; but its membership is, in fact if not in intention, confined to upper- and middle-class women, and its claim to speak in the name of the women of England, who number many millions, with a great working-class majority, is quite inadmissible.

He was referring to the fact that their evidence had been thus, he says, accepted at Baird and Bridgeman. Mary Allen was another obvious target here.

The discussion of a lady's garments, in public at any rate, would not in the ordinary course of events strike me as being a useful proceeding, but in the present case there is justification in that the lady started the discussion herself, and moreover the matter has certain psychological implications which have a very direct bearing on the question under review. The lady in question recently visited America, and was reported, on both sides of the Atlantic, as having said that she had not worn a skirt for six years.

There are some people who accept eccentricity of this sort as being representative of the 'modern' woman, but it is a libel on her to do so; it is difficult to suppress people who are possessed of a congenital desire to make fools of themselves, and left alone they will do little harm, but when their pretensions to a representative character are endorsed by official bodies, a protest must be made.[3]

Had he eavesdropped at Bridgeman or read the consequent report thoroughly, he surely would have realized that he had little to worry about on that score.

Mary Allen proceeded merrily on her way with the life full of the action she had always craved. In the mid-twenties she stood for Parliament as a Liberal candidate but was defeated, wrote her first book, learned to fly, set up a Women's Emergency Corps during the General Strike (Mrs Pankhurst was one of her first volunteers, she proudly reports) and continued with her speaking tours abroad, visiting Holland, Poland, Hungary, Czechoslovakia, Egypt, Finland, France, Germany, Greece and Brazil. Turkey also figured on one itinerary, but, just as she was about to leave Athens for Istanbul, a member of the British Diplomatic staff issued her with a 'semi-official warning'. Apparently the recent abolition of the veil had caused some unrest, and it was thought that Mary Allen's appearance in uniform, which she herself pointed out probably to them resembled that of a man, might "be used by certain fanatical elements in Istanbul to arouse mob passions".

18

The Savidge Case

One April evening in 1928, a fifty-seven-year-old ex-MP and well-known writer on financial affairs was sitting under a tree in Hyde Park with a twenty-two-year-old valve-tester from New Southgate. According to two plain clothes police officers, what they were doing there was reasonably likely to offend against public decency, so they were arrested. "I am not the usual riff-raff, I am a man of substance. For God's sake let me go!" exclaimed the gentleman, Sir Leo Chiozzo Money. But the police would not do so, and he struggled violently all the way to the station where he kept demanding that he be allowed to telephone his good friend the Home Secretary, who turned out to be not at home.

The following morning, at Marlborough Street Police Court, Sir Leo asked for a remand so as to arrange for their defence. This defence turned out to be so effective that the magistrate, Mr Henry Cancellor, decided that, having heard Sir Leo, he had heard enough – there was no need to distress the lady. He dismissed the case, gave £10 costs against the police and criticized the manner in which the police brought these cases. Sir Leo's defence was a simple one: he denied the charge. He also claimed that police had failed to obtain the services of a witness he had requested – a man who had chased after them, after the arrest, to give Sir Leo his umbrella. The police denied this. When asked why they had not asked the man themselves, they pointed out that they did have their hands rather full at the time and that they did not really think of it.

The police hierarchy was astonished by the magistrate's decision, which they thought wholly unfair. The man with the umbrella, by Sir Leo's own admission, must have been at least thirty yards away from the original incident so could scarcely be regarded as a witness. The magistrate had not only debarred cross-examination of one of the co-defendants but also had not stated a reason for dismissing the case. The bias manifested by the magistrate, wrote the Divisional

Superintendent, presented an alarming prospect from the police point of view, and he urged a retrial. Police solicitors were consulted, but, while admitting that they believed the evidence of the police officers, they felt there was nothing could be done.

But it was not to end there. Sir Leo had many influential friends, and, on 7th May 1928, a question was asked in the House of Commons as to what the Home Secretary proposed to do about a case where two persons of good repute and position were thus charged, then costs given against police. The Home Secretary, Sir William Joynson-Hicks, replied that he had to consider with the appropriate authorities whether the police officers were guilty of any perjury or breach of duties. Two days later the papers regarding the case arrived at the office of the Director of Public Prosecutions for his consideration. It was made clear that if he decided not to prosecute police (of previous good character), the Home Secretary must be in a position to satisfy Parliament that there was no case to answer. The papers were marked urgent.

The file was not put through the registry of the DPP in the normal manner, so it was a personal letter he wrote to the Commissioner of the Metropolitan Police asking him to depute one of his most experienced officers to make some enquiries about the case. The best man, Horwood decided, was Chief Inspector Collins, who had the appearance of a benign bishop, thirty-two years' service and ninety-three judges' commendations to his credit.

The Director of Public Prosecutions personally instructed the Chief Inspector to interview first the Chief Inspector at Hyde Park Police Station as to the character of the two officers, then the officers themselves, Miss Irene Savidge (the lady in the case), Miss Egan, who introduced the pair so would have knowledge of the extent of their relationship, and finally Sir Leo. It was pointed out that there could be no come-back on the couple, despite any such evidence revealed, as they had been acquitted.

Collins had been told that the matter was urgent, so that very evening he saw the Hyde Park Chief Inspector and the two hapless constables. The following morning, having tried and failed to obtain suitable interviewing accommodation at New Southgate Police Station, he sent a car to collect Miss Savidge and bring her to the Yard, should she agree to come. The Chief Constable in over-all charge agreed to this move on condition that they were accompanied by the lady Inspector.

The lady Inspector in question, one Lilian Wyles, was waiting at

Marylebone Court for a case of indecent exposure to be heard. In her book *A Woman at Scotland Yard* she tells how Collins, when collecting her from the court, had railed against the ridiculous instruction that a woman should accompany him, and was furious at having to wait for her. His manner towards her was generally rude and peremptory, but then she was used to that from her male colleagues.

When Miss Savidge was on her way from her place of employment to the Yard, she asked whether she might go home and change before continuing as she was in her working clothes. Collins refused the request. After they arrived at the Yard, the Chief Inspector told Wyles sharply, "You can go, that is all," and only thanked her for coming, she reports, when she had given him "a look". But she was worried about leaving the young woman and told him how he could get in touch with her should she be needed again. She did not hear from him again until the following evening, when she found his manner had changed markedly. He was now affable and friendly, told her that he had a successful interview and that he was sorry he had not got in touch with her to take Miss Savidge home but that it had been very late when they had finished. It transpired that the Chief Constable had been furious when he learned of the lady Inspector's dismissal from the scene and sensed trouble. He did not have long to wait.

Sir Leo's solicitor not only refused to allow him to go to the Yard and insisted that the Chief Inspector come to his office to interview his client but he refused to allow any "roving questions as to his past history and his relationship with Miss Savidge". After the consequent fruitless interview, Collins duly reported this stonewalling to the DPP, who wrote a stiff letter to the solicitor, insisting that Sir Leo spare a little more of his time to give the officer fuller information and threatening that, if he did not, he (the DPP) must take "other steps". In fact, no further steps were taken, except by Sir Leo.

On the same day as his meeting with Collins, the attention of the House of Commons was drawn to the circumstances under which the Metropolitan Police conveyed a young woman named Miss Savidge to Scotland Yard without giving her the opportunity to communicate with her friends or legal advisers, and subjected her there to close and persistent examination regarding a case already tried and dealt with by the court.

Next day Inspector Wyles was whisked from under the dryer at the hairdressers straight to the House of Commons, where a hot debate on the Savidge Affair was being conducted. A Home Office official pumped her about the case. She was tempted, she admits, to gain revenge for the years of insults, frozen faces and icy indifference from her male colleagues but declares herself instantly ashamed of such thoughts. Consequently, she gave brief answers which "did no harm to Mr Collins".

After being interviewed by the Home Secretary, Inspector Wyles was confined in a glassed-in chamber behind the Speaker's Chair and guarded by a large constable. Curious MPs peered in at her and, the following morning, the papers reported: "Miss Irene Savidge in the House as Debate proceeds". After she was released from her cage and was being escorted towards a car, one MP, "an excited little man", seized her hand and, "in a voice trembling with emotion, exclaimed, 'Justice – dear, dear child – you shall have it'."

The papers were soon full of Miss Savidge's terrible ordeal, and an enquiry was the inevitable result. The Savidge Case rocked the Metropolitan Police, but, according to Wyles, it rocked Chief Inspector Collins much, much more. Looking very pathetic, he had tried to reach her when she was in her glass box at the House of Commons, but the following day his old manner suddenly returned, and he instructed her to sit down and make a statement, which he would dictate. She then, she says, told him exactly what she thought of him, and that she would make her own statement and it would be similar to the one already in the hands of the Home Secretary. In a small voice he asked her what she had said. She told him that she had told the truth about her own small part in the affair, "and of you, nothing but good, which you did not deserve". As the enquiry approached, he clung to her, and she was allotted the task of keeping him calm. If he was to get upset, he might lose his temper while giving evidence, and the fatherly, benign countenance would disappear to reveal "the purposeful and forceful individual he was".

It was a glittering affair: Sir Henry Curtis Bennet KC (who had defended Sir Leo at Magistrates Court) and Sir Patrick Hastings KC, appearing for Miss Savidge, with Mr Norman Birkett KC and Mr H.D. Roome for the police (the costs of Miss Savidge's counsel, £2,449.7s.8d were to be paid by the Receiver of the Metropolitan Police from public funds). The accusations against the police were vague and wide-ranging, but in particular they were charged with not allowing her to go home and consult her parents before being interviewed and that during the unchaperoned interview Collins's behaviour had alternated between undue familiarity and aggression. Also, that he had made improper remarks to her such as, "Now you are really a good girl, and you never had a man, have you?* But there are several things one can do without really sinning: do not be afraid to tell us, as we are looking after you," and that whenever she replied, he distorted and altered what she had said to suit his own purposes. In addition, not only did he frequently grasp her arm and look into her eyes and say things like, "My dear Irene, are you sure of this?", but then, looking straight into her face, he sat next to her and put his arm round her and grasped her hands so as to ascertain how she and Sir Leo had been sitting.

The original police evidence had stated that Sir Leo had his hand up Miss Savidge's dress, and Miss Savidge had her hand on Sir Leo's person. The Chief Inspector had questioned her as to whether Sir Leo's clothes were "undone in a certain manner" and whether his hand was up her skirt. To clear up some details, Collins had asked her to stand up so he could see the length of her dress and asked her what was the colour of her petticoat? When this last had been revealed in the House of Commons, one MP had shouted, "A damned shame!" Further, when tea had been brought and there had only been one spoon, Collins had said, "Now Irene, will you spoon with me?"

By the time the day of the enquiry arrived, Wyles claims, this much-feared detective had become as timid as a mouse, his mood swinging from elation to depression. He confided in her all his fears to such an extent that she could not wait for it to be over. When the day for his evidence came, the Chief Constable reiterated the instruction that she must keep him calm at all costs, and to this end she even refused him a tot from their "small stock of cheering liquid of which I constituted myself bartender". He acquitted himself well, and so did Lilian Wyles, saying that Sergeant Clark had come for her at the court and taken her to New Southgate; that Irene Savidge had not asked to go home but merely remarked that she was feeling untidy and that she had reassured her she looked all right; that she had said to Collins at the Yard, "You will wish me to stay unless Miss Savidge will be all right with you," and that Miss Savidge had volunteered, "I will be all right."

It is difficult to exaggerate the sensation this case caused and the amount of publicity it generated. Every single word of every day's proceedings, which interminably covered the same tedious ground was reported verbatim in *The Times*. There were tightly-packed pages of it, broken up with only the odd sub-headings, such as, "THE

*After arrest she had gone to a doctor to be medically examined and found to be *virgo intacta*.

SUITABILITY OF NEW SOUTHGATE", "ASKED WHETHER HER MOTHER KNEW" and "USUAL PRACTICE FOLLOWED". One matter was kept right out of the proceedings – the question of whether the pair had in fact been acting indecently. One person was also kept out: Sir Leo Money. As newspapers, Parliament and persons of substance all agreed, neither it nor he was germane to the matter in hand.

The findings of the enquiry were, that although they disapproved of the practice of taking voluntary statements from persons who were unaware of what the consequences might be and had had no opportunity to seek advice, Collins was not guilty of hectoring Miss Savidge: he had merely been paternal since she looked so childlike. One must take into account the unblemished record of Collins and the circumstances in which the charges were made, i.e. after a midnight interview with Sir Leo, directly after she had seen the police, and a night for reflection on what she had said. Although childlike, Irene Savidge was nonetheless intelligent, of quick perception and quite capable of looking after herself. They made several recommendations as to the future conduct of such cases, and among them was the suggestion that when police took a statement from a woman on matters "intimately affecting her morals", another woman should always be present unless she expressly requested otherwise. (It had also been revealed that Miss Egan had had the greatest difficulty in ensuring even that her brother stay while she herself was being interviewed.)

The report was issued by two members of the tribunal. A third member, Labour MP Mr Hastings Bernard Lees-Smith, so strongly disagreed with the other two that he issued a minority report which declared that Miss Savidge was telling the truth and the police lying, and, according to Tancred, many social workers present agreed with this. He did go along with the other two in that a second woman should always be present at such statement-taking.

Nonetheless, Collins was let off the hook and returned to his duties and soon became "once again the same Chief Inspector, full of zeal, drive and bustle, with this difference: he was from then on prudent when it came to dealing with women". Indeed, he recounted to Lilian Wyles with glee an incident where he had been sent to investigate a murder "in the country", where local police were itching for him to interrogate the suspected woman, but he not only refused to go anywhere near her until a policewoman was present but then allowed only her to remain during the interview, much to the local police's chagrin. He did not make the next rank of Superintendent, but he did acquire substantial damages as settlement of a newspaper libel against him with regard to the case.

As for Lilian Wyles, this case proved a turning-point for her, and from now on she was accepted by the men of the CID. What is curious is that while she appears to have lied for her colleagues at the tribunal (and who could blame her or them when truth and justice had been held in such contempt by their betters), she chose to tell the truth (or agree with Miss Savidge's statements) in her book. When the book was published in 1951, there must have still been many people around who would remember the Savidge affair and her evidence. And, since she claimed that Collins had since become a "real friend", why did she now choose to reveal the truth of his behaviour? She also introduced a new element when she said Collins picked her up and accompanied them in the car; something not even Miss Savidge had claimed.

Subsequent to the case, two long articles on 'Police and Public' were published in the *Observer*. The writer, J.L. Garvin, insisted that women should now take an equal part in all police matters "peculiarly concerning their own sex", and every woman voter should insist on this. Further, since there were four Assistant Commissioners and women made up more than half of the population, "either one of them ought to be a woman, or a woman ought to be added to their number; and the sooner the better." The suggestion has not yet been taken up.

Another Marlborough Street magistrate, Frederick Mead, was, however, still maintaining a state of war with women police. A year earlier, in October 1927, *The Policewoman's Review* had reported that the question of suitability of women for police duty had again been opened by Mr Mead, the magistrate at Marlborough Street Police Court, who apparently objected to policewomen giving evidence of a disagreeable nature. Later, in 1929, there was another incident. When a certain WPC Ritchie was sent out in plain clothes, she was accosted by a man. She, and her companion, WPC Hill, ignored him and walked on, but he followed them and, touching WPC Ritchie on the arm, said, "Hallo dearie." They turned their backs and walked away, but he followed and persisted in pestering her, whereupon they arrested him for insulting behaviour. As I pointed out earlier, there is no specific charge when the offence occurs this way around.

The case appeared before Mr Mead, who promptly discharged it, on the grounds that there had been no breach of the peace, and though it might have been "insulting" it was not "threatening and abusive". (The charge was "Using threatening, abusive or insulting words or behaviour with intent to provoke a breach of the peace or whereby a breach of the peace is likely to be occasioned" – contrary to Sec.54: Metropolitan Police Act, 1839.)

But he had gone too far this time. The Commissioner's legal advisers thought the obligatory joining of the words "quite ridiculous and wholly unarguable". What is more, another point Mead had made, that a police officer cannot be insulted so that a breach of the peace may occur was untenable.

Probably the reason that the police reacted so strongly was, that of all the Metropolitan Police powers, this was their most sacred. It could be exercised in many and diverse incidents to which no particular statute applied, so much so that, even in my day, it was affectionately referred to as "The Breathing Act". It gave us room to breathe, saved our faces and stopped ugly violence developing before an actual breach of the peace occurred. However, we were strongly discouraged from putting ourselves forward as insulted parties. Police officers get insulted a great deal more often than people imagine, and we could have been always arresting people. A man of Mr Mead's experience should have realized the value of the power he was attacking, but obviously his judgement faltered whenever he was faced with women police. (Also pertinent, perhaps, he was now eighty-two years of age.) Police began assiduously searching files for comparable cases, but while this was going on, Mr Mead was interviewed once again and "almost admitted" that he would not make such a decision again, and the matter was dropped.

19

The Static Years

In August 1928, partly as a direct result of the Savidge case, a Royal Commission on Police Powers and Procedures was appointed. Among those giving evidence was Edith Tancred, who was continuously active in promoting the cause of women police, as was the National Council of Women whom she was representing. A bevy of Chief Constables from areas as divergent as Cardiff City and Rutland County also said their piece. Naturally, methods of taking statements from women was very much on the agenda.

The Chief Constables who did not have women police, such as Norfolk, Rutland, Middlesbrough, Staffordshire and Essex, all told more or less the same story. No difficulty had ever been experienced, and if they did need women to sit in on statements, policemen's wives or, as in Essex, a very respectable married woman living nearby, would suffice. In any case, women did not like telling such things to other women.

Wales still had no women police. The Chief Constable of Radnorshire felt that there was no need for them but that a woman should be present at such statement-taking for the safety of the male officer. The Chief Constable of Cardiff was totally opposed to women police, thinking them incapable of dealing with sexual crimes. However, there was soon to be a Question in the House of Commons, by Sir Robert Thomas of Anglesey, as to whether the Home Secretary was going to do anything about a report from Cardiff's Chief Constable concerning the association of white women with Asiatic and coloured seamen in the dock area. One male MP thought that employing more British seamen on British ships was the solution, while Lady Astor felt that women police would be the best preventive measure! Neither step was taken.

North Wales was also currently coming under pressure to appoint some women police. The North Wales Association for Friendless Girls asked for them in Merioneth, then Rhyl (during the season), but the Chief Constables reported that need had not arisen, and the matter was dropped.

Royal Commission witnesses from forces which had women police gave, rather naturally, favourable evidence. Sir Charles Rafter, Chief Constable of Birmingham, thought his six an unqualified success and said he wanted more. Major F.L. Stanley Clarke of Gloucestershire declared, "I must honestly say I think they have proved their value." He had backed his judgement by not only taking on another four but recently giving them all motor-cycles so that they could get about all over the county, to deal with women and children whenever possible, and he found "ordinary women and girls" quite prepared to give their statements to women police in preference to men. His "Flying Squad" of policewomen received much publicity, not all of it encouraging. On 4th February 1929 Janet Gray, the Lydney policewoman, sped happily across the pages of the *Sunday Graphic* oblivious of the headline, "DO WE WANT WOMEN POLICE?", just above. But the *Sunday Express* was pleased that there was not now a lonely byway or lovers' lane in the county which was not patrolled by them, and *The Policewoman's Review* felt their presence lessened the serious dangers to girls who accepted motor rides from unknown men.

A slightly chill note was struck by the Chief Constable of Leeds who, after mentioning to the Commission that his three plain clothes women had little time to do much else than take statements, since sex crimes were on the increase in his area, admitted that they had managed to fit in some enquiries for the Ministry of Pensions with regard to the misconduct of widows.

The Commission recommended that all sex statements should be taken by women and that more women police should be employed and used where possible for escort duty, searching etc, but be given the opportunity to do general as well as special work.

Scotland had not been represented on the Royal Commission as, after their 1924-25 Committee on Sexual Offences against Young Persons, the Scottish Office had issued a circular stating that, among other things, women police should take such statements when available. The Scottish women were now enjoying one considerable advantage over their English sisters: in 1927 the Scottish Police Federation had agreed to represent them.

Late in 1929 another deputation organized by the NCW and others found its way to the Home Office. Miss Tancred urged the appointment of women police for duties recommended by the Committee on Sexual Offences Against Children (England and Wales had had a separate one), the Street Offences Committee 1927 and the Royal Commission. Miss Peto spoke on their training and organization, which she said should be standardized and organized and not just left to chance as it was then (many women received no real training). The Home Secretary said he would think about it.

These were rather lean and static years for the women police, their numbers and status changing little. *The Policewoman's Review*, which Mary Allen had launched in May 1927, probably helped keep spirits up. Obviously there was still money available to the WAS, as the magazine was quite an ambitious creation, printed on glossy paper and liberally sprinkled with well-produced photographs of serving women police. One shows Dunning inspecting the Worthing Police, with a policewoman and her motor-cycle well to the fore. Articles on the existing women police, energetically canvassed opinions of Chief Constables and lady magistrates, abound. There was even a piece on 'The Custody of Women Prisoners' by C. Nina Boyle, though it is not up to her usual standard and clearly utilized long-gone experiences. The magazine also, it must be admitted, served the growing megalomania of Mary Allen. Subscribers were treated to an endless flow of photographs of her strutting around the world.

There had been other attempts at a magazine. As early as September 1915, *The Police Review* offered women police the platform of *The Policewoman*, price One Penny. Woman Patrol Miss E.M. Royle was appointed Assistant Editor, but the project faded out in 1916. In June 1919 the Women Police Service issued *The Whistle*, which, they stated, had previously been issued, though not in its present printed form, with the assistance of *The Police Chronicle*.

As is often the case, the most intriguing items in *The Policewoman's Review* are the casual snippets. From them we learn that Manchester women police have taken part in a raid on a manicurists; that Colchester's policewoman has now been joined by her sister; that the duties of Eastbourne's lady include giving special attention to postcards in shops and keeping observations on fortune-tellers and clairvoyants, and that Hertford's two women are trained at their police headquarters like the men but are given additional instruction on special subjects by the Chief Constable. From the foreign department comes the news that the higher-ranking women police in Prussia rejoice in the title '*Polizeigefängnishauptwachmeisterin*', which, literally translated, means 'police station head female police sergeant'.

In September 1927 the handsome features of Captain P.J. Sillitoe,

Chief Constable of Sheffield, appeared on the cover alongside a picture of his three policewomen, two of whom had seen service with the WAS in Cologne. Sillitoe was a firm believer in the necessity and usefulness of women police and had asked for them in his first command in Britain, the East Riding of Yorkshire, in 1925. He put them in Bridlington to help cope with the high incidence of sexual offences there in the summer, since he felt that women complainants would confide more readily in a woman officer. Sheffield already had some when he arrived, and now, he told the readers, they were fully sworn in, patrolled, did escort duties and plain clothes work, took statements from women and children in cases of indecency and attended court in all cases when women or children were being tried. The statements were well taken, and, contrary to the opinion recently expressed by a Chief Constable, he said, he found that the truth was usually elicited. "I, therefore, reiterate that I believe in Women Police, given the right type of highly-educated woman, and I incline to the opinion that where their appointment has not been a success, it is because this type has not been selected." He admired Mary Allen, possibly because she was a person of action like him and, also like him, unafraid. The WAS had resumed training, which had dropped off since Germany, but advised recruits that they could not guarantee them a post. In 1928, fortunately for the future of women police, Percy Sillitoe was willing and able to accept one of the latest WAS trainees, Barbara Denis de Vitré.

Miss Denis de Vitré came from a moderately prosperous background and had been attending a course on social welfare at Manchester University when she saw one of the WAS appeals for recruits. After her six-week course with them, she was so impressed by the possibilities of police work that she knew straight away that it was the only job in the world for her. In Sheffield she dealt chiefly with the many shoplifters and was soon receiving a commendation for her work from the city justices. Miss Peto recalls her in those days as "very fair, neat and shy".

Dorothy Peto had left Birmingham in 1924, after her father had died and she needed a job which allowed her to be at home more often. She handed over her duties to that early BTS trainee Mildred White, who had confidently expected to spend fifteen years getting to know the people of Salisbury. Despite her pessimism at Baird, she had by now been made sergeant. She had lost none of her bite and, to Peto's delight, made her acceptance of the Birmingham post conditional on her attestation there and the retention of her rank. Miss

Peto's next three years were spent as a travelling organizer for the National Council for Combating Venereal Disease, and, while doing it, she took the opportunity to look up policewomen all over the country. In 1927, when Mabel Cowlin retired from the post of Director of Liverpool Women Patrols, Miss Peto took over. Liverpool had stuck to their Women Patrols, who worked full time but on a semi-official basis with a grant from the city. However, Mabel Cowlin claimed that they were regarded as policewomen by Liverpudlians.

Among the suggestions the 1929 NCW deputation made were those that a woman should become a part of HM Inspectorate and that a senior woman officer should once more be put in charge of the Metropolitan Women Police. A few weeks later it was announced that Miss Peto had been offered the job as Staff Officer, on a year's experimental basis, "with duties of an advisory rather than executive nature". She promptly took a leaf out of Sergeant White's book and said she would accept only if she was sworn in. When she arrived for duty, she reminded them of their promise, and the Assistant Commissioner, A Department, sent for the attestation book and did it there and then. "Now," she says, "for the first time, I was a fully-fledged police officer!"

Her joy was short-lived. She was put into offices staffed only by civil servants and was not given a uniform, which made her realize that if she had not pressed for attestation she might have remained a civilian herself for that first year. Although she was "very sore about the whole business", at least she knew she was a police officer, and that reassured her. The lack of uniform did not worry her since, until the outbreak of the Second World War, her male colleagues of Superintendent rank and above did not normally wear their uniforms except on ceremonial occasions, "so I did not look out of character in a plain tailored suit and felt hat, with shirt, collar and tie, such as had been my normal wear in the Birmingham CID".

Miss Peto's brief was to examine the position of women police and advise the Commissioner on an expansion programme, as they had, at last, been promised some increase in numbers from their current forty constables, five sergeants and two inspectors. However, during that first year she was mainly observing and getting to know people. She also observed, as she put it, "an outstanding problem which coloured the work of the police" at that time: the huge influx into London of the unemployed. Men, women and children came pouring in in search of work and slept out in doorways, parks and squares and along the Embankment. The special interest of women police during this period was the stranded girl who could so easily drift into a life of prostitution just so as to eat. The Middle Walk in Hyde Park was a fruitful venue as, at almost any time, it would be "filled with youths and girls chattering in Welsh or in the dialects of the North and West". Little could be done officially, for there were no suitable laws guarding children and adolescents, and, if they did not respond to unofficial help, there was nothing for it but to wait until they had committed some offence. As it was, Miss Peto and her women did what they could, trying to get the girls into the crowded hostels, obtaining tram-passes for them while they looked for work, and so on. Ideally, they would be returned home, but, as she pointed out, there was not much sense in that if those at home were workless.

On 9th June 1930, Miss Peto was asked to sit on the Police Council Committee, which was about to draft the first regulations appertaining to the employment of women police. When the Police Council had sat earlier that year, they had refused to consider the subject but had now been pressured into it by women MPs, the NCW and particularly Edith Tancred, who had pointed out that it was not so difficult: all they had to do was implement the recommendations of Baird and Bridgeman, that would form the basis.

In 1932 Lord Trenchard took over the Metropolitan Police just as Miss Peto was coming to the end of a second probationary year. It was suggested, casually, that the simplest thing, if she did not mind, was just to let the probation run on another year. She did mind and protested very vigorously that it was illegal to keep a constable on probation for more than two years. Within a few days she was transferred from the secretarial department and given the rank of Superintendent in charge of women police. Before Trenchard would agree to the promised augmentation, he insisted that the women prove themselves, and to this end they were concentrated on one of the four districts of the Metropolitan area. If they proved their value now, he promised, he would up the number by a hundred to 150. The experiment was to last two years.

During that time the Children and Young Persons Act 1933 came into being. The ever-vigilant NCW had attempted to get included that the care of children in custody should always be passed to women police. They did not succeed but did manage to make sure that, while in court, children must be looked after by women. When the bill came into force, Mr Howgrave Graham, head of the civilian department in which Dorothy Peto had languished so long, took steps to ensure that all reports and correspondence concerning children or young persons were channelled through A4 branch (women police) which allowed them to develop close co-operation with Juvenile Courts and Local Education Authorities. From then on Miss Peto had two passions: the first had always been the welfare of her women police; now she had the Children and Young Persons Act as well.

The experiment was a success but, due to the difficulties of the times, augmentation proceeded at a slower pace than promised. While Miss Peto was doing her first two years, Miss Denis de Vitré left for Cairo and, a month later, was made a Head Constable in Cairo's women police. She was soon supervising brothels and the registration of prostitutes and, for a time, did some undercover work for the narcotics bureau. But the main task of her and her colleague, Helen Hoskyn, was to raise and train a branch of the Egyptian women police, largely to help stamp out the heavy drugs traffic prevalent at the time. C.R. Stanley, in his excellent profile of her, *The Purpose of a Lifetime*, relates how policing in Egypt was a sometimes dangerous pursuit but that Barbara was an ideal companion to have in a tight corner, " ... one who could be relied upon to use a revolver with good effect when necessary ... but life was hard and an inadequate salary and miserable living conditions compelled her resignation in April 1932".

When she returned to Britain, she became Leicester City's second policewoman, replacing the first, Eileen St Clair Sloane, who had just left after three years' service. She was lucky to get the post, employment of women police in the provinces being at a new low. The recent regulations for women police had not altered local discretion. In fact, when they were sent out, they were accompanied by one of the Home Office's circulars which assured the constabularies that they were under no compulsion to employ women police – these were merely the rules should they wish to do so. Most forces did not. Economy cuts were being proposed in policemen's pay, and the Police Federation and Chief Constables Association were demanding that women police recruiting be halted. The NCW kept fighting, but, despite a spontaneous deputation of male MPs in December 1932, local discretion remained. This time the Metropolitan Women Police were better off, since they were growing, albeit only slowly.

Constable Denis de Vitré's main employment at Leicester City was, again, catching numerous shoplifters, but she was soon also assisting the CID on arrests and raids where females were involved. She did good work too bringing abortionists to book and in one particular case posed as "a woman well advanced in pregnancy", to this end –

with the aid of a well-placed pillow. When it came to the arrest, she was "pretty severely knocked about" but hung on until help arrived. In 1936 she was made sergeant and in 1937 organized the first national women police conference. The women were not allowed to discuss their conditions of employment at this conference, and, since the Police Federation of England and Wales still refused to represent them and they had no one on HM Inspectorate of Constabularies, they were in a helpless and hopeless position. By 1939 only forty-five out of 183 police forces were employing women, and a sixth of those women had not yet been sworn in. London now had about the same number they had reached in 1921.[1]

20

To War Again

When was this lady going to be interned? the Labour MP for Colne Valley asked in the House of Commons in June 1940. He was referring to Mary Allen, a Fascist, "and proud of it".[1]

In January 1934 Mary Allen had gone to Germany where she had met and talked with Hitler and Goering. Before going she was interviewed by the *Evening Standard*, and she told them:

> I am going to see Herr Hitler at his invitation. I am anxious to learn about the truth of the position of German womanhood. I am certain it is not correct that they have been totally banished from public life. I think I shall find that Hitler has disbanded only those who were politically unreliable. It would be a mistake to ban women completely from public life, but I realize that many of them would be more suitably employed at home.[2]

Unsurprisingly, she found she was right. Hitler had even disbanded German women police because they were "not of his political persuasion". To keep them would have been like enrolling Communist agents, who would not take the oath of allegiance, in the British Police Force, Hitler had pointed out to her. She had found him sincere and an idealist and regretted the propaganda against him in Britain, which could have the same Communist threat over it within six months, if Hitler fell. At his suggestion, she had inspected the 'Communist exhibits' collected by the German police and then in the Secret Police Headquarters "rather like the Black Museum at Scotland Yard". This had made her realize from what fate he had saved Germany during "the recent uprising". Mary Allen was, above all, a patriot, and Hitler's message got through to her. She also knew a leader when she saw one.

Hermann Goering, "stern in action, a magnificent airman and fluent speaker", had reassured her that he was going fully into the matter of appointing 'Nazi policewomen' and was fully in agreement with her that, if appointed, they should wear uniform. "No one can do official work without the right to wear uniform," he said. "It inspires confidence and ensures authority. It divides the policewoman from the *agent provocateur* and the spy." Which, she said, were her sentiments exactly.[3] She became a Fascist, supporting both Hitler and Franco.

The Question in the House in 1940 had been provoked by the fact that the Women's Auxiliary Service had been represented by Mary Allen on the Advisory Council of the Women's Voluntary Services for Civil Defence. The Home Secretary reassured the questioner that neither Mary Allen nor any member of the WAS had attended a meeting of this organization since January of that year. In fact the WAS had been suspended for the duration,[4] and the last word on them comes from the kindly Miss Peto in her memoirs: "During the Second World War, I came across probably the last survivor of Miss Damer Dawson's Women Police Service on night duty in charge of the homeless and stranded who found shelter in the crypt of St Martin's in the Fields.[5] I used to call in there on New Year's Eve after visiting women police on night duty, and we would sing in the New Year together with the words of 'Auld Lang Syne'."

Mary Allen was not interned. If she had been, it would have been the final ignominy considering that five Metropolitan Women Police had been put in charge of the women internees on the Isle of Man.

As the war had approached, history had repeated itself as it always seems to. The NCW had attempted to get women accepted as Special Constables but the Government had procrastinated. The Chief Constable of Staffordshire took things into his own hands and, in August 1939, appointed twenty women specials, taking them on full time after the war broke out.[6] But he was very much in the minority for, although their employment had remained static in the thirties, their general reputation had waned, and resistance to them grown. This was partly due to something of an anti-feminist backlash and was probably also related to the economic situation, since the Police Federation still insisted they be employed as extra to the regular police force, which made them seem like an unnecessary luxury. Their chief offence, however, seems to have been not looking good.

In January 1933 the cover of *The Policewoman's Review* sported a photograph of Gracie Fields dressed as a policewoman in her latest film, 'Looking on the Bright Side'. An accompanying New Year message from the star herself advised readers that, when people criticized their uniform, they should show them this picture. Earlier, Edgar Wallace had written to the paper praising the women police but asking why they had to wear that dreadful uniform. The offensive garb was not that much different from its original form. Skirts were shorter, and flat shoes had replaced heavy boots, but the hat, especially in proportion, was more pudding-basin than ever in most forces, and the general effect was slightly weird. Consequently they became something of a music hall joke, and sometimes the joke seemed pretty silly. "HAS A POLICEWOMAN ANY SEX IN HER OFFICIAL CAPACITY?" asked the *Daily Mail* in all seriousness, above an item which described the dilemma of a Reverend Austin Lee who had been about to give his seat to a policewoman on a crowded train "when a doubt assailed him that she might consider it an insult to her uniform". He had not resolved "this knotty problem" when the train arrived at the next station and he had to alight.[7] But much more damaging than this coyness was the sniping in the courts which continued despite the suppression of Mr Mead.

In 1929, when a policewoman had arrested a drunken man, she had been rebuked by the magistrate and warned of the dangers, and in 1930 another magistrate suggested that it must hurt a man's feelings to be arrested by a woman. Later a question was asked in the House of Commons as the result of a bookmaker's being convicted of assaulting two women police while trying to escape from them. Would not, the MP wanted to know, the Home Secretary give instructions that in the future women in plain clothes should not be called upon to perform a duty which put an unfair strain on the man arrested and which might be dangerous to themselves. The Home Secretary declined, but the sniping went on. At one stage in 1932 a Recorder at the Old Bailey was prompted to say, "I hope there will no longer be ignorant clamour against women police. In my view there should be women police in all cases concerning women and children."

They were still appreciated in some places however. Hove's Constable Mabel Read (WPS trained and ex-Gretna) had already been commended by local magistrates in 1928 for her detection and arrest of a "persistent walk-in thief", and in 1937 she was again complimented for her "astuteness and alacrity" in arresting (with the help of a boatman) a man stealing from beach huts. Like those other ex-munitions women police Constables Tonra and Sandover of Cheltenham, Mabel Read received a Silver Jubilee medal in 1935.[8] But, generally, resistance to women police grew within most police forces which did not have them, and the rumours that they were being used as "rubber heelers" (on internal investigations against other police)[9] did not help their cause.

Although dilatory about allowing women to become specials, the Home Office was eager for women to replace men in the police clerical, telephonist and driving jobs and, consequently, inaugurated the Women's Auxiliary Police Corps – a body not looked upon with a great deal of favour by many women police supporters, who felt they would be employed as an alternative to women police proper by forces who wanted to resist taking them on permanently but might be under pressure to appoint some women as the war went on. This did happen, but in the long run it could be helpful to the women police cause, since some forces thus took on their first women employees and, finding the experience nowhere near as horrific as they expected, were converted to the employment of women police. One of the first to take them on was a Welsh Constabulary, Cardiganshire, whose Chief Constable was soon paying them tribute for their good work, especially in the control and search of enemy aliens. He was particularly fortunate here, since a woman police sergeant taken on with them spoke German.[10] The North Riding of Yorkshire also began employing women for the first time. "Being a primarily agricultural county, policewomen had not, before the war, been thought necessary," it states in *The First Hundred Years of the North Riding of Yorkshire Constabulary, 1856-1956*. They do not do things by halves in Yorkshire. Once they had made the decision to take on forty WAPC, they went further by attesting twelve of them and putting them on motor patrol duties unaccompanied by men. The women turned out to be much more successful in this area than had been expected, their history declares with endearing honesty, and goes on, "The WAP Constables who were employed on motor patrol duties, although many were well below the physical standard now expected of policewomen, were not afraid of interrogating suspects and made many arrests, particularly of deserters of both sexes."

The NCW and other organizations continued to press strongly for more regular women police on the grounds that they were still not employed by many forces for the protection of women and children and on war-time grounds of the usual growing prostitution, increasing juvenile crimes and evacuee assistance. The Police Federation and many Chief Constables continued their stout opposition. It must not be assumed that this was merely blind prejudice, said a leader in *The Police Review* of 16th August 1940. It was just that the ways in which women could be usefully employed were strictly limited, due to their comparatively frail physique and "because they are women". Shortly after the latest bland refusal to allow women police representation by the Federation, the same journal published a sympathetic leader as the result of a letter from a male reservist complaining that he had no voice, due to non-representation.[11]

The pressure to appoint women police continued apace, but only on behalf of the English and Welsh Constabularies. The Scottish Constabularies and the Metropolitan Police were felt to be progressing satisfactorily. Ever since the sex statement circular in the mid-twenties, women police in Scotland had developed entirely as plain clothes officers (the WAPC saw the re-emergence of uniformed women north of the border). Shortly after his appointment to Glasgow Constabulary in 1931, Sir Percy Sillitoe had upped the strength of the women to fifteen and raised their wages. He also acquired Janet Gray, "the Lydney policewoman", who became his first woman sergeant. The other big cities, Edinburgh, Dundee, Aberdeen and Ayr, acquired one or two, as did Lanark and, in 1935, Dunbartonshire, which made Scotland's numbers up to twenty-eight.

Glasgow's fifteen women, Sir Percy told *The Policewoman's Review*, generally assisted the detective staff as much as possible and were "great assets to us males". In addition, he felt that their very presence was a protection for the men. In fact, their work was an amalgam of uniform and CID work. They patrolled streets and parks dealing with anything that came up, from street accidents to pickpockets, and visited or did observations on brothels, shebeens (illicit liquor shops), dance-halls, theatres and those picture houses. Women and children were, of course, their particular province, and they were particularly effective, the city's report for 1934 stated, in cases of palmistry and shoplifting.

When the war started, Sillitoe quickly launched into the recruiting of WAPC. Both his wife and daughter became members, his wife being instantly raised to the rank of Assistant Commandant – "a flagrant example", says A.W. Cockerill in his book *Sir Percy Sillitoe*, "of the nepotism of which Sillitoe was guilty on more than one occasion". Nonetheless, I expect Scottish women police were grateful for his continued support. He was not alone in this; women were regularly praised and encouraged in the yearly reports of HM Inspector of Constabulary for Scotland. In the year ending 31st December 1939 he said: "The more one gets to know of the policewomen's work, the more one appreciates their helpfulness, kindness and acts of humanity. They have delicate duties to carry out, and credit must be given to them for the tact and ability with which they do their special work." By the middle ot 1940 their displacement was Aberdeen two; Ayr two; Dundee two; Edinburgh two; Glasgow fifteen; Kirkcaldy two; Motherwell and Wishaw two; Paisley two; Dumbarton one; Lanark six and Renfrew one.[12]

In July 1939 *The Picture Post* published six pages of pictures on 'The Life of a Policewoman' which might have been termed 'The Recruitment and Training of the Metropolitan Women Police', for it was nothing less than a sales job. The Press, of course, took what they could get from the police in those days and what they wanted were more women recruits "of the right type" to bring them up to their new establishment of 155.

During the thirties Miss Peto had worked very hard to extend their duties. Instead of always sending one male and one female officer on women prisoner escorts, she persuaded the Assistant Commissioner Crime to allow either one or, if necessary, two female officers to do the job. She had women court officers appointed to busy magistrates courts such as Marlborough and Bow Streets. On seeing rows of police officers waiting to collect errant juveniles from remand homes and escort them singly across London by public transport, she devised the Juvenile Bus scheme where they all travelled together with one male and one female escort. (I rather wish she had not done that. I used to hate that duty, one had to be up so early.) But, most important, she saw that her officers were deeply involved in the implementation of the Children and Young Persons Act and built up the A4 Index of 'stray or missing girls' which was to become the backbone of their work, particularly in central London.

By the start of the war, the establishment was up to 136, and it was hoped they would soon reach their new target. A great deal of unnecessary wastage occurred due to the resignation on marriage rule officially introduced in 1931. Once the war had started, this rule and some others were set aside, and some women, previously affected, rejoined. Mrs Wills, née Wakefield, who had left in 1921, applied despite being a year over the new limit of fifty-five. Miss Peto assured her she was just the type of woman for whom they were looking, but rejected her just the same. "I should have waited until the following day and seen Clayden," she told me with a laugh, "I'd have stood more chance with her" – which is probably why she was usurped by Miss Peto. Clayden was something of a favourite with the women, "kindly, sympathetic and human", one told me. "Oh, she was a pet," said another. Though Miss Peto had a nice sense of humour, she was not a flippant person,[13] and she expected loyalty and high standards from her charges, doubtless always having in mind how constantly on trial they still were. But she cared about them and was never too grand to relieve them on loo duty at a ceremonial. Despite the fact that she was tall, masculine and increasingly eccentric, the men also liked her, partly because she was always so willing to guide them through the intricacies of the Children and Young Persons Act. "I don't think she removed her uniform, except to sleep, for the whole war," says one of her constables of that era.

Part of the reason the WAPC received a less than enthusiastic welcome from Miss Peto was not their work, which she admits they did well, but because their uniform so resembled that of the proper women police and they tended to wear it with less circumspection. Worse, they carried shoulder-bags. As she remarks in her memoirs: "It has always seemed to me that a police officer with a shoulder-bag is a complete anachronism. If she has anything of value inside it, she either risks losing it in a rough and tumble or is hampered by having to think of its safety. On the other hand, if it only contains a handkerchief and – which heaven forbid – her make-up, let her put these things in her pockets and leave the bag at home!" However the 'proper' women police were not exactly unencumbered, particularly at the start of the war when, as well as their tin hats and gas-masks, they had to cart around haversacks containing their anti-gas clothing. The swift donning of anti-gas trousers presented something of a problem, and instructions were soon issued that, in the event of a gas alert, the women police should step smartly into the nearest doorway, pull on the trousers and then remove the skirt over the top of them. Then they were to place the removed skirt into the haversacks "for future resumption". Miss Peto does admit that the haversacks also proved useful for the odd book or packet of biscuits, as were the tin hats: "I remember that once, when on my way off duty with a pound of pears in my tin hat, the air-raid warning sounded just as I was changing trains at Piccadilly Circus Underground, whereupon I clapped my tin helmet on to my head, shooting the whole pound of pears around me onto the platform, where I left them and hastily jumped into the train!" WPC O'Leary remembers the lovable Clayden returning to the Yard quite exhausted after a day's station visiting and complaining how heavy the helmet and gas-mask became when she found a large tin of pilchards tucked between the two. She had bought them on the way to work and had been carting them around with her all day, unsuspecting.

During the early days of the 'phoney war', the Queen spent an afternoon at one of the two women police residences, Pembridge Hall Section House at Notting Hill Gate. Like all official buildings, it was heavily sandbagged around the entrance – so heavily that, when one of the WPCs fell headlong down the stairs while carrying her bedding into the protected basement, it was found to be stretcher – as well as bomb-proof. The girl, who was thought to have injured her spine, had to be extricated through the slit which had been left in an almost vertical position. Fortunately her spine was found to be intact, and the entrance was enlarged to cope with further eventualities. Confidence in protective measures was not enhanced by the discovery that the building was situated so directly over the Central Line of the Underground that the line could be seen through a gap in the protected basement floor. (When I lived there, you could hear each train go through, and the whole building shook each time.) However, the Defence Department, while filling in the gap, persuaded them that this was an advantage rather than the reverse, for the tunnel would absorb much of the blast if a bomb fell on them.

Soon all was ready for the Queen's visit. Miss Peto had been down to the Yard with a specimen of the type of teacup which would be offered Her Majesty and had it passed by the Acting Commissioner A Department, and the dig-for-victory onion sets in the front garden had been arranged in the form of a Union Jack. Unfortunately there was no sign of the expected crowd since somebody had forgotten to inform the Press. Women sergeants formed a guard of honour; "we lesser mortals were kept in the background," recalls one WPC. Somebody had also forgotten to warn them that women in uniform were expected, in those days, to salute and curtsy at the same time. On the whole Miss Peto was rather relieved that they had not known; and they happily saluted.

One of the women Queen Elizabeth made a point of greeting was the six-foot Annie Matthews, affectionately known as "Big Ben". She was one of the originals who had joined in 1919. Lilian Wyles called her "the perfect policewoman" because she "embodied strength, wisdom and an immense charity in a rugged exterior".[14] Annie had become well-known in Hyde Park in the previous years, where one of her tasks was to keep the poor children from bathing in non-bathing areas where they were likely to be injured by broken glass, tin cans etc. (The famous picture of the WPC chasing the naked children is said, by some, to be of Matthews. Others say it was ex-WPS, ex-munitions Florence Howell.) Wini Gould, who was a rookie working with the experienced Matthews, remembers her being pushed in the Serpentine:

A few days previously a man had seen Annie chasing the children away and told her that, if he saw her doing it again, he would push her in. He was a wealthy, well-educated man, but a bit of a crank, and didn't understand.

I was standing talking to Annie and we were both facing the water, waiting for her relief to arrive, when suddenly she was pushed from behind into the water. The water was right up to her waist and Annie couldn't swim, there was consternation. The water was cold and she went blue – she was some fifteen years older than me. "Hold on to him, Gould," she cried, and I did. Annie struggled ashore, and we marched him back to the station. I thought the people round about were going to tear him to pieces. I can't recall what happened to him, but we didn't have any more trouble with the kids. Annie was ill for a time after that and when she did not appear in the park the children would ask where she was.[15]

But Annie's exploits in the park were not the reason for the Queen's interest: she had once been a housemaid at Glamis Castle.

Pembridge escaped the bombs. "I remember seeing all Bayswater alight one night as I went home," says ex WPC Mary Roberts, "and I expected the worst," but the section house was still intact. Mary was in West End Central, however, when a landmine struck, bringing down the heavy double front doors on some unfortunate PCs on duty there. One PC was killed, and several were injured, as were some civilians and Mary. She had been cut by flying glass, making her, she thinks, the first Metropolitan woman officer to be injured. She with others helped dig out those who were trapped; Miss Peto, on hearing of the incident, took the car round and had her night-duty women driven home.

After the flying bombs had begun, WPC Law, attached to the Central CID, was at home getting her lunch when one fell into the playground of a primary school nearby. The pupils had been sitting outside at tables in the sun and "a few moments after the explosion," Miss Peto relates, "children came drifting through her door, into the hall and up the staircase, dazed and begrimed, clinging to the stair-rail like a flock of bewildered sparrows, whilst she tended one, who lay gravely wounded on the floor below them."

Another morning Inspector Violet Butcher was on her way to visit her officers at Rathbone Place Police Station, just north of Oxford Street, when she saw a flying bomb check and stoop over her destination. She reached the scene a few minutes later but could do nothing for WPC Bertha Cleghorn but hold her hand until she was dug out from the debris. Bertha died next day in the Middlesex Hospital, where she had spent many hours guarding attempted suicides and ailing women prisoners.

21

"Must be Pretty – and Tough"

Shelter patrols were part of the duty of police in those days, and in the large ones women police were supplied on a regular basis to help keep order and give general assistance. One of the biggest was at the Midland Railway Goods Depot, just off Leman Street, where each loading bay housed a different nationality and was stacked with furniture and cooking utensils. Other large ones were, of course, the underground stations. Miss Peto found her lack of sense of smell a comfort while visiting her women stationed in them. They were stuffy and, packed with hundreds of bodies, soon smelled quite dreadful. But she was not unaware of the discomfort of others and tried to get them relieved as often as possible. She would ask the accompanying WPC what the smell was like. In some of the early, makeshift set-ups with minimal toilet facilities, the smell was pretty horrible, one WPC remembers, "but she was intent on getting all the details". Even when her charges were loaned out to clubs office or the CID, Miss Peto would try to keep an eye on their welfare. "She used to ring up the senior male officers when I did plain clothes duty on clubs," the same WPC told me, "to make sure I wasn't having to indulge in too much alcohol."

As Lilian Dawes had been used on clubs in the twenties, on the principle of a man and woman being less conspicuous than men alone, so they continued to be used even in the Second World War, this time on less glamorous 'bottle parties'. Soon after the war began, the police magazines were full of the way bottle parties slipped through a loophole in the law, evading licensing and gaming regulations. Their secret was mobility. Normally, before any action is taken against such activities, observation is kept on the premises for several nights. But these 'clubs' would be in a different private house or flat or empty premises each night, and a grapevine would tell people where that was to be. It was decided to bring the Defence Regulations into play, but the difficulty still was to find out where the next party was to take place. However, one Saturday afternoon WPC O'Leary, who was on a brothel observation in Knightsbridge but had just realized that her prostitutes had gone away for the weekend, noticed a great deal of coming and going at nearby premises. She had done a lot of club work and thought she recognized one of the people, so she grabbed a cab and said, "Follow that car." Eventually she arrived at some empty premises where the party was taking place. The 'guests' had first been given one address where they had been passed on to the second. She got a message back to the station, and a raid took place. "The court was packed when it came up," she recalls, half with police wanting to get a look at the participants and see how the case went, and half with party organizers with similar professional interests. The accused pleaded guilty and were heavily fined, and things were never so easy for them after that. Eventually WPC O'Leary's cover was blown as far as club work was concerned. Back in uniform, she was picking her way through sleeping bodies in an underground station when she saw a group of people sitting up staring at her: they were friends of the owner of the last club she had been instrumental in prosecuting and knew her well as a customer. "They could hardly believe their eyes!"

The Second World War also saw some increase in the numbers of Metropolitan women in the CID. In 1933 three women had been attached to the CID in C Division (the West End) to deal with cases involving women and children and to be loaned to other divisions when necessary. Of course, the mere idea of women detectives had provoked witty Press articles. They would be most effective, said one, under the heading 'A Fair Cop', if they donned "maiden's blush chiffon and a hat from the Rue de la Paix", but the trouble was, they were, after all, still women and so must let their hearts rule their heads. What would happen when they began falling for the miscreants they had arrested? "Would she bite the bullet and reach for the handcuffs with a low choking sob? Or will she throw Honour to the winds and urge her surprised but gratified prisoner to beat it while the beating is still good?"[1]

Despite this problem, ten more women were authorized for the Metropolitan area in 1940. It was then admitted that women in plain clothes had been proving most useful shadowing IRA suspects "without themselves being noticed". Further, since the blackout, they had "proved their capacity and courage" in dealing with bag-snatchers and pickpockets, some of whom operated from cars — 'motor bandits' as they were then termed.[2] In fact they had been used as decoys. WPC O'Leary, who was only five feet four inches tall and of slight build, and so often used on plain clothes duties of various kinds, recalls walking the streets of South Kensington waiting for her handbag to be snatched.

Though their involvement was small, numerically the CID women had naturally become mixed up in some of the more famous cases of their day, right from the start. In 1923 Glasgow's Ellen Webster befriended a Mrs Newall who was charged with the murder of a newsboy. Though Mrs Newall had spoken to no one since her arrest, she whispered her thanks to Ellen before she was led away after being found guilty and sentenced to be hanged — the last woman in Scotland to be executed.[3] Lilian Wyles was, unknowingly, almost instrumental in the conviction and hanging of another woman and her lover. She had been instructed to stay in the room at Ilford Police Station with the woman and listen to what she said.

> She was agitated and excited, keeping on pacing the room and gazing from the window. She wanted to know why she must stay in that room, and in the station; why could she not go home? As she looked from the window which overlooked the station yard, she had a clear view of the side door of the station, and the door of the CID office which, in those days, was across the yard opposite the station proper. Then she turned impatiently from the window, so did not see issuing from the station a group of men, the DDI, two sergeants and another young man who was a stranger to me. They walked slowly by the window where Mrs Thompson had been standing. Later she was to get a glimpse of that young man. Then her hand flew to her mouth, there was a slight scream, and Mrs Thompson moaned; "Not that, not that! No. No! Why did he do it? Oh, God!" The strange young man was Bywaters.

Lilian Wyles was also deeply involved in 'The Horse with the Green Tail' case which, she felt, illustrated the almost casual, almost cavalier, handling some policemen used to give to sexual assault cases. A thirteen-year-old girl, after having been sexually assaulted by soldiers in the Horse Guard stables (she had been taken there to see 'the horse with the green tail'), poured out her hysterical story to a police inspector and was directed to the nearest police station. But even Lilian Wyles admitted that women did not always get the full facts out of other women. It was very difficult; many, rather naturally, hated telling the plain unvarnished facts. "I was seduced from the path of virtue," one victim insisted to her and refused to elucidate further, remarking that anyone with education would understand what she meant. The police were merely being dirty-minded, it was often suggested. "Seduced", Lilian Wyles found, was a favourite, all-embracing word used by officers of the female military police in the Second World War – at least until they had been properly trained. They were merely trying to be kind, of course, and to save the victims from 'reliving' their awful experiences, but it was of no use in law.[4]

Mary Roberts found her fellow policemen on C Division both helpful and protective. Attitudes towards women police were improving again, as was indicated by the approving manner in which incidents involving them were now reported and the attitudes of the Marlborough Street Magistrates. As *The Times* reported on 7th October 1943:

A POLICEWOMAN'S LOT

A woman police constable of Hyde Park Station was commended by Mr J.B. Sandbach, KC, the Marlborough Street Magistrate, yesterday for arresting an American soldier and a civilian at the meeting ground in Hyde Park on Tuesday. After she had arrested the soldier and was taking him through the crowd, a building operative started an argument with the soldier and struck him. The soldier retaliated, and as the civilian was about to continue the fight the woman constable arrested him as well.

And *The Police Chronicle and Constabulary World*, reported on 21st January 1944 what appears to be almost a re-enactment of some First World War scenes. A Liverpool City policeman had gone into licensed premises to separate two fighting men and found himself surrounded by a hostile crowd. WAPC Maudsley had seen his plight, sent for further assistance and ploughed in too. She was congratulated for her "brave action" by the Chairman of the local bench. Later that year the same journal was telling with gusto how a Glasgow City policewoman, Mary Brown, when taking part in the capture of four youthful van thieves, had knocked one of them down, and out, when he had the temerity to resist arrest. She too had been congratulated by the local Sheriff.

By January 1944 there were many more attested WAPCs (1,093 out of 4,247) than regulars (335 out of 348) in England and Wales. Many Watch Committees and Chief Constables still adamantly refused to appoint either regular women police or WAPCs. Suddenly, in 1944, the Home Office dropped the velvet glove and told them that police forces in areas where troops were stationed must appoint women police or it would be done for them under defence regulations, and sent HM Inspectors around, "seeing where the greatest need is". A leader in *The Police Chronicle* of 5th May commented on the "lively discussion" this provoked in various areas. Soon its pages were heavy with advertisements for women police or WAPCs nonetheless. When a lady member of King's Lynn Town Council congratulated them on changing their minds, there were cries of "We were forced!", and West Suffolk decided that it was "no use kicking against the Home Secretary's views". Many held out, including Cardiff, and Grimsby's "lively discussion" resulted in the Town Council three times refusing to confirm the Watch Committee's Minutes because, though the Town Council had instructed them to appoint women, they had taken no action. Admittedly, suitable women proved difficult to acquire at this late stage, though possibly some Constabularies used this as an excuse. Sillitoe, who had just taken over in Kent, and immediately put in for twenty women, seemed to have no difficulty finding his first ten, though it is true that some went there from other forces so as to avoid prejudicial attitudes. He also had the advantage of Inspector Barbara Denis de Vitré who had been manning a mobile canteen amid the smoking ruins of Coventry for part of the war and had just been acquired by Sillitoe to recruit and train his new women's force.[5]

One of the areas in which Miss Peto found it most difficult for her women police to be accepted was on ceremonial duty, either on crowd control or as part of the procession. She had been pleased that they were to be included on a Royal Police Review in the mid-thirties until she discovered that they were not to march alongside the men but to be tucked away in a group with Colonial policemen beside the Royal Box. Her first breakthrough was an occasion during the Silver Jubilee celebrations for George V when The Mall was closed to all but LCC schoolchildren and policed solely by her women. Lilian Dawes diverted traffic from the roundabout outside the Palace, and Annie Matthews pointed out the royal grandchildren peeping out of a Palace window, much to the delight of the children. All went well, and at the next event, the King's funeral, the women were put on ceremonial duty though confined to mingling with the crowd in Hyde Park and not lining the route. The last public occasion before Miss Peto retired made up for this, when a detachment of women police, alongside WRAF, ATS and WRAP, led the VE Parade along The Mall, "fists swinging to well above the shoulders in military fashion, as we proudly saluted Their Majesties on the Royal Stand in Constitution Hill".[6]

Miss Peto's place was taken by an outside appointee, the forty-one-year-old Miss Elizabeth Constance Bather, who, she admitted, had to stretch a little to reach the required height of five feet four inches. The daughter of a Winchester housemaster, Betty Bather had, before the war, been the youngest JP in Hampshire and a member of the local council. In 1939 she had joined the WRAF, quickly attained the rank of Group Officer and later been loaned to Canada to help form a woman's branch in the Canadian Air Force. On returning to England, she was appointed Senior Staff Officer at Bomber Command Headquarters. She was also, the *Daily Mail* of 5th December 1946 remarked inconsequentially, a moderate smoker and liked the occasional gin and lime. Miss Bather had joined late in 1945, done three months' initial training, spent another three on division getting practical experience, then acted as Miss Peto's assistant, with the rank of Chief Inspector, for six months.

It was fortunate for the appearance of the Metropolitan Women Police that she arrived just then, for the uniforms were being redesigned, and Betty Bather, very smart herself, helped come up with something very presentable. The whole issue was taken most seriously. Sir Harold Scott, the then Commissioner, remembers attending a 'fashion parade' with the Home Secretary Chuter Ede. The new uniform was all part of a recruiting drive. Sir Harold supported women police, felt they were hampered by their concentration on sexual matters and the still-suspicious attitude of many of the men, and had decided to raise their numbers to three hundred.[7] Soon, everything the Metropolitan women did was news, particularly any arrests, attempted arrests or signs of toughness. Strength and femininity were the two requirements always juxtaposed. "Must be pretty – and tough,"[8] said one headline, and Miss Bather recalls the Press always wanting photographs of pretty policewomen practising judo.

Things were also looking up for the provincial women. In 1945 Miss Denis de Vitré was appointed to assist HM Inspectorate of Constabularies on matters relating to women police. It was one of those fortuitous amalgams of the right person being in the right place at the right time. "De V", as she was happy to be called to lessen the difficulties of her unwieldy name, was probably the most popular senior women police officer the service has produced. She had charm, humour and bubbling enthusiasm. "Everybody loved her, the men too," says an ex-Leeds policewoman simply. "She treated everyone with the same degree of friendliness and respect,"[9] says one of the men. Above all she was a woman of great determination, and she was to need it. True, some of the Constabularies, such as the North Riding of Yorkshire, who had not employed women until they had taken on

WAPCs, were now taking them on as regulars — some with less good grace than others. The Watch Committee records of York City Police reveal "fierce opposition" to the appointment of their first woman, Mary McLaren, in 1945.[10]

The new assistant to HM Constabularies also felt that the work of women police was too narrow and too involved with sexual offences which, quite apart from being boring and restricting, gave the women a pretty jaundiced view of the opposite sex. She persuaded Chief Constables to take a wider view of their potential and, most important, to allow them to train with the men. Previously, their training had been very hit-and-miss, only London, Glasgow and Birmingham having training schools they could attend. Many women were expected just to pick things up as they went along. More barriers fell. The resignation on marriage rule was dropped (Scotland kept theirs until 1968);[11] the Police Federation, with a little pushing from the Home Office, consented to represent the women; Liverpool disbanded their Women Patrols and replaced them with women police, and, in 1948, "de V" was made an Assistant Inspector of HM Constabularies. What they were asking for was "a sort of lady Sir Leonard Dunning", the Chairman of the Bridgeman Committee had remarked. Now they had one. Unfortunately the real Sir Leonard did not live to see it; he had died in 1941.

22

Towards Equality

The newsagent inspected me closely. Finally he enquired, "What sort of ad?"

"Oh ... model," I replied vaguely.

Everything went quiet while the other customers gave me the once-over, taking in my disastrous red rinse, which I was only too aware did not harmonize too well with my currently fashionable salmon pink duster coat.

"Well, that would cost about thirty to fifty bob ... depends."

He was not happy about me, I could feel it.

"Er ... thanks. Thanks very much. I'll think about it," I said, and fled. Though I had obviously been handpicked for this job, I was really not much good at it and wished they would not ask me to do it, but my non-police appearance and demure expression usually confused people; probably even more so given the combination of hair and coat.

Like WPC O'Leary, I was five feet four inches tall, slight of build and attached to West End Central so, while not being in the CID, I was often loaned out to them or to uniformed officers doing plain clothes work on clubs, brothels or bookies. I sat for hours in steamy cars, was worn on the left arms of rather small policemen while sauntering through Soho and even danced a nifty foxtrot, all in the name of duty. Not usually on my own merits but as a cover for the man doing the job, although I did have to give evidence when the case came to court.

Inevitably, much of the West End work centred around vice. The object of my enquiry about a model ad had been to discover whether Soho newsagents might be planning to be living on immoral earnings now that the new Street Offences Act would prevent the prostitutes selling their wares on the streets. An increase in the number of shop window ads for Models, French Lessons, Swedish Massage and Strict Governesses had already been noted and, given that the usual price for shop window advertisements was about two shillings each, and a board of them at the quoted price would fetch in around £25 (I was earning £6 a week), it seemed that they would.

In those days prostitutes lined central London streets. Some of us policewomen arrested them; we all searched them if they had stolen from clients or there was no matron to do so when they had been brought in for soliciting. Once I had to carry out a search to determine whether one of them was indeed a woman; he was not.

We also took the case histories and fingerprints of the new girls and found them as likeable or dislikeable a group of people as any other. Occasionally, if we felt a mutual regard, we would give them a discreet smile or barely perceptible nod next time we moved them on, which they would return with equal care. I think we largely accepted the double standard about them and their customers but we were annoyed when we heard about the male officers arresting the female half of an indecency case (some prostitutes took their clients down dark alleys) while letting the male escape.

We were often sent up to Shepherd Market to move on the elegant Mayfair prostitutes from the vicinity of Lady Astor's home. She would phone in and complain about them and, since she liked to see women police because, we were told, "she saved us", off we would go, cursing and not knowing what they were talking about.

But the backbone of our work in the West End was picking up missing girls and approved school absconders. Each day, before we took off onto the streets, we would peruse our notice boards for any new faces or old, familiar ones. Their photographs (usually copied from small, blurred family snapshots) had been sent out with their descriptions, aliases and brief personal details by A4 Index at Scotland Yard, now a large and sophisticated database run entirely by women police but proving useful to male officers as well.

Chances were that the juveniles would change everything about themselves except, of course the colour of their eyes (and sometimes relatives even got this wrong), so we used these descriptions as guidelines only. It was irrelevant whether they had run away from Aberdeen or Bromley in Kent; such was the pull of London's West End that there was a good chance we might find them having a wash in Piccadilly Circus Underground station toilets half an hour later. They were more conspicuous than they imagined, even when "lost" among the subsequent crowds on the streets, with their youth and aimlessness, dirty feet, general "slept rough" air and smell.

Once we stopped them, as casually as possible, and asked them a few questions, we would try to find our way through the welter of lies we received in return. Where possible, we took them to a police box to check on their supposed personal details with A4 Index. The women police at the other end would try name, alias, scar indexes and so on. There was even a date of birth index because girls might change their year of birth to an earlier year, to pretend they were older and so beyond our justification for stopping them, but leave the day and month unchanged. If these checks failed the A4 girls would make a few inspired suggestions, giving us further points to check, or merely a run-down on those juveniles just "out".

If we felt fairly certain we were on to something we would ask the girl to accompany us to the station. We would ask nicely, particularly if the A4 girl had said of the butter-wouldn't-melt girl, "By the way, she's violent." Later, at the station, tearful reunions with parents often took place, even when the girl had still been denying her suspected identity until her mother walked through the door. Some would even deny that the woman *was* their mother despite her protestations to the contrary. How much and how well many people lie is one of the most shocking things to a new police recruit.

If they had run away from home but parents refused to take them back or were obviously not coping with their recalcitrant offspring they would be taken to juvenile court as being in need of Care or Protection. We did not do this blindly; we were always aware that we could be creating more hardened delinquents. If they were absconders from approved schools or borstals, they would be handed over to the escort sent to pick them up.

Occasionally young runaway boys came into our area. Two Manchester lads aged fourteen and fifteen once turned up at West End Central at 10.30 one night and told me they had run away from home that morning. Fortunately, the West End glamour had soon faded with the light. However, fifteen-year-old Arthur had already drifted into criminal and predatory homosexual company (for girls the promiscuity or prostitution had only to be heterosexual to count as a sign of being at risk) before I spotted him wandering around Great Windmill Street in Soho. His mother had not reported him missing and he had been gone from his London living-in job for nearly a month so I dealt with him as needing Care or Protection. His home difficulties were sorted out and he went back to mother and some local supervision. This side of the work was later to develop, with many more young boys picked up.

Only the occasional drug users came our way but this, too, was to change later. Drugs *had* once been a problem in the area – during and after the Great War. To help break up the cocaine ring that had formed among lower-grade prostitutes using West End loos as dressing rooms Mrs Stanley selected a policewoman (possibly Lilian Dawes or Violet Butcher) to pose as a prostitute and mingle among them.[1]

Our work rarely involved families and young children although I did deal with a couple of abandoned babies, one of which had been left on a pew in a church where it was found by the startled vicar. But in the force's more residential areas women police frequently dealt with child neglect and battered wives, and sorted out family quarrels.

"After the pubs shut on a Friday and Saturday night we would get a procession of wives in," said one ex-East End WPC. When she asked one wife to show her bruises the woman opened her mac to show herself to be stark naked. She had run so fast she had not even stopped to put on her shoes. The police were, the WPC admitted, much more concerned about any children the woman had left behind in the man's care and would escort her home to see if they were all right. If they were, they would advise the wife to turn up at magistrates' court the next morning. "Of course, she never did. 'Never interfere in husband and wife disputes' was one of the 'rules' we were taught, the theory being that she would always change her mind and probably turn against you to boot; besides, 'she quite enjoyed it really'."

Stella Condor, in her book, *Woman on the Beat*, tells of one 3-year-old boy who did not survive the experience of having an unchecked and brutal father. His final assault on the boy was not reported by the very pregnant and terrified mother, and only just by a neighbour who had known what was going on for some time but was concerned not to be thought interfering. She had heard the child screaming that morning.

> There, in a large double bed, lay a child, his tiny, dark face a vivid contrast to the whiteness of the bedspread. He did not so much flicker an eyelid when we came in, but remained gazing ahead of him ... Even in his present state of shock, you could see he was a lovely child. He had black, curly hair, large brown eyes and a little snub nose ... As gently as possible I pulled back the sheets. The child was wearing only a cotton vest, and, at the sight of that pitifully thin body and legs covered in bruises, I winced.

The little boy's sister told her that daddy had hit him with a belt that morning. He died half an hour after reaching hospital, of multiple injuries including broken ribs which had brought on pneumonia.

At West End Central one of our number was always on reserve

duty at the station to deal with any matter which arose regarding women or children: a mother bringing her daughter in for us to speak to; a boy wanting us to find his girlfriend who had run away to the bright lights; a CID officer wondering if we could "get anything out of" a woman prisoner that he had not managed to extricate. Members of the public brought in all their problems. "I don't know who I am," one woman told me, "I can't even remember my name." "Please stop my wife having sex orgies with other men", wept a middle-aged man.

A high proportion of the people who wandered or were brought in to police stations were mentally disturbed. In most cases police listened to their complaints about neighbours who were sending electric currents through the walls or who had murdered their budgies; took a message to pass on to MI5 or gave them a small area of the division on which to keep an eye, then sent them on their way, if not happy, at least a little relieved. Some, however, were violent and/or unable to look after themselves. Many with whom I came in contact were middle-aged ladies who blew their final fuses at their places of employment and either threatened other workers or became embarrassingly amorous towards their boss. When sent out to these we had to stay with them until the mental health authority attended, which could be an exhausting and harrowing experience: trying to take scissors out of their hands as they roamed a workroom, or listening to them finally telling their office chums what they thought of them, or even preventing them from removing their clothes – a particularly female trait, this.

One variation on this theme was a woman who had walked into some offices, insisted she lived there and not only refused to leave when the startled manager tried to disabuse her of this impression but became hysterical and violent. It transpired that she had attended court that morning for a separation order which, to her surprise, her husband had contested. For some reason this proved the last straw just as she happened to be passing those offices. Fortunately, she regained her equilibrium shortly afterwards.

We were always called on when women needed to be escorted anywhere. This could entail anything from taking a drunken old derelict to a hostel after the last public transport had stopped to looking after female witnesses in a murder case or picking up or dropping a prisoner in some far-flung corner of the UK – usually at short notice or none at all. "You're going to Wales" they told me when I arrived for late-turn duty at 3 p.m. one afternoon. And in Wales I was that night, clutching a toothbrush someone had dug out for me and holding on to a very sexually precocious 15-year-old who had done her best to seduce every male on the train: I think I did a good job of protecting her. Another time, having been warned the evening before, I travelled to Newcastle-upon-Tyne and back in one day (seven hours each way then) – hard luck that I had had a date that evening.

Apart from our specialist work, once out on the streets we dealt with anything that came our way: drunks, accidents, illnesses and endless direction-giving – sometimes to none-too-polite recipients who regarded us a public amenity much like a signpost. In fact, we did everything the beat policeman did – except control traffic points, of which there were several on our patch. We did sort out the odd snarl up we came across – very badly in my case – and handled a couple of regular school crossings. However, two of our women: a gutsy and likeable Australian girl and an ex-Roedean pupil, actually enjoyed directing traffic and would follow up the Mayfair school crossing with an hour or so on the busy Park Lane point, allowing the PC to go for a cup of tea. Needless to say, they were very popular.

We did do the occasional summons for parking within the precincts of a pedestrian crossing, but not for speeding since we were not allowed on traffic cars. Oddly, back in the thirties, WPC Winifred Gould had been so employed soon after the introduction of the thirty-mile-an-hour limit. She had sat in the front of an unmarked car as part of a "family", clutching a board marked "POLICE – STOP" to be raised at the opportune moment. In the back sat a young policeman wearing a school cap. She usually only acted as a witness until one day the male sergeant said "This one's yours, Win", as a taxi sped past. She gave her evidence so well, she recalled later, that the driver changed his plea to guilty and the magistrate, Bernard Campion, referred to her as "the original Gertie, the girl with the gong".[2]

By the time of my service (1954–60) women police were included in crowd control at all central London ceremonials and premieres; we smaller women were particularly popular with the crowds because they could see over our heads. Rather than being tucked away we were, in fact, often placed in prominent positions so we got a good view of the proceedings. This was partly because we were a little spoiled and partly because we were thought to brighten the scene, particularly those of smart appearance, and we were still rare enough to attract interest. I admit that at five feet four inches I could not supply the buttressing power of a male officer (minimum height five foot eight) but there were several strapping six-foot policewomen and quite a few weedy policemen.

In 1953 Commissioner Sir Harold Scott echoed the thirties Silver Jubilee experiment by putting women police in charge of 30,000 school children viewing the coronation from the Victoria Embankment. They made a good impression then, and did so again at the school kids' demo in 1972 when they looked after Trafalgar Square. Their presence there, Commander Shirley Becke was to claim, prevented violence and diminished the status of the demonstrators.[3]

The attitude of the men towards us women officers at West End Central was generally excellent. The fact that we were twenty women (mostly in their twenties) among 600 mainly equally young men probably helped and, unlike their predecessor Frederick Mead, the magistrates at Marlborough Street and Bow Street were never less than charming to us. If anything, we received preferential treatment, we were pets.

Our Woman Inspector was Florence Pike; she had been in charge of the aliens interned on the Isle of Wight during the war. But this did not account for the stream of German ladies who called in at West End Central and sometimes accompanied us around the beat. This was due to the good work done by Metropolitan Women Police Inspectors Kay Hill and Sophie Alloway who, in 1945, had been seconded to the Public Safety Branch of the British Occupation Zone, which included Hamburg, Essen, Dortmund, Münster and Cologne.

Despite Goering's half-promise to Mary Allen, the Nazis had not reformed uniformed women police but developed a woman's CID (the WKP) who were, by 1944, 600-strong. Many of these were scattered during the war's aftermath. Some were denounced and some removed during the various bouts of deNazification. The two British women officers had the job of rebuilding the uniform branch and a smaller, plainclothes, section. Later they were joined by two other British women and by the time the last of them left in 1948 the uniform branch had become 447 strong and there were eighty-nine women detectives. In 1949 "de V" was asked to visit the American Zone to advise on women police and, in 1951, Miss Alloway and Miss Hill were invited back to a conference of West German Women Police where they were publicly thanked for their "fair and understanding behaviour" when in control.[4]

In 1957 the kindly Winifred Barker took a group of about fifty women from all over the UK to Cyprus in the hope of making "murder mile" a little less murderous. (Due to the Greek Cypriot fight for independence from the UK and union with Greece, and Turkish resistance to that, members of the British forces and police were being killed.)

"Does a smile keep the peace better than a gun?" asked the *Sunday Graphic* under a picture captioned: "WOMAN'S TOUCH IN MURDER MILE". Woman Sergeant Joan Coke, "veteran of ten years' service in Cardiff Docks", was shown directing traffic in notorious Ledra Street in Nicosia but exercising "none of the toughness associated with Tiger Bay". The policewomen were greeted with curiosity rather than hostility, the paper reported. "You see they aren't used to women doing any kind of man's job," remarked Sergeant Elizabeth Preece from Newport.

Indeed, the locals must have found it a rather astonishing move particularly since the male officers were armed and female ones were not. They went about normal women police duties, even in rural areas, amid some level of natural distrust from the Cypriots. But before leaving they recruited Cypriot women into the force.

Certainly defusing violence had been one way we women police felt we made up for our lack of muscle power. Men were less likely to attack us because a) they had no idea whether we could throw them over our shoulders and so make them look foolish and b) the penalties would be higher, due partly due to our sex but also to our reputation for fairness.

Our other trump card was that we lacked the aggression that we sometimes saw escalating minor incidents into major ones. Quite apart from their ego problems, some men do just love a good fight, particularly those they are liable to win. One East End WPC told me that the merest hint of a pub brawl would result in a mad scramble of policemen trying to get in on it. "They would be hanging onto the sides of the van." Once there they would pile in with glee and grab anyone in sight. Mind you, it was ultimately effective: "Pubs would clear immediately if they heard that the police had been called."

However, times became more violent and as women's status and independence grew, their protection in public (it had always been OK to hit them in private) diminished.

"Men will hit women in public now," a senior provincial policeman told me, "and we are losing a lot of women recruits due to the violence which they did not expect to be so bad."

Of course it was difficult to judge where true concern ended and bigotry began; that same force had a proud record of curtailing opportunities for women. What was certain was that something should be worked out before a sweeping ban was introduced in the name of protection and inability to do the job. Possibly, raising the minimum height for women to the same as that of the men or making sure the women were very well trained in self-defence? My training on that score had been pretty perfunctory.

There certainly had been no shortage of evidence of women's bravery. In 1947 Detective Sergeant Alberta Mary Law was awarded the King's Police Medal (she was the first female recipient) for acting as a decoy to a man who not only snatched women's handbags on Tooting Bec Common but savagely assaulted them as well – as he did the Sergeant.

In 1955 Sergeant Ethel Bush and Constable Kathleen Parrott (two of the many policewomen who had walked the lonely lane on this job) suffered serious injuries when decoying a violent sexual attacker. They both received the George Medal. The following year Pat Stacke and Pat Gair walked country lanes night after night, successfully luring a habitual and very violent rapist known as "The Beast". During 1964–5 many policewomen had the unpleasant and dangerous job of offering "certain services" to passing motorists in the hope of catching "Jack the Stripper", the perpetrator of the "nude murders".

Women had also come in for their share of life-saving awards, such as the Lancashire policewoman who forced a live home-made bomb from a man's grip and removed it to safety. However, the exaggerated media attention that any positive physical action by a policewoman always received did not help her, particularly when the incident was well-embroidered. I was dying to meet a colleague reported to have "brought down a smash and grabber with a flying rugby tackle". She had, in fact, turned a corner and come upon members of the public holding onto this little man who had done the deed. And that is what she, a very honest person, told anyone who asked her about it.

Unsurprisingly, this extreme publicity irritated the male officers whose brave acts did not get half the attention. The Met's Margaret Cleland, whose daring, much-publicized rooftop rescue in 1966 of a small child from a father who was threatening to jump, taking his son with him, reported subsequent antagonism from her male colleagues.[5]

The spirited Stella Condor described such an incident, which even caused her boyfriend to desert her. She had been escorting a prostitute under arrest to the police station when a man had rushed up to her yelling, "Quick officer, stop that van." It was a stolen department store pantechnicon and, while it was at the lights, she jumped onto the running board, opened the door, dragged out the driver and marched him to the nearby London Pavilion Cinema to phone the station. Meanwhile, her prostitute prisoner appeared with two policemen in tow. The newspapers were soon enquiring about her clinging to a sixty-mile-an-hour van. "PC STELLA GETS HER MAN!" proclaimed one headline. Rather droll considering that her boyfriend had given her up (so she was told) because he could not stand the teasing.[6]

Despite the excessive real-life attention, women police were all but ignored in fiction and drama at this time. If featured at all, they would be escorting weeping women whom male officers had arrested or helped, or typing away in the background with an occasional trip into the foreground to pin a message on a notice board. On the rare occasions they were given something to do they were often shown to be problems in themselves, the fact that they were women altering the storyline. At other times, their role was to be rescued from a fate worse than death – by a policeman of course. Rarely were they shown doing an ordinary, straightforward police job. As Superintendent Janice Jeater (then deputy head of a division of the Metropolitan Police) pointed out to the *London Evening News* of 28th January 1978, "the women's role is never adequately portrayed on TV". By then, (except in Northern Ireland) women were technically equal to men in law, the Sex Discrimination Act having been passed back in 1975.

In 1961 Miss Barker took over control of the Met women from the retiring Chief Superintendent Bather. Six months earlier "de V" had died of cancer leaving women in the provinces without a strong voice. Two years earlier she had given an excellent speech at the General Assembly of Interpol which, together with the British report on women police, had persuaded many foreign police authorities to begin employing women for the first time.[7] The following year, women got their first foothold in HM Scottish Inspectorate when Superintendent Janet Gray, the highest-ranking woman in Scotland, became an Assistant Inspector, though only part-time due to the small number of women police in that country.[8]

Women had been filtering into the CID in small numbers for several years, mainly because they were essential to giving men good cover in some jobs and useful for other more tedious ones like handling shoplifters. But some uniformed officers had already shone in this field. In 1941, when on a missing person enquiry, Ivy Robinson had "got a feeling" about the lodger next to the missing girl's home.

She took her suspicions to the CID who eventually arrested him for murder. Similarly, in 1949, Sergeant Maud Lambourne began to sense something wrong with the man she was interviewing about a missing person, Olivia Durand-Deacon, and, since he turned out to be John George Haigh, who had murdered that wealthy woman and then dissolved her body in a bath of acid, she turned out to be right.

So it was beginning to seem that Margaret Damer Dawson was wrong in her assumption that women would not make good detectives. Indeed the head of a reputable security firm told me he found women much more observant than men.

In 1959 Detective Sergeant Margaret Heald made an especially good impression with her work on the Messina Brothers vice case. Ten years later three women police were included on the Kray enquiry and in the mid-seventies women were added to the group of "birdwatchers" staying at a Welsh farm while keeping an eye, not on lesser-spotted feathery creatures, but on humans manufacturing a massive amount of LSD. The job was named Operation Julie after one of the officers involved.

Detective Sergeant Shirley Becke and Detective Constable Daphne Skillern, the two female CID officers at West End Central in my time, were renowned for the stylishness of their obligatory hats. Both were destined for higher things. In 1966 Mrs Becke succeeded Miss Barker as the head of the Metropolitan Women Police, which was now around 600-strong. She sought more opportunities for her women officers in dog handling, traffic, special patrol groups and so on but the problems of rank structure and promotion remained. Women could only find initial promotion from within their own small department and there was, Becke noticed, a lingering unwillingness to place women in charge of men, which ruled out most of the higher ranks.

A complication was added by the introduction of Juvenile Bureaux in 1969. There had been a deliberate effort to involve men in this but that meant that they began invading "the small area of work the women had taken as their own" and the bureaux were put under the Community Relations Branch – which was headed by men.

Commander Becke was already of the opinion that women's police specialities had become a straitjacket and she, and Commissioner Sir Robert Mark, decided that integration (already in the wind) was the only solution. So, in 1973, two years before the Sex Discrimination Act was passed, the Metropolitan Women Police ceased to exist as a separate branch and became part of the main force.[9]

The first Metropolitan mounted policewoman put in an appearance in 1970 but early integration moves were also being made in other forward-looking forces such as Lancashire. The move to equality was underway but it was not going to get an easy passage.

23

Equal at Last?

Many policewomen welcomed the enhanced opportunities integration offered them. Others, especially those with long service, did not. They had enjoyed the specialist role they had trained for and hated seeing their areas of expertise now neglected and, it seemed, often deliberately ignored by the police service. Apart from its effect on the welfare of women and children it was insulting to give the impression that their previous work had been unimportant.

"Unlawful sexual intercourse no longer seems to take place," one policewoman told *Police Review* editor Doreen May. "Before integration the local social services knew who to talk to and now they don't. Only the other day a probation officer said, 'How we miss the policewomen!'" Contact with problem families was lost as was some of the expertise about handling sexual offences such as rape – an omission which was to come back and bite the service. Some new young policewomen resented that they were expected to handle rape cases without the requisite training and that they were dumped on them when they wanted to be doing more fast-paced things like catching burglars.

Occasionally the blindness to the success of women's police work in the past was ameliorated. A central London Sergeant told me that when it was realized that runaway juveniles were still coming into the area but were no longer being sought out and sent back home she was quickly put in charge of a squad, staffed by both sexes, for this purpose.

At the same time a backlash against women's equality had begun. Concern was voiced at Police Federation and Superintendents' Association meetings that the service was being flooded with women who had not, they claimed, got the physical strength to do the job. It was a subject tackled by Doreen May in the *Police Review* of 12th May 1978 when she interviewed women from four forces: Greater Manchester, Surrey, Suffolk and West Yorkshire. They felt that there was often too much stress placed on this physical factor and that any incident involving them received undue publicity. "'We could quote unhappy incidents involving men,' said one. 'It's psychological,' said another, 'if there's a fight they would rather have a five-foot-seven man who just scraped in under height regulations than us. I asked a male colleague how many fights he had been to since Christmas. He told me one and moaned that he'd had a policewoman with him. He was like a rake – she was six feet and built like a tank. If you work in a group of men and there's one a lot weaker, you would bear this in mind if you went to an incident. Some of us are stronger than some of the men.'"

Some women found themselves more protected than they had been before integration. One senior woman from a northern force told me that many station officers who had young daughters refused to send women out to potentially violent situations but kept them protected in the stations. Others said, "They are being paid the same as men, let them get on with it." A Superintendent complained to me that he had had a woman in tears to him because she was afraid of going out on night duty while a woman admitted to the *Police Review* that she *was* afraid but claimed that many of the men were more so but would not admit it.

In 1979, the first edition of this book was published and, at the same time my Saturday Night Theatre BBC Radio 4 drama *Against All Natural Instincts* was being produced.[1] The title was Marlborough Street magistrate Frederick Mead's opinion on women doing police work. The play described the clash between Nina Boyle (Prunella Scales) and Margaret Damer Dawson (Anna Massey) when the latter collaborated with the male authorities by helping enforce a curfew on "women of a certain class". The Met police magazine *The Job* sent along a reporter and photographer[2] and I invited Sergeant Audrey Mattison. She was in charge of the gaoler's staff at that court which, by then, had three female JPs, a female clerk of the court and a female usher, not to mention women lawyers coming in and out. All, of course, contrary to their natural instincts.

However, integration was still causing some serious hiccups. As ever, with the development of the British women police, how they progressed depended much on the force in which they served and the attitudes of its senior male officers.

In 1977–8 the number and displacement of women in the Lancashire Constabulary was:

Chief Inspector: 1, Personnel Department, HQ

Inspectors: 1, Training School, Hutton Hall; 1, in charge of a section of a Division; 3, Divisional Foot Patrol

Sergeants: 10, Juvenile Bureau

Constables: 100, Divisional Foot Patrol; 62, Juvenile Bureau;

3, Seconded to Regional Crime Squad; 3, Divisional Detectives; 3, Drug Squad; 3, Special Branch; 2, Mounted Branch; 4, Traffic Patrol; 1, Crown Court; 1, Scenes of Crime; 2, Prosecutions Department; 1, Headquarters Control Room

TOTAL: 201

TOTAL FORCE ESTABLISHMENT: About 3,000

Thus, while some women were doing reasonably well, others were still having a bad time and, to help support the latter, *Police Review* asked me to collate and write a weekly page for women police. For this, I gathered women police news and specialist firsts, the more ludicrous press reports such as the breathless account of Rome's female police being given Baby Berettas, "ideal for the dainty feminine hand"; snippets on women police history and general police oddities and news. The first of these pages appeared in November 1980, and they continued until May 1982, morphing from "For Women Police Officers" to "Joan Lock Talking About" as I began to feature more general police subjects.

Meanwhile, I began to tackle some of the women police's problems in full-length *Police Review* features, enquiring how they were faring generally, exploring their progress in breaching the barriers surrounding specialist branches such as dog handling; changes in press depiction of them; their maternity and child care problems; and examination of their counterparts in some other countries.

In July 1986, when equality had had time to settle in, I gathered together a group of interviewees for a BBC Radio 4 documentary on the subject. The programme's title was *A Man's Job Alone?*, the phrase being part of that statement made by a Police Federation representative before the Bridgeman Committee in 1924 (but without the question mark). Women police officers taking part were a WPC, an ex-WPC, an Inspector, a Chief Inspector and a Commander. Other interested parties were Doreen May, ex-editor of *Police Review,* and academics Ken Russell and Sandra Jones. Sandra had recently completed a report (*Policewomen and Equality)* for the Home Office in which she took a look at the medium-sized county force of "Medshire". At that time there was a popular BBC TV series, *Juliet Bravo*, which featured a female inspector, Kate Longton, played by Anna Carteret whom I chose as the programme's linking narrator.

I opened with what the women police thought of their depiction in that TV series. Essex's Inspector Maureen Scollan was worried that Kate didn't seem to want to delegate but do everything herself while Hampshire's WPC Sandra Sinclair thought they made crime-solving look too easy but at least the kiddies now shouted, "Oh look! There's Juliet Bravo!" which was an improvement on "pig" or "Miss Piggy". The Met's Commander, Jenny Hilton, one of the country's two senior women police, liked the series for its humane feel and because the characters were well developed.

These female officers had found that the public reacted quite naturally to their increased presence on the streets – unless a male officer was present. Then, they would speak over or around them to the man, even if the woman officer had initiated the contact and the male officer was clearly a rookie. This would even occur, found Kent's Chief Inspector Sullivan, when she was clearly in charge of an event. They also discovered that the male public did not like being arrested or summonsed by a woman, particularly if the offence implied some criticism of their driving skills. However, drunks would still try to chat them up.

Leicester Polytechnic lecturer Ken Russell pointed out that, given their current numbers, there should now be twenty-five women police in senior positions rather than two. Indeed, in some forces the highest rank held by a woman was Sergeant. Jenny Hilton, one of those two senior women, admitted that "objective data" did suggest that even she had been held back due to her sex. Maureen Scollan reported that when she had appeared before promotion boards she had been asked personal questions about her relationships with men and her marriage prospects to which male officers would not be subjected. Jenny Hilton now sat on boards herself and had found that women applicants presented themselves very well and were self-confident but reluctant to take on an argument, probably because they were so conditioned to be nice and agreeable. It was harder to hold back women in the Met because their first two ranks were achieved via exams alone. There was no board – the hurdle at which women in other forces fell.

When promoted Superintendent, Jenny Hilton had expected resistance from subordinates such as "dyed in the wool sergeants and inspectors. "But," she said, "in some ways, rank overcomes gender.""

In fact, it had been those of the same rank who seemed to feel more uncomfortable with her. "But eventually one gets known for oneself, therefore it's no longer important what one's sex is."

Their high rate of wastage on marriage was often held against women police. The rate of loss was now declining but in her "Medshire" interviews Sandra Jones had discovered that some intended police spouses had put pressure on women to resign before they married, and it didn't seem to be just the worries about their safety which troubled them.

"In almost every station I have been in there were war stories about covering up for male colleagues when the wife rang in and there seems to be a sort of macho culture which condones this activity . . . the policeman who is married to a policewoman then comes to fear that she may also be drawn into this kind of cultural or extra-mural activity."

When she returned to work after giving birth WPC Sandra Sinclair found herself under attack from her male colleagues and eventually she sat them down and made them come right out with their comments. "And we got 'well you should be at home with your baby, you shouldn't be back at work, you're taking money from a man.'"

She returned, with difficulty, after having a second child and found the comments were now more financial: "the money you and your husband are rolling in" etc. Becoming a mother, she felt, had definitely made her more relaxed and better able to cope with police work. She cited a moment concerning a cot death – something she herself had dreaded – when the mother would not let go of her baby's body. After talking to the woman for over an hour she offered the baby to Sandra. "I felt then, that was it, I was back where I belonged."

By contrast, West Yorkshire's Jenny Cromack had decided that she *must* choose between family and the job she had always wanted and really loved, and was bitterly disappointed it had come to that. She had spent her last eighteen months in CID and had become much engrossed in dealing with cases of fraud.

As for the strength factor, Inspector Scollan had not only found her lack of physical strength a problem when doing riot training but also felt that she had been unable to make herself heard. (This lack of power in the female voice was also mentioned when I looked into the employment of women as dog handlers. Of course, most women were unaccustomed to adopting loud and commanding tones.)

Chief Inspector Sullivan (actually, newly-appointed Superintendent Sullivan) was not in favour of using women on the front line in public order situations but thought it vital that they be trained to cope, pointing out that during the miners' disputes it had been women police who had been left holding the fort and emphasizing that there was no reason why a riot could not have erupted there.

The careless, even almost deliberately vindictive, manner in which integration had been handled in some forces was attacked by ex-*Police Review* editor Doreen May. It was clear that it wasn't only the women police who had suffered due to this but the female public whose needs had been so cavalierly shrugged off.

"They came in and found the women police offices had been turned into storerooms overnight and tragically a lot of files had been thrown away because the attitude was, right, you're integrated, and the result was a lot of expertise in dealing with rape and child assault victims was lost." (Following a long period when new young WPCs were just expected to instinctively know what to do in sexual assault cases, there were now attempts to send them on special rape and sexual assault courses during their first few months' service.) However, Maureen Scollan pointed out that "in a lot of cases it's too late. You've made your mistakes and you might have spoilt an enquiry because you don't know how to take a proper rape statement and you don't know how to take samples because in some cases the average police surgeon needs to be led."

Even this sudden concern had been more or less forced upon the police service after the subject had exploded onto the television screens in January 1982, when three male Thames Valley officers were seen cruelly haranguing a woman who claimed she had been raped.[3] There was a public outcry about the harassment. "Police bullies who raped this woman in public", was a typical press comment. The Home Office issued new guidelines on the handling of rape victims by police. A couple of months later I trawled rape crisis centres to find out how these guidelines seemed to be working. The answers were mixed, the constant refrain being that it depended on which police station and in which officer's hands the victims ended up.[4]

And were women finally being allowed into the specialist branches? On the whole it seemed not, particularly into those with a macho image such as traffic or dog handling. Senior officers would just "let it be known" that they wouldn't entertain female applicants, explained Sandra Sinclair. A "Medshire" Superintendent had told Sandra Jones that, as it would be unlawful for him to refuse to allow a woman to apply to be a dog handler, he had a word with the head of the section and they decided just to point out what an unpleasant and difficult job it was. Many women got the message and stopped applying for entry into certain specialist branches. However, Jenny Cromack did admit that there were some women who were happy just to get an office job and sit there until they started a family which gave the men the impression that they all just wanted a cushy number.[5]

The following year, in 1987, Sandra Jones's book, *Policewomen and Equality: Formal Policy v Informal Practice,* was published. I wrote a review of it in which it is clear that I was angry about what I had read and had been hearing elsewhere. Not only, I pointed out, was there little progress on promotion, continued blockage of entry into specialist branches, curtailment of vital operational experience, and unofficial (i.e. illegal) entry quotas in many forces but, worst of all, there remained the constant carping about women police, with the unedifying spectacle of even senior officers apparently feeling safe enough to make the most sexist remarks without fear of retribution.[6]

With more married women now staying on, maternity leave and child care became a much-aired problem. In January 1987, I spoke to several police mothers on the subject who told me of their particular difficulties. While pregnant, due to the physical risks of the job, they had either to be given nine-to-five inside jobs, which could cause resentment with colleagues, including fellow policewomen, or be sent on maternity leave early. The other problem was managing child care around shift work which could be complicated (or sometimes eased) if the husband was also a police officer. (Incidentally, the piece was given my best ever *Police Review* cover with a delightful photograph of an attractive young policewoman and her two children.)

Several of the interviewees and correspondents were positive and offered good advice on how to cope, while admitting there had been bad moments and that it was hard. Opportunities for job-sharing or part-time might help, some felt, but there were also some sad letters from those who had been unable to make it work. As one remarked, "Even before she was born I felt my job slipping through my fingers."[7]

Meanwhile, it was with matters of life and death that their Northern Irish sisters were concerned. It was a replay of the Cyprus situation. The male officers of the Royal Ulster Constabulary were armed. The female officers (first admitted into the force 1943) were not. The reasoning was the same as in Cyprus: if they were armed they would become targets for assassination and also be less effective in dealing with the welfare of women and children. The former reason was of no small import. By November 1986, 230 male and five female officers had been killed but, an RUC spokesman told me, there had been "no clamour from women officers for guns".[8] However, I do recall one female officer saying that she had made herself familiar with firearms (they were given no official training) and that she had practised reaching across a male officer with whom she might be patrolling to grab his gun as he fell. A sobering thought.

The women were caught in a double bind. The force was made up of regular RUC officers and Reservists[9] and, in 1980, the Chief Constable, Sir John Hermon, had decided that all full-time reservists should be armed. However, he was not prepared to change the no arms policy as regards women. This meant the phasing out of full-time women reservists. Thirty-one of them took their sex-discrimination case before the Industrial Tribunal for Northern Ireland and two of them on to the European Court of Justice where they won and they received compensation. A further Industrial Tribunal case brought by 310 officers was settled out of court, with claimants receiving sums ranging from £1,000 to £5,600 each. Reporting this latest victory on 10th November 1988 *The Times* added a rider: "Last night police sources indicated that the RUC policy of not arming women officers was unlikely to be changed in the foreseeable future."

It was five years later, in August 1993, when it was announced that armed women police were to be on the streets of Northern Ireland by the following April, starting that October with a small number restricted largely to driving duties. Duly, on 1st April 1994, a sobering photograph of an RUC woman appeared in the *Police Review*. She was carrying a pistol and a Heckler and Koch sub-machine gun. By that time, six RUC policewomen had been killed and eighty-eight injured in terrorist attacks.[10]

Interestingly, later that year, in an announcement about taking steps towards a more acceptably representative force, the Province's police authority linked the need for the appointment of more women (then one in ten of the force) to that for more Catholics (thirty-eight per cent of the population but only eight per cent of the force). This equality linkage was going to recur in the rest of the UK, but with ethnic minorities.

Inevitably, due to their increased presence, women police on the mainland had also been killed on duty, as had their male counterparts. In 1983 WPC Jane Philippa Arbuthnot died when an IRA bomb exploded in Knightsbridge. The following year, WPC Yvonne Fletcher was murdered by gunfire from the Libyan People's Bureau in

St James's Square and, in 1997, Met WPC Nina McKay was stabbed to death during an attempt to detain a violent man. Worse was to come later.

When, in 1993, I again looked at the specialist department problem I pointed out that DCI Jackie Malton, who had "inspired" the character DCI Jane Tennison in the current rave success TV programme *Prime Suspect,* had explained to the public that the male chauvinist attitudes depicted were now outdated and added that the status of women officers varied according to the force and department they worked in, which was still true.

Sandra Jones, who had researched "Medshire" in the early 1980s, now told me that current research suggested that little had changed. One woman Sergeant who had finally made it into her chosen branch thought that matters had in fact improved. However, methods of keeping women out had become more subtle – such as setting unnecessarily high physical standards unattainable by most women.

HM Inspectorate claimed that the CID situation in twelve forces they had studied appeared promising but a closer look revealed that the women's roles were often narrow. Even after acceptance the battle was not always won. "There is still a great deal of resentment," one long-serving female dog handler told me sadly. Another added, "The antagonism is largely down to the old sweats but this can be picked up by the younger men, particularly when in packs."

Others took a more positive view. "I've never been held back in anything I've wanted to do, either by management or the system," claimed one middle-ranking officer who had served in several specialist departments. "In fact I've had a lot of support." But *she* noticed it was the young male PCs who seemed to have the most to prove. If anything the job was more macho than when she joined. But not only women suffered. "You know coppers – they'll always seek out the weakest one on the shift." It did help a woman, she added wryly, if she was halfway pretty or had a forty-two inch bust. "You can't eliminate gender traits." Another woman told me: "One girl I know is totally ignored by her department. They have even gone as far as sliding the door closed in her face when she is trying to get in the van."

More women were complaining about sexual inequality and sexual harassment and this was regarded as a positive sign. However, a disturbing development was the number of cases being settled out of court, which meant the message was not getting out and those responsible were not being punished. And, of course, a complaint could always rebound on the complainant. The name of one of a group of women who had accused a senior officer of indecent assault became known. "As a result", reported a female sergeant, "she was hounded, being told, 'You've broken this man's career.'"

Many female officers saw no problem and were scathing about wimpish colleagues who complained about harassment or were overly sensitive to male attitudes. Others had mixed feelings. "I don't suffer any," one Met officer told me, "but then that's my personality. They wouldn't dare." But she admitted that while half of her felt the complaining women were feeble, "the other half thinks, why should the men get away with such behaviour?"

An ongoing problem for many women officers was getting the right uniform and equipment for the job. Being given a handbag instead of capacious pockets for your notebooks, and straight skirts you couldn't run in rather than trousers, was par for the course. "They yell that you are not keeping up while you struggle along in a protective suit that is three sizes too big and a helmet that is falling over your eyes."[11]

A Sergeant who joined Thames Valley in 1995 recalls that there was only one female-size stab vest amongst twenty to thirty male vests. It was much too large and covered the equipment at her waist. Being automatically precluded from putting in doors or taking part in the planned arrests of violent individuals also hampered her until she tackled her skipper and asked why. "From the day I challenged decisions things completely changed for the better. We all have the same training," she points out, "and in many cases us girls were able to talk down violent individuals."

At times when writing my *Police Review* pieces supporting women police I had the feeling that I was just whistling in the wind but, I was later to discover, at least two of them did have some consequences. The first, "How Long Must She Wait?", published on 11th September 1987, asked when were we going to get a woman chief constable. The world's first woman police chief in a major city was Penny Harrington, who in 1985 was appointed to lead the police in Portland, Oregon. Delighted, I had interviewed her by post and via tape recordings. But the careers of US police chiefs can be fragile and within eighteen months she had been brought down by a powerful police union and was suing the city on several counts.[12]

I started by pointing out that, fifteen years earlier, Tony Judge, founder-editor of *Police*, the journal of the Police Federation of

England and Wales, had commented: "In the current climate Britain will have a woman prime minister long before the first chief constable is appointed." Given that Mrs Thatcher had become prime minister in 1979 and it was now 1987 he had certainly been right about that. Now he said, "Within ten years without any question – probably five." Many women fitted the current senior officer mould of spells in academe interspersed with short refresher courses in practical policing. Indeed, he was "amazed" that no women had appeared on shortlists so far. "But they will."

I included the comments on promotion to chief constable made during my radio programme by Commander Jenny Hilton: "I think that things will change dramatically over the next five years. Some very good women we have at Inspector, Chief Inspector level will start to come to the top." Chief Inspector Sullivan had not been so sure despite her own recent promotion. "To be honest I don't see a woman being chief constable this century."

One person I did not consult for the feature was Merseyside's Assistant Chief Constable Alison Halford, who at the time was the highest-ranking woman in the country. I felt she had been subject to sufficient attention so I would give her a rest. Shortly after publication, an uncommissioned article landed on the desk of *Police Review* editor Brian Hilliard. It was titled "Until the Twelfth of Never" and it was written by Alison Halford. In it, she commented that the inability of some very senior men to cope with a woman of comparable rank was quite bewildering. In some ways, they felt threatened; thus she was given no support, guidance or empathy, as would be afforded a newly promoted male Assistant Chief Constable.[13] Both Brian and I were amazed that Halford had put her head above the parapet to such a degree.

She later admitted that after the article's publication her force had been "humming". Her Chief Constable, Sir Kenneth Oxford, had told her that he didn't mind but that it had not gone down well with the Home Office. Her *Police Review* article was to come up several times during her investigations of her seemingly stalled attempts to climb further up the ladder. However, due to various disciplinary accusations against her she was suspended from duty in 1992 – eighteen months after she had begun a sex discrimination case against Merseyside's Chief Constable James Sharples, the Home Office, Regional HMI Sir Philip Myers and Northamptonshire Police Authority.

At the EOC Tribunal the *Police Review* article was brought up again and Halford responded that she had felt impelled to write it because my piece had been so "cosy" so "grossly misleading" in contrast to the reality she had experienced . (In her book, *No Way Up the Greasy Pole,* she states that Joan Lock had prophesied there would be a woman chief constable in ten years.[14] Not true. I prophesied nothing, merely recorded the opinions of others. The "within ten years" was from the much-respected and long-experienced Tony Judge. "Not this century" had been another opinion.)

Halford's Equal Opportunities Commission Tribunal continued for two years, attracted huge publicity, and was finally settled out of court.[15] Afterwards, a fellow crime writer rang me to exclaim, "I didn't realize all this was your fault" and sent me a double-page spread on the case in the *Daily Mail* of 18th July 1992, which included the following bemusing statement:

> Ms Halford believes the world might not have heard such stories (of the accusations against her), and certainly didn't need to, but for the chain of events which followed publication in the *Police Review* in September, 1987, of an article by former policewoman Joan Lock which pondered the question would there be a woman chief constable in her lifetime?

(At least I was pondering now, not prophesying!) Anyway, some good may have come out of the whole affair. At last, the selectors appeared to be considering the merits of female applicants more carefully and, three years later, in July 1995, Pauline Clare became the UK's first female Chief Constable when she was appointed to lead Lancashire Constabulary. Two years on, Elizabeth Neville became Chief Constable of Wiltshire Police and another two years saw Jane Stichbury leading Dorset Police.

More have followed since, with some forces appointing women twice. The first in Wales was Barbara Wilding (South Wales Police) in 2004, and the first in Scotland was Norma Graham (Fife Constabulary) in 2008.

The second of my *Police Review* pieces[16] that had some consequences described the International Association of Women Police with which Damer Dawson had been involved all those years back. I had been a member for several years as had a handful of British women and one or two had spoken at their conferences. However, eleven of the association's twelve regions were in North America and Region 12 (for a time run by Gail Thomson of Lothian & Borders) covered the rest of the world so "International" seemed something of a misnomer. I pointed out that they now wished to rectify that situation by attracting more of us foreigners and I gave the contact details. Tina Martin of Derbyshire Police greeted the news enthusiastically and determined to form a British chapter, even going over to the US to find out how. She was also keen to take a British contingent to the 1987 annual conference, which was held in New York. I helped whip up more interest with a couple more *Police Review* features[17] and go they did, looking very smart with their bowler hats, white gloves and neat navy uniforms.

The British Association of Women Police[18] (affiliated to the IAWP) duly materialized. I was involved in some fledgling events and when they hosted the IAWP 1996 Annual Conference in Birmingham (the first outside North America) I took along a panel of female crime writers. I eventually lost touch with them until out of the blue I received an invite to their twentieth anniversary bash which was being held at the House of Lords on 23rd November 2007. There, I and the two other founder members (Tina and Carolyn Williamson, who had both picked up the baton and carried it forward with such hard work) were made much of and it was great to see so many confident happy policewomen now holding down responsible jobs.

Was I the one who had written that piece asking when we would have a woman Chief Constable, asked the association's president, Julie Spence? When I answered in the affirmative, she grinned. "Well, I'm the fifth." (She was then heading Cambridgeshire Constabulary and was attracting some approving attention.)

The BAWP magazine *Grapevine* reported in autumn 2007 that the number of women police had now risen to twenty-three per cent, and that, back in 2001, the Home Office had acknowledged their importance by funding an official national co-ordinator, enabling them to put themselves on a firmer footing and to recruit more members. They were now regularly consulted on issues affecting women and had representatives on numerous Home Office working parties.

By then, there were about 200 firearms officers in the UK, and at a Home Office equal rights conference BAWP's Liz Owsley pointed out that force-issue guns were too large for most women's hands so they could end up shooting themselves or each other.[19] The BAWP also took up uniform and equipment issues – vital subjects, with knives and guns continuing to put the lives of officers at risk.

In 2005, when responding to an alarm at a travel agents, West Yorkshire Constables Sharon Beshenivsky and Teresa Milburn were met with gunfire from the escaping robbers. Sharon was killed and Teresa badly injured. Similarly, in 2012, when responding to a burglary report, Greater Manchester Constables Nicola Hughes and Fiona Bone were greeted by a hail of bullets and a hand grenade in a deliberate death trap set by a man who hated police. One officer was killed instantly, the other died later. At least no-one claimed that their sex had made them more vulnerable, rather it was the question of whether our police should be armed that came to the fore.

To help women keep up in other ways, the BAWP also held training courses and gave annual awards for outstanding achievements. Things were looking up.

But conditions can change unexpectedly. At the time of writing, the whole British police service is in turmoil. Massive budgetary cuts have meant the slashing of personnel, particularly at the higher ranks such as Superintendent and Chief Superintendent. Pay rates are being restructured, giving higher rates to specialists, front line officers and those who do shift work while cutting those of others. Officers can no longer count their years of service as a reason for pay increases. Some have seen a drastic reduction to their income and their pension rules rewritten.

In addition, police stations are being sold off (including Scotland Yard) and direct entry applicants with no police experience are to be shoe-horned into senior jobs, helping block the path of those climbing up the hard way.

According to speakers at the recent Federation conferences women police have already been affected by all this – to their detriment. The Home Office figures of March 2012 showed that there were no women of ACPO[20] rank in seventeen out of forty-three British police forces. As Professor Jennifer Brown of the Manheim Centre for Criminolgy said, "Austerity is allowing people to do all sorts of things that would otherwise not be acceptable", while Jayne Monkhouse, the Federation's equality advisor, pointed out that the occupational segregation of roles such as firearms work, which were still largely carried out by men, would mean that female officers could expect to earn 93.4p for every pound earned by their male colleagues. Citing the Federation's Woman's Reserve survey of 3,407 female officers, Brown claimed that over forty per cent of them had considered leaving and over seventy per cent were very worried about the financial impact of the Winsor report.[21]

Some Met women with families have the additional problem of having found homes they can afford outside the force area so they are having to commute long distances to work while budget cuts lead to less work flexibility and thus more stress. "They are all really desperate to get out," an ex-WPC told me, "and are counting the days until they can go." Home Counties forces are facing a different dilemma: a migration of numbers of experienced officers into the Met for higher salaries due to London weighting, as well as many leaving for better-paid private sector jobs.

What is certain is that the British police in general are very demoralized, not just by reduction in their earnings and overwork due to their dwindling numbers, but also by the feeling that they are no longer able to do their jobs properly. There are nowhere near sufficient numbers to police a busy town centre on a Saturday night and, said one female officer, "It's embarrassing going to a victim hours late and trying to explain why you have not arrived sooner."

Ironically, most of the senior police officers in crime dramas now seem to be women. I've also noticed that whenever a police force needs to apologise for some misdemeanour they often use their senior women as spokespeople, presumably relying on the softer touch. Plus, of course, the person in the Superintendents' Association hot-seat is now a woman: the newly-appointed President, Irene Curtis. She is also worried about the present Superintendents being overworked due to their diminished numbers, plus the effect that direct entry officers may have on the lower ranks who will be taking orders from someone who (in this mainly operational role) has no idea what it's like out there.

As for female officers' chances, Irene Curtis admitted, "We have not got a sustainable way of improving the representation of women at the moment."[22]

But it is not all doom and gloom. As well as Irene Curtis's appointment, three more women Chief Constables were taken on in 2013: Debbie Simpson to Dorset; Suzette Davenport to Gloucestershire and Justine Curran to Humberside, which makes a total of twenty-two since Pauline Clare broke the sex barrier back in 1995. A West Midlands Inspector, Shindo Barquer (a tireless recruiter of women police and raiser of awareness about honour-related crimes, the complexities of arranged marriages and domestic violence) recently won two Asian Women of Achievement Awards (Public Sector and Chairman's)[23] and the police witness who made the Levenson Inquiry on phone hacking sit up and take notice was Deputy Assistant Commissioner Sue Akers QPM. Sue, who ran three of the linked enquiries on the subject, was described by the *Independent* as "her own woman" and "not to be messed with"[24] and was generally felt to have much outperformed the senior policemen who appeared.

Despite losing its Home Office grant due to cuts, the BAWP continues its good work (although necessarily in a more limited fashion) under the new President, Assistant Commissioner Cressida Dick, and is to host the IAWP 2015 Conference in Cardiff. Last year, they held their twenty-fifth anniversary celebrations at the Scottish Parliament Buildings.

The following day, the Scottish Women's Development Forum was attended by Scottish women police who, during their previous ten years, had upped their overall numbers by ten per cent to twenty-eight per cent. But now, as well as cuts, they are facing the additional complications of a newly amalgamated force structure. Instead of eight separate forces and a Crime and Drug Enforcement Agency they now have one national police force: Police Scotland. However, speaking at the Forum, Kenny MacAskill MSP, Cabinet Secretary for Justice, assured the women that it was important that the new service still retained a representative workforce.

"A better gender balance within the Scottish Police Service will enhance service delivery. It is not just the right and moral thing to do, it is essential if we are to deliver the benefits of reform."[25]

Sir Stephen House, the man heading this new force, declared that among his priorities would be improving the investigation of rape and the tackling of domestic violence. However, only one (Deputy Chief Constable Rose Fitzpatrick) of his ten-strong operational Executive Team is a woman. House claims he wants to help more women reach higher rank and, when tackled, suggested he would be delighted if he eventually handed over control of the service to a woman.[26] Given this start, it seems unlikely.

"There will be no rollback on equality", promised the new Minister for Equalities, Lynne Featherstone, in a speech to the Fawcett Society in 2010. But she has now moved on to other things. However, Irene Curtis, the new President of the Superintendents' Association, has been making waves by advocating not only a return to "common sense policing" but an end to the "macho, white, middle-aged male culture" of the UK's top ranks by the appointment of more women, ethnic minorities and also some of the excellent men who don't fit the accepted mould.[27]

It is impossible to predict what the outcome of all the changes will be but it is clear that the women will still be in there, fighting for their rightful place in the police service.

Glossary of Abbreviations

CLAC   Criminal Law Amendment Committee
DORA   Defence of the Realm Act
NCW   National Council of Women of Great Britain and Ireland
NUWW   National Union of Women Workers
NUWSS   National Union of Women's Suffrage Societies
NVA   National Vigilance Association
QMAAC   Queen Mary's Army Auxiliary Corps
WAS   Women's Auxiliary Service
WAPC   Women's Auxiliary Police Corps
WFL   Women's Freedom League
WLGA   Women's Local Government Association
WPS   Women Police Service
WPV   Women Police Volunteers
WSPU   Women's Social and Political Union.

F   Fawcett Library
IWM   Imperial War Museum
LM   London Museum
PRO   Public Record Office
(Wom Coll   Women's Collection)

Selected Bibliography

The Pioneer Policewoman, Commandant Mary S. Allen OBE (Chatto and Windus, 1925)

Lady in Blue, Mary S Allen OBE (Stanley Paul and Co. Ltd., 1936)

The Memoirs of Miss Dorothy Olivia Georgiana Peto, OBE (unpublished), March 1970, The Metropolitan Police Historical Advisory Board

A Woman at Scotland Yard, Lilian Wyles BEM (Faber and Faber Ltd., 1951)

Woman on the Beat, Stella Condor (Robert Hale, 1960)

The British Police, J.M. Hart (Allen and Unwin, 1951)

A History of Police in England and Wales, 1900-1966, T.A. Critchley (Constable, 1967)

Annals of an Active Life, Gen. the Right Hon. Sir Nevil Macready, Bart. GCMG KGB (Hutchinson and Co, 1924)

Scotland Yard, Harold Scott (Deutsch, 1954)

The Story of Scotland Yard, Sir Ronald Howe (Arthur Barker, 1965)

The Hidden World of Scotland Yard, Guy R. Williams (Hutchinson, 1972)

Sir Percy Sillitoe, A.W. Cockerill (W.H. Allen, 1975)

The Suffragette Movement, E. Sylvia Pankhurst (Longmans Green, 1931)

Rise Up, Women!, A. Rosen (Routledge and Kegan Paul, 1974)

Unshackled, Dame Christabel Pankhurst (Hutchinson, 1959)

The Militant Suffragettes, Antonia Raeburn (Michael Joseph, 1973)

Women on the Warpath, David Mitchell (Cape, 1966)

The Home Front, E. Sylvia Pankhurst (Hutchinson, 1932)

Defence of the Realm Manual AUG-1918

Hansard

Parliamentary Committee on the Employment of Women on Police Duties HMSO, 1920 (The Baird Report)

Home Office Departmental Committee on the Employment of Women on Police Duties, HMSO, 1924 (The Baird Report)

Home Office, Police Post-War Committee. 2nd report HMSO 1947

Inquiry in regard to the interrogation by the police of Miss Savidge (Tribunals of Inquiry (Evidence) Act, 1921). HMSO, 1928.

PAMPHLETS

Women Police, 1914-1950, Edith Tancred (The National Council of Women of Great Britain, 1951)

Women Police (The Women's Freedom League, 1922)

The Women Police Question (The League of Womanhood, 1925)

Women's Freedom League, 1907-1957, Stella Newsome (The Women's Freedom League)

Nina Boyle, Cicely Hamilton (for the Nina Boyle Memorial Fund)

The Purpose of a Lifetime: a profile of Barbara Mary Denis de Vitré, OBE, Clifford R. Stanley (Barry Rose, 1972)

The History of the Official Policewoman (NCW, 1922)

Bi-Annual Reports of the Women Police Service, 1915-19

Bi-Annual Report of the Women's Auxiliary Service, 1920-21

Annual Reports for the Bristol Training School for Women Police and Women Patrols 1917 and 1918

The Vote
Votes for Women
The Whistle
The Policewoman's Review
The Job
Metropolitan Women Police Association Newsletter
Police Review
The Police Journal
Police Chronicle

Notes

CHAPTER ONE

[1] Detail about dorothy bags and stones only, *The Militant Suffragettes*, p. 104.

[2] Information on this incident from *Lady in Blue*, pp. 14, 19-21. However *The Times* report, 13th July 1909, says that Agnest Carson and Florence Cook broke the Home Office windows. Mary Allen is mentioned but not her windows.

[3] *The Times*, 13th July 1909.

[4] *Votes for Women*, 16th July 1909.

[5] *Lady in Blue* pp. 13 and 14.

[6] Mrs Sparboro's statement to Mrs Baldock in Holloway Prison, July/August 1906, as quoted in *The Militant Suffragettes*, p. 22.

[7] Information on the time in prison from *Lady in Blue* pp. 17-21; Gladys Roberts' diary as quoted in *The Militant Suffragettes*, p. 110, and 'Hunger Strikers' an item in *The Bristol Echo*, 4th September 1909.

[8] *Votes for Women*, 6th August 1909, and Gladys Roberts' diary, *op. cit.*

[9] *The Suffragette Movement*, pp. 310-11, and *The Militant Suffragettes*, 113.

[10] Mrs Blathwayt's diary (a Bath WSPU supporter) 31st July 1909, quoted in *The Militant Suffragettes*, p. 113. "Annie Kenney expects to be taken soon herself."

[11] *The Vote*, 25th July 1913, and an unidentified newspaper cutting headed 'River Speech to MPs'. Effects of Edith Watson, courtesy of her son, Bernard John Watson.

[12] Nina C. Boyle in *The Vote*, 23rd May 1913.

[13] *The Vote*, 15th August 1913, notes that Great Britain is lagging behind the USA and Canada who are employing policewomen.

[14] *Lady in Blue*, pp. 15, 21, 22 and 25.

[15] Police Report, 1st December 1916, MEP02 1710 PRO, but the attitude of Mr Mead is dealt with at some length in further chapters.

[16] *The Vote*, 19th September, 10th and 17th October 1913.

[17] 'Mob Law in Park', item in 'Our Point of View', *The Vote*, 29th May 1914,

gives an example of alleged lack of protection in which police allow a gang to smash up the WFL platform at Hyde Park Corner and to assault their members without interfering and later, when a Mrs Cubley attempts to apply for a summons for this assault, claims she is "grossly insulted" and "driven away without redress" by the magistrates.

18 *The Times*, 14th July 1914.

19 Information for incident, *The Vote*, 17th and 24th July 1914. *The Times, op cit.* N.B. I have used *The Vote*'s versions of the false names; those in *The Times* differ slightly.

CHAPTER TWO

1 *The Vote*, 28th August 1914.

2 Recruitment details, *The Vote*, 21st and 28th August 1914.

3 IWM Wom Coll EMP VI 41 see 15.

4 Evidence of Margaret Damer Dawson before 'Baird Committee', 905.

5 Obituaries: WAS REPORT 1920-21 and the *Daily Telegraph*, 22nd May 1920. *The Pioneer Policewoman* and *Who Was Who*.

6 Obituary, *Daily Mirror*, 21st May 1920.

7 *The Pioneer Policewoman*, pp. 10 and 13.

8 *The Pioneer Policewoman*, p. 17.

9 Hilda M.K. Neild writing in the *Weekly Dispatch*, 22nd July 1917, says "pressure of work" forced Nina Boyle to "put the management into other hands".

10 Letter to the Criminal Law Amendment Committee from the Commissioner, July 1914. PRO MEP02 1608.

11 Quoted in an undated and unsigned precis of the activities of the three organizations. PRO MEP02 1608.

12 Interview with Commissioner and his training assistance. Margaret Damer Dawson's evidence before the Baird Committee. 907/930/931.

13 *The Pioneer Policewoman*, p. 20.

14 *Daily Graphic*, 25th November 1914.

15 An obituary on Mary Allen in the *Daily Telegraph*, 18th December 1964, stating she was the first, brought letters from Edith Watson 29th December 1964, with her September claim and Mrs Henrietta Robley-Browne 4th January 1965, of July, which seems unlikely since they were not formed until August. In an unsigned statement on the Women Police Volunteers (the Imperial War Museum asked all the women's organizations to present details of their stories after the war), it states that Nina Boyle chose and first wore the uniform and also mentions the Press attention when Edith Watson appeared at the Old Bailey. IWM Wom Coll EMP VI 41.

16 From notes in the effects of Edith Watson where she says she was "one of the first".

17 As 4: 907.

18 Representatives of these organizations signed a letter to *The Times*, 13th

October 1914, announcing the inauguration of the patrols and asking for donations.

[19] Mrs Creighton wrote to Mrs Franklin on 27th June 1913, saying she would rather speak on 'How purity teaching can best be given' than history which she had not taught lately. F: AUTO Vol. II.

[20] Ray Strachey in *The Cause* tells how she was a signatory to a very damaging anti-woman's suffrage letter in 1889, saying "the emancipatory process has now reached the limits fixed by the physical constitution of women." On 18th February 1903, Lady Frances Balfour wrote to Mrs Fawcett saying that Mrs Creighton was complaining that the council (probably that of NUWW) had passed a resolution supporting women's suffrage "because she was not there to keep them in order". F: AUTO: VOL.1B, but by 14th February 1914, she was making a speech in the Albert Hall, declaring herself for emancipation as it would be good for society. As much "for the sweated worker as the cultured lady" but that it must be done "by noble means". 'Woman's Suffrage' speech published by the National Union of Women's Suffrage Societies. L.M. Suffrage Collection. 50.82/332.

[21] As 18.

[22] Report of his speech "yesterday" to a meeting of women in Church House, Westminster. *The Times*, 18th October 1914.

[23] *The Times*, 17th November 1914.

[24] Which were in force between 1870-83 and under which prostitutes in garrison towns were compulsorily registered, medically examined and, if necessary, treated. Opponents of the acts, such as Josephine Butler, held that they encouraged white slave traffic.

[25] Information re Plymouth Watch Committee, WFL actions etc from *The Vote*, 16th and 23rd October and 6th November 1914.

[26] *The Vote*, 27th November 1914, states that "many men of Lord Kitchener's Army stationed at Belton Park gave Miss Boyle an attentive hearing".

CHAPTER THREE

[1] Personal details of Miss Harburn from her obituary, *International Women's News*, January 1964; *The Pioneer Policewoman*, pp. 28-9, and interview with relatives.

[2] *The Pioneer Policewoman*, p. 29.

[3] Letter from Nina Boyle to Mr Asquith, Prime Minister, quoted in *The Vote*, 23rd October 1914, suggests that, rather than impose so many restrictions on women, they might just get the troops to exercise "a little elementary self control".

[4] As 2, p. 31.

[5] *Grantham Journal*, 19th December 1914. In *The Pioneer Policewoman*, p. 27, Mary Allen says that the Women's Central Committee of Grantham elected a sub-committee to establish a fund to maintain the women police.

[6] J.C. Carlile in *Folkestone During the War*, p. 151 (published by F.J. Parsons, Folkestone).

[7] She is referring to the fact that, she claims, the civil and military police are to be the sole arbiters of who is a prostitute and could abuse this trust. In the same leader she cites such a case.

[8] As 2, p.35.

[9] WPS REPORT, 1915. The report does not give venue of the 'cases' but it's most unlikely that it is anywhere else.

[10] Miss Damer Dawson's evidence at Baird, 908.

[11] *Op. cit.*

[12] See *The Vote* 1st, 8th and 15th January 1915.

[13] Letter, 14th January 1915, quoted in *The Pioneer Policewoman*, p. 37.

[14] Edith Watson (unpublished account in her estate) claims these three "resigned". Damer Dawson (Baird 909) and Mary Allen (*The Pioneer Policewoman*, p. 15) that all but two of the WPV sided with them and so they resigned the name of the force. Certainly Eva Christie stayed with the WPV – see further entries in *The Vote*.

[15] Entry 11th June 1915 in *NCW Women Patrols, 1914-20*, IWM Wom Coll EMP 42.7.

[16] As 10, 912.

[17] As 2, p. 44.

[18] As 9.

CHAPTER FOUR

[1] Letter to Superintendent Wells from Ida Beaver, London Organizer of the Women's Patrols, and M.G. Carden, Hon.Sec. of the Central Women's Patrol Committee. PRO MEPO 2 1608.

[2] Letter, 29th October 1914, PRO H045 10806.

[3] PRO H045 10806.

[4] As 15, Chapter 3.

[5] *The Times*, 13th October 1914.

[6] *The Times*, 31st December 1914.

[7] Letter, 8th January 1915, PRO H045 10806.

[8] Extracts from Organizers Reports of May and June 1915, PRO H045 10806.

[9] Damer Dawson/Baird 999; *Miss Peto's Memoirs*, p. 16, and *The Pioneer Policewoman*, p. 154.

[10] Letter from Damer Dawson to the First Commissioner of HM Office of Works (who controlled the parks), 4th June 1915. PRO MEPO 2 1608.

[11] Report from Hyde Park Police Station. PRO MEPO 2 1608.

[12] As 1.

[13] Note he added to 11.

[14] As 11 in Chapter 2.

[15] As 8.

[16] As 8, plus extracts for January and March 1916. PRO HO 45 10806.

[17] *Miss Peto's Memoirs*, p. 11.

[18] As 16.

[19] Letter, report and memo. PRO MEPO 2 1608.

[20] In her books Mary Allen admits that police often protected them and that police and prison officials were much kinder to them than were the general public.

[21] Letter from Commissioner to Home Secretary, 19th July 1916. PRO HO45 10806.

[22] *Miss Peto's Memoirs*, p. 29, and other sources.

CHAPTER FIVE

[1] Note by Acting Superintendent Short on a report on the incident from Hyde Park Police Station and answer to the Chief Constable's query, 17th July, 1916. PRO MEPO 2 1708.

[2] Letters and Police Reports, July and August 1916. PRO MEPO 2 1708.

[3] 23rd August 1916, PRO MEPO 2 1720.

[4] *The Pioneer Policewoman*, p. 42.

[5] His evidence before the Baird Committee 2579.

[6] 22nd September 1916. PRO MEPO 2 1710.

[7] PRO MEPO 2 1710.

[8] As 5: 2581.

[9] Report from Vine Street Police Station, 1st December 1916. PRO MEPO 2 1710.

[10] As 5.

[11] Report on incident from Vine Street Police Station, 4th January 1916, PRO MEPO 2 1710.

CHAPTER SIX

[1] WPS REPORT, 1915-16.

[2] Quoted in *The Pioneer Policewoman*, p. 38.

[3] *Miss Peto's Memoirs*, pp. 16 and 17.

[4] 30th January 1917. PRO HO 45 10806.

[5] In a letter to Sir Edward Henry from Damer Dawson, 16th November 1916. PRO MEPO 2 1608.

[6] *Op. cit.*

[7] 'The Day's Work of a Policewoman', IWM Wom Coll EMP VII 43.

[8] PRO MEPO 2 1710.

[9] 13th February 1917, PRO HO45 10959.

[10] As 7.

[11] 4th August 1917.

[12] In a list of serving WPS in *The Pioneer Policewoman*, the only King at a small unit is Sergeant King at Erith: she has only two constables, so it's probable she started out as a constable there.

[13] *The Home Front*, p. 340.

[14] 27th September and 4th October 1918, as quoted in *The Pioneer Policewoman*, pp. 74-5.

[15] *Annals of an Active Life*, p. 316; Macready tells of how he gives them cars.

[16] As 15, Chapter 3. Entry 16th May 1918.

[17] As 10, Chapter 3. 1028.

[18] Home Office report 'Measures for dealing with Prostitutes' mentions the serious outbreak of VD at Folkestone and the 'new regulation' to cope with it. PRO MEPO 2 1720. *N.B.* DORA Regulations which specifically related to prostitution were 13A, 14 and 40D. The 'curfew' in Grantham and Cardiff was brought about by Regulation 13 which was meant for controlling the movements of the civilian population.

Other information in this chapter comes from the joint evidence of Mary Allen and Margaret Damer Dawson at Baird, and Mary Allen's two books.

CHAPTER SEVEN

[1] Minute by Assistant Commissioner, A Department, on File, dated 16th October 1916, PRO MEPO 2 1710.

[2] *Miss Peto's Memoirs*, p. 29.

[3] The *Daily Telegraph*, 9th June 1917, and as 15, Chapter 3, entry 22nd May 1917.

[4] PRO MEPO 2 1710.

[5] Letter to *The Times*, 26th February 1917.

[6] As 15, Chapter 3, 11th April and 7th May 1917.

[7] Letter to the Commissioner from Mrs Carden, 17th December 1917. PRO MEPO 2 1608.

[8] PRO MEPO 2 1710 and 1608.

[9] *Op. cit.*

[10] IWM Wom Coll EMP VI:42.1.

[11] PRO HO 45 10806.

[12] WPS REPORTS, 1915-16 and 1916-17.

[13] *The Pioneer Policewoman*, pp. 97-8.

CHAPTER EIGHT

[1] *The Vote*, 15th December 1916, 7th and 28th September 1917.

[2] *The Vote*, 9th April 1915.

[3] *The Times*, 22nd and 27th March 1915.

[4] *The Vote*, 9th April 1915.

[5] As 11, Chapter Two.

[6] 'Suffrage and Politics: 9 (Women's Freedom League)', Wom Coll IWM.

[7] *Weekly Dispatch* articles, 15th and 22nd July and 19th August 1917.

[8] WPS REPORTS and as 15, Chapter Three, 8th November 1915.

[9] From Margaret Damer Dawson's speeches as reported in *The Times*, 15th March and 11th October 1916.

[10] As quoted in the *Southport Visiter*, 15th May 1917.

[11] From a circular by the Rev. Ernest Houghton, Rector of St Stephen's, Bristol, as quoted in *The Times*, 14th October 1915.

[12] *Weekly Dispatch*, 27th November 1916.

CHAPTER NINE

Most of the information in this chapter is from *Miss Peto's Memoirs*; Mrs Joseph's and Mrs Young's combined evidence at Baird and 'NCW Women Patrols 1914-20', see 15, Chapter 3, BTS Annual Reports 1917-18, with the following exceptions:

[1] Damer Dawson's evidence at Baird 999.

[2] *The Times*, 22nd July 1914.

[3] Report of the Patrol Meeting (following the NCW AGM), 4th October 1917. Wom Coll EMP 42.1 IWM.

[4] Appendix 111 'Liverpool' by Mabel Cowlin in Edith Tancred's booklet *Women Police, 1914-1950*, published in 1951 by the NCW. Met Police Library.223 Store.

[5] PRO HO 45 10806.

[6] PRO HO 45 10962[A].

[7] Birmingham: Evidence of P.C. Collins, Birmingham City Police, at Baird, 1831-46 and WPS Report 1916-17. Lancashire: Evidence of Chief Constable Lane of Lancashire at Baird. Birkenhead: As 10, Chapter 8.

CHAPTER TEN

[1] Letter from the Commissioner to Mrs Stanley, 2nd November 1917, quoted in 15, Chapter 3.

[2] As 3, Chapter 9.

[3] PRO HO 45 10806.

[4] PRO MEPO 2 1608.

[5] As 3.

[6] PRO MEPO 2 1710.

[7] A letter to S.W. Harris, 28th August 1918, asking him to inform the Home Secretary that he is sorry that Chamberlain could not attend "this morning's Cabinet when Regulation 40D was discussed" – one of the DORA regs. re prostitution. PRO HO 45 10806.

[8] PRO MEPO 2 1748.

[9] *Miss Peto's memoirs*, p. 22.

[10] 'Report on Drinking Conditions among women and girls in Woolwich and District' and applicable corres. PRO MEPO 2 1710.

[11] PRO HO 45 10962A.

[12] *The Pioneer Policewoman*, p. 24; Damer Dawson at Baird/937 and 15, Chapter 3.

[13] *History of Police in England and Wales*, pp. 185 and 187.

[14] As 15, Chapter 6.

CHAPTER ELEVEN

[1] *Miss Peto's memoirs*, p. 32.

[2] *Lady in Blue*, p. 50.

[3] *Op cit*, p. 53, and WPS Report, 1920-21.

[4] *Annals of an Active Life*, p. 415.

[5] *Daily Mail*, 4th October 1918.

[6] PRO HO 45 11067. Dated 2nd November 1918, initials indecipherable.

[7] IWM Wom Coll EMP VII 43.

[8] His letter to the Bridgeman Committee, 1924.

[9] *The Pioneer Policewoman*, p. 128.

[10] A feature in *Time and Tide*, apparently by a WPS spokeswoman, states that all of the second batch of twenty were WPS; Lilian Wyles, in *Woman at Scotland Yard*, says there were "quite a number" of ex-WPS recruited, while the *Manchester Guardian*, 19th March 1919, claims that "most of the new class" (the second) were ex-WPS. In a letter to Lady Norman, 4th November 1918, Damer Dawson mentions the Commissioner's request and her compliance, IWM Wom Coll EMP VII 43.

[11] *A Woman at Scotland Yard* p. 25.

[12] "B. Clayden" appears among the constables listed as doing duty there: *The Pioneer Policewoman*, p. 28 and I have presumed this to be her.

[13] *Miss Peto's memoirs*, p. 66.

[14] PRO MEPO 2 1759 18/11/18.

[15] Quoted in 4, p. 398.

[16] Lilian Wyles' evidence at Baird.

All unattributed quotes from Miss Peto and Lilian Wyles come from their books as above. Most other information in this chapter comes from these books and Lilian Wyles' evidence at Baird.

CHAPTER TWELVE

Unless otherwise stated all the information and direct quotes in this chapter is from the Baird Committee Report with the following exceptions:

[1] From the report on her, and Mary Allen's, evidence to the sub-committee on women police and women patrols, mentioned in previous chapter. PRO HO 45 10962A.

[2] Canteen and Recreation Hut built by Canadian YMCA. Americans had the Eagle Hut. WPS did duty at both, helping to keep order, looking after men under the influence etc. See *The Pioneer Policewoman* and *Lady in Blue*.

[3] Chief Constable Lane did admit that, when preparing their evidence for the Committee, they had discovered that, in fact, the women did not have rent allowance, but insisted this was purely an oversight which was now being put right. His evidence at Baird.

[4] *The Pioneer Policewoman*, p. 132.

[5] Foreword by Miss Peto to Edith Tancred's pamphlet *Women Police, 1914-1950*.

[6] Edith Tancred's statement at the Federated Training School's Deputation to the Home Office pressing implementation of Baird. 25/2/21 PRO HO 45 11077.

CHAPTER THIRTEEN

[1] Letter from Miss Peto to Home Secretary, 29th October 1919, plus minutes on file. PRO HO 45 10962A.

[2] PRO HO 45 11067.

[3] As quoted at Baird by Margaret Damer Dawson.

[4] As 2.

[5] WPS REPORT, 1920-21. They also claim that in the subsequent (uniforms) court case in February and March 1921, "he attended the police court on two or three days, in case it should be necessary to testify as to his identity." But they still do not name him.

[6] PRO MEPO 2 1710.

[7] During my own service this was given as a reason for our not carrying truncheons, we thought jokingly – but we were unaware that it had been said seriously by Mrs Stanley.

CHAPTER FOURTEEN

[1] PRO HO 45 11020.

[2] *Daily Chronicle*, 28th and 29th July 1920. The *Bristol Times and Mirror*, 12th August 1920.

[3] PRO HO 45 11077.

CHAPTER FIFTEEN

Most of the information in this chapter is from the WPS annual reports; Mary Allen's books (including the quotes from the official diaries of the policewomen in Ireland); Margaret Damer Dawson's obituaries (she died 18th May 1920); her death certificate, and *Miss Peto's Memoirs*, with the following exceptions:

[1] As 16, Chapter Two.

[2] In *Annals of an Active Life* Macready tells how he impressed on Lloyd George the necessity of appointing Horwood because he was worried that someone inexperienced and without talent would get the job, p. 427.

[3] PRO MEPO 2 1710. (In a file minute he first suggests "taking what steps we can", 2nd July 1919).

[4] *A Woman at Scotland Yard*, pp. 100-101.

CHAPTER SIXTEEN

Most of the information in this chapter is from Home Office records (PRO HO 45 11067 and 11077) and Hansard, with the following exceptions:

[1] *A Woman at Scotland Yard*, p. 108.

[2] 'First Interim Report of the Committee on National Expenditure', 1922. Known as The Geddes Report or Axe after the Chairman, Sir Eric Campbell Geddes.

[3] In her memoirs (pp. 42-3) Miss Peto says that Horwood had no use for women police and that Geddes therefore got a ready welcome from him.

[4] In a memo (27th December 1920) on the first deputation re the implementation of Baird, Dunning says that the Commissioner is urging adoption of recommended pay rates or service would suffer as they were resigning, and that a third of them were widows with children. PRO HO 45 11077.

[5] The *Manchester Guardian*, 21st March 1922.

[6] 'Women Police' published by the Women's Freedom League. F:396.5:351.74.08.

CHAPTER SEVENTEEN

Information on Germany: *The Vote*, 13th April and 3rd August 1923; the *Yorkshire Evening Post*, 14th April 1924; interview with Miss Harburn's relatives and *The Pioneer Policewoman* and *Lady in Blue* (extract from the latter).

Information on the US: 'Women Police Abroad' by Edith Tancred, *Police Journal*, 1931, pp. 175-87; *Daily Chronicle*, 7th November 1924; *The Pioneer Policewoman* and *Lady in Blue* (extracts from the latter).

[1] *The Times*, 30th August and 1st September 1922.

[2] 'County of Gloucestershire Constabulary. Women Police – A Brief History of the growth of the Department', the Chief Constable of Gloucestershire's Report to the Standing Joint Committee, 2nd July 1918 and 15th October 1918, and PRO HO45 10962A.

[3] *The Women Police Question* published by The League of Womanhood. LM:30.82/321. 11.

CHAPTER EIGHTEEN

Information in this chapter from the report of the 'Inquiry in Regard to the Interrogation by the Police of Miss Savidge', published by HM Stationery Office, 1928; *The Times* from 2nd May to 14th June 1928; *A Woman at Scotland Yard*; and *Women Police, 1914-1950* by Edith Tancred, published by The National Council of Women.

CHAPTER NINETEEN

Information in this chapter is largely from *The Policewoman's Review* 1927-9; *Miss Peto's Memoirs*; *The Purpose of a Lifetime*; *Women Police, 1914-50* and interviews with women police then serving, with the following exception: (1) *The British Police*, p. 145 and *History of Police in England and Wales*, p. 218.

CHAPTER TWENTY

[1] The MP, Mr Hall, stated that she had boasted openly that she was a Fascist and proud of it.

[2] *Evening Standard*, 29th January 1934.

[3] *Lady in Blue*, pp. 150-5.

[4] *Daily Herald*, 26th April 1945.

[5] The WPS, then the WAS, had worked there, helping girls on behalf of the Charing Cross Vigilance Association, since 1917.

[6] *Police Chronicle and Constabulary World*, July 1941.

[7] Quoted verbatim in *The Policewoman's Review*, March 1930. Date of extract not given.

[8] *The Policewoman's Review*, 1928-37.

[9] There were questions in the House of Commons about their being used on 'internal security', and there were still echoes of the rumours in my day.

[10] *Police Review*, 26th July 1940.

[11] *Police Review*, 31st January 1941.

[12] *Police Review*, 23rd August 1940.

[13] Shirley Becke, as quoted in Miss Peto's obituary, 'The Guiding Light of Women Police', by George Gray, *The Job*, 8th March 1974 (transposed).

[14] *A Woman at Scotland Yard*, p. 90.

[15] As quoted in 'Win the Rebel', an article by Peter Simmons in *Warren* Magazine of No 4 District of the Metropolitan Police.

Other information from *Miss Peto's Memoirs* and interviews.

CHAPTER TWENTY-ONE

[1] 'A Fair Cop' by K.R.G. Browne, in the London *Evening News*, as quoted in *The Policewoman's Review*, July 1930.

[2] *The Times*, 9th January 1940.

[3] *In Appreciation* by Jean Marshall. *Guardian*, magazine of the former Glasgow City Police, summer 1973.

[4] *A Woman at Scotland Yard*, pp. 122, 133 and 148.

[5] *The British Police*, p. 144; *Police Chronicle and Constabulary World*, 1944, and *The Purpose of a Lifetime*.

[6] *Miss Peto's Memoirs*, p. 115.

[7] Various newscuttings and *Scotland Yard*, p. 221.

[8] *Sunday Times*, Johannesburg, 18th April 1948.

[9] 'Policing's Own Major Barbara' by Frank Elmes, *Police Review*, 19th January 1973.

[10] Peter N. Walker, Press and Public Relations, North Yorkshire Police.

CHAPTER TWENTY-TWO

[1] In *A Woman at Scotland Yard*, pp. 76-7, Lilian Wyles relates this story but does not say who the policewoman was: however, Miss Peto in her memoirs

(p. 30) states that Lillian Dawes and Violet Butcher were employed in drug-trafficking detection when they were still Special Patrols.

[2] As note 15, Chapter 20. (*Gertie the Girl with the Gong* was the title of a popular song which went "I'm Gertie the Girl with the Gong, and I saw your car speeding along. If you go over thirty, then Gertie gets shirty. And tinkles a tune on her gong.")

[3] *London Law Enforcement – The Feminine Angle:* essay by Cmdr Mrs S. Becke QPM, Metropolitan Police Library 2543, March 1973.

[4] *Miss Peto's Memoirs* pp. 147.

[5] "Why I'm sorry I won the George Medal", *Daily Mail*, 20th October 1976.

[6] *Woman on the Beat*, Stella Condor, pp. 64–8.

[7] *The Purpose of a Lifetime.*

[8] See Note 3, Chapter 21, and "Woman on the Beat" by Jean Marshall, *Guardian* (Glagow City Police Magazine).

[9] As note 3, and "Metropolitan Uni-Sex" by Shirley Becke, QPM, Commander, Metropolitan Police, *The Police Journal*, July/September 1973.

CHAPTER TWENTY-THREE

[1] Broadcast, 25th November 1978.

[2] *The Job*, 24th November 1978.

[3] *Police*, a fly-on-the-wall BBC TV documentary on Thames Valley Police, 18th January 1982. It won a BAFTA for the best factual documentary series.

[4] "Rape and the Police", *Police Review*, 20th May 1983.

[5] *A Man's Job Alone?* BBC Radio 4, broadcast 21st and 22nd July 1986.

[6] "Not Yet One of the Boys", *Police Review*, 27th February 1987.

[7] "Mothers in Law" and "A Career Beyond Maternity" *Police Review*, 30th January 1987 and 31st August 1990.

[8] RUC reply to my request for information on women police, 26th November 1986.

[9] Full- and part-time.

[10] *Independent*, 12th August 1993.

[11] "Prime Prospects" and "Bravo Juliet", *Police Review*, 14th May 1993 and 28th July 1995. "Forces struggle to end canteen culture", *The Times*, 9th September 2000.

[12] "The World's Highest Ranking Policewoman?" and "World's First Woman Police Chief Resigns", *Police Review*, 27th September 1985 and 4th July 1986.

[13] *Police Review*. 9th October 1987.

[14] Alison Halford, *No Way Up the Greasy Pole* (Constable, 1993), pp. 71–2; 87; 102; 221–45.

[15] Ibid, p. 11.

[16] "Turning the Pages", *Police Review*, 6th September 1985.

[17] "Going International" and "Preparing for New York", *Police Review*, 11th July 1986 and 14th November 1986.

[18] BAWP. Originally the British Association of Women Police but later

changed to the British Association for Women in Policing to better reflect the membership, which has always been inclusive of police staff.

[19] *The Times,* 27th April 2010.

[20] Association of Chief Police Officers.

[21] *Police,* March, May and June 2013.

[22] *Police,* May 2013.

[23] *Grapevine,* Summer 2010.

[24] *Independent,* 3rd March 2013.

[25] *Grapevine,* Spring 2012.

[26] BBC News Scotland, 31st March, 2013.

[27] *Police,* February 2013; *Mail Online,* 18th March 2013; *Lancashire Evening Post,* 19th March, 2013; *Telegraph Media Group,* 18th March 2013.

Index